PIONEERING
THE **VOTE**

PIONEERING

THE **VOTE**

THE UNTOLD STORY OF SUFFRAGISTS IN UTAH AND THE WEST

NEYLAN McBAINE

SHADOW
MOUNTAIN

For Elliot, who is dedicated to all of the
"thinking women" in his life.

Visit us at shadowmountain.com

Library of Congress Cataloging-in-Publication Data

Names: McBaine, Neylan, author.

Title: Pioneering the vote : the untold story of suffragists in Utah and the West / Neylan McBaine.

Description: Salt Lake City : Shadow Mountain, [2020] | Includes bibliographical references. | Summary: "A history of the suffragist movement among the pioneers who settled the West, in particular members of The Church of Jesus Christ of Latter-day Saints"—Provided by publisher.

Identifiers: LCCN 2020009532 | ISBN 9781629727363 (hardback)

Subjects: LCSH: Wells, Emmeline B. (Emmeline Blanche), 1828–1921—Fiction. | Women—Suffrage—Utah—History. | Women—Suffrage—Pacific and Mountain States—History. | Suffragists—Utah—Biography. | Suffragists—Pacific and Mountain States—Biography. | Mormon women—Utah—Biography. | Mormon women—Pacific and Mountain States— Biography. | LCGFT: Biographies.

Classification: LCC JK1911.U8 M33 2020 | DDC 324.6/230978—dc23

LC record available at https://lccn.loc.gov/2020009532

Printed in the United States of America

Lake Book Manufacturing, Inc., Melrose Park, IL

10   9   8   7   6   5   4   3   2   1

"THE STORY OF THE STRUGGLE FOR

WOMAN'S SUFFRAGE IN UTAH IS THE STORY

OF ALL EFFORTS FOR THE ADVANCEMENT

AND BETTERMENT OF HUMANITY, AND

WHICH HAS BEEN TOLD OVER AND OVER

SINCE THE ADVENT OF CIVILIZATION."

—DR. MARTHA HUGHES CANNON,
first female state senator in Utah
and the United States

"MOST WOMEN'S SUFFRAGE AND

FEMINIST HISTORIANS HAVE ALMOST

ENTIRELY IGNORED THE WEST."

—SANDRA L. MYRES,
historian

PREFACE

On August 26, 2020, we celebrate the centennial of the Nineteenth Amendment, the constitutional amendment that extended voting rights to American women. There are currently several museum exhibits in Washington, D.C., honoring the centennial of the Nineteenth Amendment and the suffrage movement that led to its passage. There are newspaper editorials, important new books, documentaries, and celebratory events. But almost all of these fail to seriously consider the role of the western states and territories in delivering suffrage triumphs up to fifty years before the amendment. And none honor the fact that this year, on February 14, we also marked the 150th anniversary of the first female vote under an equal suffrage law, which happened in the unlikeliest of places: Utah.

On February 14, 1870, Salt Lake City resident and twenty-three-year-old schoolteacher Seraph Young was the first American woman to cast a ballot with suffrage rights equal to men's. Two days earlier, the Utah Territorial Legislature had granted women the right to vote in "all elections," and Utah women went to the polls to exercise their new right in a municipal election that very week. Wyoming, Colorado, and Idaho also were home to trailblazing men and women in the fight to recognize women's right to contribute politically. In fact, by the time the Nineteenth Amendment extended women's voting rights across the nation, all of the states that had already granted full suffrage to their women were in the West. Glaringly, the first thirty states to join the Union were the last to grant full suffrage rights.

There has been extremely little scholarship examining why such a radical movement as granting women political voices found its first triumphs in the western states and territories. As historian Sandra L. Myres notes, "Most women's suffrage and feminist historians have almost entirely ignored the West. Writers have concentrated on the national suffrage leaders and on the history of the movement in the eastern states. Western suffrage votes are treated as some sort of aberrant political behavior rather than as part of the mainstream suffrage movement."

Some historians explain the West's behavior by noting the spirit of innovation that was both common and necessary in the frontier West. To survive and thrive, frontier dwellers had to put aside the expectations and traditions of their Eastern counterparts. While it is true that the relationship between the frontier experience and the women's movement is important, this theory oversimplifies the motivations and political forces driving the first suffrage triumphs.

This book proposes that one reason the suffrage leadership of Utah, Wyoming, Colorado, and Idaho is not more fully explored is because the forces that drove the movement in those areas are now uncomfortable and even foreign to contemporary audiences. Each of the first four suffrage wins was the result of specific local pressures that have little resonance in our modern world. For example, the fight for the vote in Utah was inextricably intertwined with the fight over polygamy, the practice of a man taking more than one wife. The federal government demanded its extinction, while the Utahns demanded both freedom of religion and the right to govern themselves. The women of Utah, the vast majority of whom were members of The Church of Jesus Christ of Latter-day Saints and some of whom were in plural marriages, sought the vote to prove they were independent, unoppressed, and intelligent agents of their own wills. But the specter of polygamy overrode any voice that might have carried their message down through history.

Wyoming, Colorado, and Idaho each had their own forces at work as well, and some, such as racism and the movement to ban alcohol, are also hard for us to unpack today. In contrast, the suffrage movement of the twentieth century—from 1910 to the amendment's passage in 1920—captures our imagination much more easily. We feel kinship with the moral rightness that we see in the last decade of the fight: women should participate in our civic governance because it is *right*, because women are people too. We are captivated by the mass media images that arose from the new century's consumer culture and the advent of modern advertising. We see in the clever slogans the birth of our own media landscape. We recognize our own brand of activism: the marches, the banners, the hunger strikes. We see reverberations even today of women chaining themselves to the White House fence, of the rage boiling just beneath the surface as we participate in annual women's marches.

Considering the powerful images and stories that came out of the twentieth-century suffrage movement, why is it important for us to cast an eye back to the nineteenth-century Western movement?

One reason is that the suffrage movement wasn't ever just about voting, and the legacy the movement leaves for us today isn't just about voting. The story of suffrage is really the story of American women transitioning from the localized influence of the domestic sphere to the broad influence and visibility of the public sphere. Through the movement, they crossed the threshold of participation into public and civic life. The movement's activities gave American women a platform on which to gain and exercise their own voices as independent agents. It allowed everyday women to become heroes and gain their first skills in organizing, mobilizing, and working together on the national stage. The typical woman living in contemporary society today takes for granted her opportunity to magnify her voice and influence. We have the suffragists to thank for that, and it was the women of the West who first exploited those platforms to give the movement a running start.

Secondly, by ignoring the activities and accomplishments of the nineteenth-century women, we fall into the anti-feminist trap of silencing women's voices. By the time the twentieth century's Progressive Era was in full swing and advocacy for the amendment was at its height, mass media and consumer culture gave women ample platforms for sending their messages far and wide. National magazines and newspapers were easier and less expensive to print and distribute; photographs evoked the emotions of a thousand words. We have to work harder to excavate the words and deeds of the nineteenth-century women. We have to cull through diaries and localized newspapers, piece together events and references from myriad sources, and rely on journalists' written descriptions of events, rather than seeing a picture of them. Many more records from this earlier time have been lost or are buried in academic collections.

But we owe it to these women to do the work of uncovering their words, even if it is less glamorous work than delving into the Progressive Era's media riches. Particularly in the case of the polygamous women of Utah, we owe it to them to genuinely seek out what they wanted us to know about them, not what Eastern newspapers or legislators said about them. We've silenced them and lost hold of their story because we don't understand polygamy, because we can't comprehend that they actually wanted to stand up for plural marriage or that they had independent agency while entwined in such a system. But by not letting them speak for themselves, we define them not by their own words, but by their marital statuses. Defining a woman by who she is married to is not fair to women today, nor is it fair to women of the past.

Lastly and perhaps most importantly, looking back at the early suffrage triumphs reminds us that the Nineteenth Amendment, as significant as it was, is actually just one milestone in a lengthy and ongoing process to recognize all Americans' rights to civic participation. It is a fallacy to recognize the Nineteenth Amendment as an ending—the end of the struggle for women's rights—or as a beginning—the beginning of women's liberation. The truth is that all the Nineteenth Amendment did was make it illegal for states, which independently govern their own voting rights, to bar people from voting on account of sex. This, of course, was crucially important, and it opened the door for most women to claim equal voting rights in every state. But in practice, many people continued to be barred from exercising their political voices because of their race, ethnicity, or cultural status. In 1924, Native Americans gained U.S. citizenship and voting rights through the passage of the Indian Citizenship Act. Neither men nor women of that community had been able to vote before then. And still, many states, including Utah, made laws and policies that prohibited Native Americans from voting for decades to come. Similarly, the passage of the Immigration and Nationality Act in 1952 finally allowed immigrants of Asian descent to become U.S. citizens and gain voting rights. And in 1965, the Voting Rights Act prohibited poll taxes, literacy tests, and other racially discriminatory state voting regulations in a long-overdue effort to protect the opportunity of African Americans and other people of color to exercise their constitutional rights.

If we correctly see the Nineteenth Amendment as simply one reference point—albeit an important and high-profile one—in the journey to bettering our country, we should also look back to the steady drumbeat of activity that led up to that point. The early examples of Utah, Wyoming, Colorado, and Idaho, although perhaps not fully understood today, offered the rest of the nation ample proof that American women could constructively participate in civic life. Without their trailblazing, the door leading to women's entrance into the public sphere may have stayed shut even longer.

When I moved to Utah from New York City eleven years ago, I didn't realize I would fall in love with my new home in the intermountain West so completely. But as a born and bred New Yorker, I also didn't realize how entrenched Americans are in the belief that all significant events happened east of the Mississippi. We harbor images of pioneers and cowboys and ranchers and gold miners, but I have found that we underestimate the way interactions between East and West in the past have forged our political, economic, and cultural structures even today. This is the story of significant events—and people and relationships and setbacks and triumphs—that have been forgotten, but which shape the country we live in now.

CHAPTER 1

'Tis asked what is a woman's sphere
How should she act her part?
Is it to wear a smiling face
To hide an aching heart?
To speak in accents soft and low
Her irate lord to soothe,
With aching brow and weary hand
His pathway render smooth?
This once was thought a woman's lot
Her only aim in life
But now she shines in every home
Companion, friend, or wife.
So, with her heart and soul combined
And conscience holding sway,
Her sphere is ever spreading out
Where wisdom points the way.

"Woman's Sphere," by Laura Hyde Miner, published in
the *Woman's Exponent*, May 15, 1895

Salt Lake City, Utah
Sunday, May 12, 1895
6:30 in the morning

Emmeline looked up from the note she was composing, put down her quill, and stretched her bony, ink-stained fingers. Finally, the time had come to leave. She allowed herself to feel a pulse of excitement. Miss Susan Brownell Anthony and the Reverend Anna Howard Shaw were, at this moment, preparing to disembark their train at Union Pacific Depot in Salt Lake City. They were just a few blocks away, and the much-anticipated weekend had finally arrived. All of the letters back and forth to the East, all of the meetings with her colleagues to plan a perfect event were finally going to bear fruit. The historic day just dawning marked both an end and a beginning. So much had happened to get the women of Utah to this point. Yet there was so much still to accomplish.

She'd been up for hours, writing final notes of encouragement to the women and men who were to speak at the weekend's Rocky Mountain Suffrage Conference. Emmeline had participated in planning numerous women's advocacy conferences over the past decades, in places as far away as Atlanta and Washington, D.C., so she was no stranger to the logistical challenges of pulling off a meeting of this scope. Advancing the interests of Utah's women, and specifically advocating for suffrage—the opportunity for women to participate in political elections—had been Emmeline's existential focus for twenty-five years. But this event was different: this was on her own turf. At this conference, she would host women she had corresponded with for years but had met only as cumbersome cross-country travel had allowed. It wasn't only Anthony and Shaw who sent Emmeline into a flutter of nerves now; it was Mary C. C. Bradford and Ellis Meredith Stansbury from Colorado, women who had done so much to shape that state's 1893 suffrage victory. Mrs. Emma DeVoe, a formidable speaker and fundraiser for women's equal suffrage throughout the western United States, would also be present. Dozens of key suffrage leaders and influencers from as far away as Tennessee and Kansas were, at this very moment, gathering to the "Crossroads of the West," as Salt Lake City was sometimes called, both to celebrate the past and plan for the future. These were women who just yesterday, it felt to Emmeline, had been critics of Utah and its women, and of her personally. *How quickly their sentiments had turned*, mused Emmeline. *How quickly they could turn again.* But this weekend, the newspapers were predicting a "good, old-fashioned love fest" as the visiting women joined with thousands of Utah women in what Emmeline hoped would be an unprecedented moment of unity.

As Emmeline looked up to the clock on the mantel, she felt the weight of the conference attendees' shared purpose rest on her shoulders. Today, they would celebrate the recent triumphs of Wyoming and Colorado entering the Union as states whose women were free and enfranchised, as well as equal suffrage recently being written into the proposed constitution for the new state of Utah. The significance of these wins, she knew, could not be overstated. The suffrage movement, already decades old, was finally breaking through the murk of fear and mire of limited perceptions of women's capacities.

Certainly, a moment of revelry was in order. But the women must quickly turn their attention to the challenges still facing women's suffrage across the nation. How would the suffragists gathered for this Rocky Mountain Conference ensure that Idaho, another primed Rocky Mountain state, soon added an equal suffrage clause into its state constitution? California too would be a critical win. And how could they fuel the movement to also catch fire in the East, where it had stalled? Were they up to the task? Or would the embers of women's suffrage they had nurtured in the West peter out before the wind could blow them east into a glorious bonfire?

It was still only six thirty in the morning. Emmeline had hardly slept, which wasn't unusual for her, but this time she had been plagued with worry in the loneliness of her single bed. Were they prepared for the crowd? Would the service provided by the hotel and her hosts be as refined as Miss Anthony usually received in the East? Would Miss Anthony be suitably impressed by how much the city had grown since her last visit? More importantly, could the tensions and suspicions of the past decades be put aside? There was nothing more Emmeline could do now. After sealing the last of the envelopes and addressing them to tomorrow's speakers, she readied herself to join the other ladies who were gathering as a welcome party at the station.

Emmeline paused, chiding herself. Her daughter Annie always told her she didn't take enough time to revel in her accomplishments. She only looked at what yet needed to be done, what she needed to worry about next. For years, staying busy had been the way Emmeline put aside the dark moods that tried to hold her captive. In moments when her Eastern childhood and early loves haunted her—the children and men she had lost, the green trees and moist breezes she no longer enjoyed—she coped by writing poetry and staying busy. Maybe it was the early, peaceful hour that prompted Emmeline to remember Annie's advice this morning and take just a moment to recognize what a historic day she was about to step into. Today, Utah—and she, Emmeline B. Wells—would host the most important women's voices in the nation. They were coming in an unprecedented show of unity, a solidarity that had eluded the women's equal suffrage movement for decades as racial prejudices, disagreements on strategy, and the practice of plural marriage in Utah had thrown a specter across women's efforts both nationally and in the West. Enough had changed over the past five years that such a conference as this was possible. This, indeed, was something to celebrate.

All that was needed was a light wool shawl, which Emmeline plucked from the peg at her front door. On this day in mid-May, the glorious Utah mountains still had snow on their caps, and there were cloudlike blossoms wafting through the air from the valley's cottonwood trees. The morning was crisp, but with a promise of warmth as the day progressed. It was the perfect time for Miss Anthony to be visiting Utah, and Emmeline couldn't wait to show her around their desert home. Utah hadn't always felt like home to Emmeline, even though she'd now lived here for almost fifty years, but whenever visitors like Miss Anthony came from the East—from the part of the country that was still a part of Emmeline's very soul—she felt a growing pride in what she and her fellow pioneers had accomplished in this valley.

Emmeline was sixty-seven years old—not young enough to sprint up the street as she might have done in the past. Now, it was adrenaline, not youth, that motored her tiny frame from her home between 400 and 500 East to the corner of South Temple and Main Street to the front portico of the Templeton Hotel, where the Utah Drag was conspicuously parked outside and the ladies were gathering.

The Utah Drag, sometimes called the Big Red, was parked on South Temple Street, its horses already pawing the ground anxiously. The Utah Drag was a large omnibus that seated about thirty people when squeezed together. Essentially a large wagon, the vehicle had a simple roof held up by thin iron pillars, five on each side, to maximize the passengers' ability to see everything around them. There were panels of cowhide that could be rolled down from the roof to protect the passengers in the case of inclement weather, but on this May morning the panels were left rolled up

4

for maximum exposure. The Utah Drag was a well-known sight around the city. Hired on special occasions to show guests around Salt Lake, the omnibus had distinctive red siding that alerted those who saw it that something exciting was coming their way.

But there were more than thirty women interested in going to the Union Pacific station, and the omnibus could not accommodate all those waiting for a ride at the Templeton Hotel. The overflow of forty additional women were busy distributing themselves between six or eight other waiting carriages. Approaching the crowd, Emmeline tacitly approved of the size of the group.

Arriving at the Templeton, she was greeted deferentially. "Good morning, Aunt Em!" rippled across the group as the ladies parted to let their tiny leader pass through. Though barely five feet tall, Emmeline was a commanding presence, partly because of her eccentric dress: she insisted on all-white dresses, tailored in an old-fashioned, rather nostalgic style, with a waistline reaching barely twenty-three inches around. She had delicate features, matching her petite figure, scarcely 100 pounds, with soft eyes whose brows dipped at her temples and gave a shadowed, faraway expression. Her lips had lost their fullness with age and now sometimes gave the impression of a disapproving frown. Her wispy white hair she wore parted and pulled back in a low bun, consistent with the style of the day but not pulled quite as austerely as some. Rather, the soft white waves added to her slightly otherworldly aura.

"Where is Ruth?" Emmeline responded to the greetings as she passed through. "I need Ruth."

"Over there, Aunt Em!" One of the younger ladies pointed to the main entrance of the Templeton, where the forty-two-year-old Ruth May Fox clearly had things under control.

Ruth had been Emmeline's choice to properly manage the affairs of the morning. Ruth was the treasurer of the Utah Territorial Woman Suffrage Association, responsible for collecting and keeping track of the money that supported Utah's suffrage campaign as well as making contributions to the national organizations to support campaigns throughout the country. Also a member of Emmeline's Reapers Club, which facilitated the social and intellectual development of women in Salt Lake

City, Ruth was the perfect protégé. She had already raised twelve children and was now ambitious for herself. Like Emmeline, she wrote poetry. Like Emmeline, she had struggled with the demands of plural marriage, or polygamy—the practice of one man having several wives. And, like Emmeline, she had been forced to provide for herself and her children. Although Ruth's husband, Jesse, had prospered for the first decades of their marriage, the recent financial crisis of 1893 had forced the Foxes to sell their dry goods business. Ruth was still in the beginning stages of her reinvention as a provider in her home and a leader in their community, but Emmeline knew that this important visit by Miss Anthony could be a watershed moment in helping Ruth develop her leadership skills.

"It's a beautiful morning, Aunt Em!" exclaimed Ruth upon seeing the small figure in white approach her. Emmeline was escorted to the front seat of the Utah Drag, the place of honor behind the driver, and she greeted friends and admirers from the omnibus as the rest of the ladies settled themselves in the various carriages.

Emmeline surveyed the scene. It was a good turnout, a respectable group. The number was plentiful, and smartly dressed. She knew that many of the ladies were wearing dresses made of Utah silk, showing pride in the local industry that had garnered such acclaim at the Utah women's booth at the 1893 World's Fair in Chicago. No member of the press would ever be able to claim Miss Anthony was not properly honored in Utah if this group was as cultured and organized as Emmeline saw here. She hoped once again that the rest of the weekend would go as smoothly.

Ruth soon had the caravan ready to leave for the train depot. There were seventy-two women in total in the welcoming party, all chatting with excitement as the horses were prepared for the four-block journey, heading west along South Temple Street to the Union Pacific station. For many of the women, it would be their first time meeting Miss Anthony. Some of the older ones remembered her first visit to Utah, in July of 1871, when she congratulated the Utah women on being the first women in all of the United States to vote under an equal suffrage law, after that law was passed by the Utah Territorial Legislature in February 1870.

That was when Emmeline had first met Miss Anthony too. Susan B. Anthony's first visit to Utah in 1871 marked an awakening for Emmeline

RUTH MAY FOX

Born November 16, 1853, in Westbury, Wiltshire, England
Died April 12, 1958, in Salt Lake City, Utah

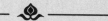

Ruth May joined The Church of Jesus Christ of Latter-day Saints in England before her family immigrated to the Salt Lake Valley when she was thirteen years old. In 1873, she married Jesse Williams Fox Jr. In 1888, her husband took a second wife. An economic collapse five years later caused the families to separate, leaving Fox to largely rely on her own abilities to support her twelve children.

In 1892, Fox started to work with women's clubs in Utah. She became the treasurer of the Utah Woman Suffrage Association and helped charter the Utah Woman's Press Club. She also published many of her own poems in newspapers.

Fox became closely involved with prominent Utah women, including Emmeline B. Wells. Together, they joined the Republican Party when the two-party system arrived in Utah. She excelled at speaking publicly throughout the valley, promoting Republicanism and women's suffrage. She successfully drafted petitions and advocated for the inclusion of women's suffrage in Utah's state constitution. In 1898 she joined the General Board of the Church's organization for young women, the Young Ladies' Mutual Improvement Association. She served as the General President for eight years, from 1929 to 1937.

and many other Utah women. But the suffrage movement was already decades old when Miss Anthony's first visit took place. A generation had already sowed the seeds of potential political emancipation of women by the time Emmeline awoke to the vision of female civic participation. Now, twenty-five years after Anthony's first visit, second and sometimes third generations of women were bonded by their dedication to the cause. Emmeline's grown daughters were now active participants, working hand in hand with other intergenerational suffragists. As the leading voice for the suffrage movement in Utah, Emmeline believed that it was just as important to know what had come before as it was to have a vision for what was yet to come. While leading her planning committee for this Rocky Mountain Suffrage Conference, Emmeline ensured that all committee members were fully versed in the history of the movement to that point. In fact, all who fell under Emmeline's mentorship were required to know the origins of the suffrage movement and, in her opinion and as supported by fame in the media, the woman to whom the movement owed the greatest debt of gratitude.

LOOKING BACK

Susan B. Anthony, the leader of the national suffrage movement and Emmeline B. Wells's own mentor, was interested in the progress of the movement in the western United States and in Utah specifically for much of her adult life. Born in 1820 in Adams, Massachusetts, Anthony was raised in a Quaker family that engaged in activism and moral questioning common to the Quakers of that time. She taught school for fifteen years before entering the activist conversation about temperance, the movement to abstain from drinking alcohol. Because she was a woman, she was not allowed to speak at temperance rallies, which caused her to be sympathetic to the efforts of Elizabeth Cady Stanton.

Stanton, five years Anthony's elder, engaged in women's advocacy as early as 1848, when she organized the first official women's rights convention in Seneca Falls, New York. Along with abolitionist and Quaker Lucretia Mott, Stanton was active in anti-slavery circles, but the two women had been denied seats (because they were women) at an 1840 anti-slavery convention they attended in London. The offense grated on them for years and planted the seed of an idea. In 1848, Mott visited Stanton and the two women finally decided to act on the idea planted during the London debacle. They drafted up a "declaration of sentiments" and advertised "a convention to discuss the social, civil, and religious condition and rights of woman." The convention was put together quickly, taking advantage of Mott's out-of-town visit. Because of the organizational haste, the two-day conference was only advertised in local newspapers, resulting in most of the 300 attendees being from the area. In a feat of last-minute organization, the Seneca Falls convention occurred July 19–20, 1848.

At the convention, Stanton, Mott, Martha Coffin Wright, and several other Quaker women presented the Declaration of Sentiments and an accompanying list of resolutions, drafted in the style of the Declaration of Independence, and they invited discussion and debate over their expressions. The Sentiments detailed the "entire disfranchisement of one-half the people of this country, their social and religious degradation," including women's inability to hold property, receive an education, retain their financial earnings, retain custody of their children in the case of divorce, and be confident and independent contributors to society. It also decried the hypocritical standards of morality demanded of men and women, a "different code of morals," which resulted in women being cast out of society for the same behavior that was tolerated and even lauded in men.

No concept presented at the convention was more controversial than the idea that women should be able to vote in political elections, thereby influencing the nature of their treatment and inclusion as citizens. Heated debate dominated the two days, with Frederick Douglass, the convention's only African American attendee, arguing eloquently for its inclusion. It was not assumed, at the time, that voting rights would be the central focus of this new movement. Dedication to temperance, educational reform, labor reform, and other areas of civic and social influence were the main takeaways from the convention. It was only later that a woman's right to vote became a symbol of her ability to control her position in society and claim her independent agency.

The document was signed by exactly 100 people: 68 women and 32 men. In hindsight of modern times, Seneca Falls is positioned as the beginning of a revolution, the "suffrage movement," one of the longest running social justice campaigns in U.S. history. It is an event that marks a "before" and "after" in the country's history. In fact, the decision to date the start of the movement in 1848 came in retrospect. About twenty years later, in 1869, when Elizabeth Cady Stanton and Susan B. Anthony teamed up to create the National Woman Suffrage Association and wanted to underscore its pedigree as the original and true suffrage organization (in contrast to the American Woman Suffrage Association headed by Lucy Stone), they pointed to the Seneca Falls convention as their origin story. Conveniently neglecting the fact that Anthony wasn't at Seneca Falls or even part of the movement until later, Stanton highlighted her own part in organizing the 1848 event in justifying her as the movement's founding mother.

Even though the Seneca Falls convention did not formally establish an ongoing structure or next-steps list, the nascent "woman's equal suffrage" movement was able to maintain its momentum because similar conferences carried forward the same sentiments, including a convention in Rochester, New York, two weeks later, which Susan B. Anthony's parents and sister attended. Anthony herself attended one of these conferences in 1851 and met Stanton, and the two women started a lifelong friendship and working relationship. Abandoning the teaching and farming jobs that had sustained her until that point, the thirty-one-year-old Anthony threw herself fully into social reform work. For the rest of her life, she lived almost entirely on the fees she was paid as a public speaker.

Until the beginning of the Civil War in 1861, conventions like Seneca Falls and Rochester were frequent occurrences in the eastern United States. And then, while the eastern part of the country had its attention focused on the Civil War, the movement to emancipate women moved west.

CHAPTER 2

There must be something we desire to gain,
A recompense for pacing to and fro;
Some sweet fruition which we would obtain,
Or greater wisdom, that we fain would know;
And this is why we toil on, and endure—
Do battle 'mid life's trials, storm and strife,
Because we feel that there is something sure,
That we shall find, within a higher life.

"At Last," by Emmeline B. Wells

Sunday, May 12, 1895
6:45 in the morning

"Mrs. Wells?"

Emmeline twisted around on her bench, looking down from her perch in the omnibus to a woman standing on the street.

"May I have a moment of your time?"

Emmeline looked into the eyes of a young African American woman, in her early twenties, who held a notebook in one hand and a pencil in the other. She was tall and quite stately in elegant dress, especially considering her young age. Her eyes were resolute and held Emmeline's gaze proudly.

"I believe I only have a moment until the horses are ready."

"I understand. Thank you, Mrs. Wells. My name is Elizabeth Taylor, and my husband and I publish the *Utah Plain Dealer*."

"Ah, yes, I have heard of it. Your husband is William Taylor, no? I have seen him at Utah Press Association meetings. You do fine work for the colored community here."

"That's kind of you to say, ma'am. We try to do our part, though of course we don't match the impact of your own paper."

"Well, the *Woman's Exponent* has been around for some time now. What can I do for you?"

"I will be covering the conference events for the *Plain Dealer*, and I'm hoping you might tell me why today is so significant to those of us here in Utah and in the West generally."

"I'm sure you received the notice that went to the press last week: This is a much celebrated gathering of delegates from states and territories in this land where women have achieved their political enfranchisement after many decades of concentrated labor. We gather now to lay the preliminary plans for an active campaign in Idaho, as well as other states in the West that are ready for their liberation."

"Yes, ma'am. I did receive that statement and we will be printing it. But I would very much like to know how *you* feel about this gathering, from your personal point of view as a leader of Utah women."

"Ah, yes, certainly." Emmeline paused to gather her thoughts. She thrilled every time she had the opportunity to speak as a voice for her people. As a self-styled poet, she knew how to tug at heartstrings with impassioned rhetoric coupled with well-crafted reasoning. "Today, on the eve of statehood," she began, with the far-off gaze of someone gathering air into thoughts and thoughts into words, "the women of the Territory of Utah—soon to be the State of Utah—stand at the forefront of the national movement to enfranchise all American women. The nation has seen how we have labored tactfully and industriously, how we have tried by every means to educate and convert the general public. As the third state to enter the Union with our women's civic rights intact, Utah, along with its western neighbors of Wyoming and Colorado, is leading an awakening that will traverse this nation as if Lady Liberty herself were thrusting her lamp into every darkened window, ushering in the light of a more civilized world. Today, those of us laboring around the nation come together to celebrate the awakening that has already started and ensure that nothing can stop it from progressing further. Miss Anthony and Reverend Shaw put their trust in us here today."

Taylor scribbled in her notebook, jotting down her self-taught

ELIZABETH AUSTIN TAYLOR

Born in 1874 in Kansas
Died March 22, 1932, in Owensboro, Kentucky

Elizabeth Austin Taylor was born in Kansas to parents who had formerly been enslaved. She arrived in Utah when she was a teenager. In 1891, at the age of seventeen, she married William Wesley Taylor, and together they raised five children. Starting in 1895, they published the *Utah Plain Dealer*, a newspaper for the black community, for more than a decade. Both Elizabeth and William belonged to both the Utah Press Association (UPA) and Western Negro Press Association (WNPA). Due to their involvement in the UPA and WNPA, William and Elizabeth traveled widely throughout the western United States. Very few articles from their paper survived the twentieth century, and so almost all that is known of their efforts to gain social and political equality in Utah is from the pages of a rival black newspaper, *Broad Ax.*

Elizabeth and her family helped establish the Trinity African Methodist Episcopal Church in Salt Lake City. Elizabeth led children's groups and participated in the literary society. William was the grand treasurer of the local black Masonic grand lodge. Elizabeth was active in the associated black women's organization, the Queen Esther Chapter of the Order of the Eastern Star.

After the devastating death of her husband in 1907, Taylor continued as editor of the paper for several more years. She continually sought for equality. At a 1909 WNPA conference, she delivered an address entitled "Is There a Future in Journalism for Negro Women?" After marrying John W. H. Morris in 1908, she helped push a resolution calling for the desegregation of Salt Lake businesses and services. Elizabeth later moved to Colorado and eventually Kentucky to be closer to her daughters, who had graduated from college and worked as teachers. Taylor was an influential voice, inspiring those in her community, pushing for social change, and promoting unity and equality for the discriminated in Utah.

shorthand as fast as she could. "What a lovely vision . . . Yes . . ." She finally looked up to the petite woman in the carriage and held her eyes again. "Thank you so much, ma'am."

Taylor disappeared back into the milling crowd. As a newspaper woman and gifted writer, she gave voice to a community that was growing larger in Salt Lake City and the West generally, but whose opportunity to reap the full benefits of social and political advancements was severely limited. For white women, meeting in public to demand additional rights of civic engagement was certainly on the margins of socially acceptable behavior in most of America, but the women put forward a vision of female inclusion that was at least within the imaginative grasp of white men. On the other hand, for most African American woman, even the opportunity to imagine those additional rights felt out of reach, not to mention the opportunity to express a vision of their own inclusion.

There were some, though, who dared to imagine and promote that vision. Elizabeth Taylor followed closely the work of Ida B. Wells, an African American newspaper woman herself and one whose example Taylor aimed to follow. Wells was born in Mississippi at the end of the Civil War but got her footing in journalism and activism in Memphis as a young adult. Soon after Taylor moved to Salt Lake City in 1892, Wells wrote several pamphlets and an exposé on lynching, which resulted in her press being destroyed and Wells having to flee Memphis. Resettled in Chicago, Wells joined other African American leaders in boycotting the 1893 Chicago World's Columbian Exposition, accusing the World's Fair leaders of locking out African Americans and portraying the black community negatively. Wells would go on to found the National Association for Colored Women's Club and be present at the founding of the National Association for the Advancement of Colored People, working concretely to share her imagined vision with others and make it a reality.

But Taylor was twelve years younger than Wells, and Salt Lake City was not Chicago, so Taylor and her husband wrestled with how a white woman's fight could eventually result in increased rights in their own community too. They knew they were in for an even longer, more exhausting battle than Emmeline, Anthony, or any of the white sorority. The *Utah Plain Dealer* would be right there every step of the way.

LOOKING BACK

Growing up in the antebellum North, Emmeline B. Wells did not wrestle with questions of race or get swept up in the abolitionist movement that was starting to boil around her. Rather, she wrestled with the decision to either pursue a promising future of worldly success or join a small community of religious visionaries who believed they were restoring Jesus Christ's true teachings after a period of apostasy. Emmeline Blanche Woodward was born in 1828 in Petersham, Massachusetts, where she was unusually well educated at an all-girls school. Receiving ample praise for her schoolwork and writing, Emmeline's earliest wish was to make something of herself: to become a well-known poet. When she joined The Church of Jesus Christ of Latter-day Saints on March 1, 1842, her aspirations adapted themselves to the embrace of her new community, and while still hoping for fame as a poet, she also wished to "be useful" to her people and to her God. It was not an easy decision, but it was aided in part by her love for her mother, Diadama, who was attracted to the young church's message. In recollecting the decision to be baptized into the new church, Emmeline explained later, "Two powers seemed to be warring with [me]. One said, 'Obey your mother, go down into the waters of baptism in the little brook that always seemed a sanctuary.' The other voice said, 'Do not heed the sayings of your mother … a brilliant future awaits you, you must not make this sacrifice.'"

Just over a year after joining the Church, fifteen-year-old Emmeline married James Harris, another fifteen-year-old member of the Church from their town, and together they left Massachusetts for Nauvoo, Illinois. Diadama stayed behind in Massachusetts to prepare her younger children for the exodus west; James's mother, Lucy Harris, assumed guardianship of the young couple. Members of the young Church gathered in the swampy river town of Nauvoo to escape the unwelcoming communities they had faced in New York, Ohio, and other northeastern states since the Church's founding in 1830.

In Nauvoo, Emmeline observed the Relief Society, the women's organization within the Church, which was presided over by Church founder Joseph

Smith's wife Emma. At the time, the Relief Society consisted of a select group of elite Nauvoo women who had taken on the responsibility of caring for the poor and guiding the morals of the growing community. It was established as a society to bring relief, as its name suggested, but it was endowed with a special vision by Joseph Smith himself, who encouraged the women to think bigger than just being a ladies' club. Smith's goal for the entire Church was to establish God's kingdom on the earth and provide the necessary knowledge and structures that allowed people to be gathered with each other and with God after earthly life. The women's group was set apart to play a unique role in that mission, acting in spiritual partnership with the structures of male hierarchy Joseph was establishing throughout the Church. By strengthening their sociality as women and caring for those in their midst, the Relief Society intended to lift women from the physical and spiritual shackles that held them back from achieving their full potential.

Although Emmeline was too young and obscure to participate in the Nauvoo Relief Society, the organization played an enormous role in the rest of Emmeline's life after she moved to Utah. It was a primary mechanism through which she later gathered the women of Utah in their suffrage efforts. Relief Society also provided Emmeline many opportunities to gain administrative skills, first as the secretary of the global organization starting in 1888 and then as its General President in the last decades of her life. Even though she was very young while in Nauvoo, her time there gave her insight into the Relief Society's earliest work and purest motivations. It was her first taste of women coming together to do "something extraordinary," as Emma Smith described their work. The Relief Society was formed just six years before the Seneca Falls convention. While Elizabeth Cady Stanton and Lucretia Mott most likely had not heard of the female religious outcasts' efforts to start their own revolution, both groups recognized that it was time to awaken women to be more active public contributors and establish social structures that allowed them to participate more fully in civic life.

Emmeline was also shaped by another communal experience in Nauvoo that reverberated throughout the rest of her life: the practice of polygamy, or plural marriage, by members of The Church of Jesus Christ of Latter-day Saints. Members followed Joseph Smith's example in accepting that plural marriage was a commandment from God, although not all were asked to participate in the practice. Despite being from mostly New England and European homes steeped in Victorian morals, some members of the Church—and almost all of its leaders—participated in the practice, but not without heartache.

In 1845, when Emmeline was sixteen years old, she gave birth to James Harris's child, a boy named Eugene who died six weeks later. The young couple's grief was debilitating and carved grooves in Emmeline's character that would never be filled, but the romantic girl still found hope in her husband's love. The couple decided that James should leave Nauvoo to find work to support his young wife, promising he would return soon and they could start a family once again.

Emmeline, living with her mother-in-law Lucy Harris, relied on Lucy to share news of James. But Lucy was cold, disappointed by her son's young bride and her apparent inability to keep a baby alive. Eventually, the letters stopped, and Lucy only shrugged dismissively when Emmeline inquired if there had been news from her husband. James never returned. After Lucy Harris too left Nauvoo, regretting her decision to bring her family into the Church, it seemed clear that Emmeline had been abandoned. The young couple's marriage was declared dissolved. The girl was left bereft and brokenhearted, becoming familiar with feelings of isolation and ostracism that would follow her for her entire life.

She was young, romantic, and filled with faithful fervor, and perhaps another girl's scars would have eventually faded with time. Not Emmeline's. Her scars remained raw and at the surface for her entire life, festering doubt and loneliness with the faintest encouragement. Emmeline was forced to relive her despair forty-eight years later when she received an unexpected package at her home in Salt Lake City. In it, Emmeline found a collection of letters, all addressed to her from James—letters that had been unearthed by a cousin in the recently deceased former mother-in-law Lucy Harris's home. They were letters of devotion, of promise, written to James's teenage bride in care of his mother, who had chosen not to deliver them to their intended audience. The horrific realization that James had in fact not abandoned her, but instead never received one encouraging or loving letter in reply to his own, incapacitated Emmeline. She then was not just scarred, but broken. She did not even write about the letters in her diary until a year after receiving them.

But she took action eventually: upon next traveling east, Emmeline made a special visit to the cemetery where Lucy now lay buried. According to an eyewitness account, "That tiny but mighty old lady stood with her arms raised over the grave and she called down a curse upon her mother-in-law that... no doubt caused the wicked one to writhe in her shroud!"

The lost potential of her first marriage haunted Emmeline for the rest of her life. The specter of her alternate life—a life in which her childhood love stayed by her side—shaped her future perceptions of herself as a wife and mother and independent woman. A half-century later, soon after receiving the letters in the mail, Emmeline reflected that her marriage to James "affected my whole after life. I cannot tell it here not even after all these years. My destiny changed or the course of my life drifted into an entirely different channel from that heretofore anticipated by me or any of mine. This was as completely a turning point as one could possibly have." But in hindsight at least, she saw the turning point as setting her on the providential path that ultimately defined her: "I was mysteriously guided and my way marked out." At sixteen, homeless and friendless in a new community, Emmeline had to become a self-reliant woman.

Abandoned at such a young age, it must have been a relief to Emmeline to discover the protective oversight of Newel K. Whitney and his wife Elizabeth Ann. At first, Emmeline was employed to teach the young Whitney children, putting to use her fancy Massachusetts education and allowing her to provide for herself. Eventually, Emmeline grew close to all members of the family. So close, in fact, that two weeks before her seventeenth birthday, Emmeline agreed to be married to Whitney as his third living wife. Whitney was thirty-three years older than Emmeline, but he offered protection and stability to the young girl. Her diaries and letters reflect a progression in her understanding of what the marriage actually meant emotionally, spiritually, and financially. Apparently, she initially viewed the union as a type of adoption—a legal agreement, yes, but, more importantly, a spiritual link to a righteous patriarch. Three years into the marriage, Emmeline wrote Whitney an impassioned letter, welcoming physical connection into their relationship too.

Whitney's first wife, Elizabeth Ann, was an especially strong influence, and Emmeline revered "Mother Whitney." Emmeline's letters from her time with the Whitneys describe a stable and happy home life. But Whitney too was a brief presence in Emmeline's life. In 1850, after five years of marriage to Emmeline, Whitney died soon after the family traveled from Nauvoo to Utah with the Mormon pioneers. Emmeline was alone again, this time with two young daughters—a permanent tether to Newel, Elizabeth Ann, and their Nauvoo home. Although only twenty-two years old, Emmeline took her destiny into her own hands, once again using plural marriage as her tool for empowerment: she approached Daniel Wells, a high-ranking Church and government official, proposing she become his sixth wife. He accepted.

By proposing to Wells and entering into her third marriage—and second polygamous marriage—Emmeline responded to a drive familiar to many nineteenth-century American women: the drive to be protected physically, to have social standing, and to have influence, even if only through her husband or in her home. The traditional gender structure of her time and place was consistently unkind to unattached women. Women who didn't possess one of the limited number of acceptable skills available to women for self-preservation (such as teaching or sewing) or who weren't tied in name and ownership to a respectable man (as a daughter or wife) often found themselves in a social no-man's land: not legitimized as either property or as an independent agent. And of course, things could go very bad very quickly for women whose lack of male attachment prompted the questioning of their virtue, or who were left with children to raise alone.

The Latter-day Saints who entered into polygamous marriages, a number estimated to be between 20 and 30 percent of the total Church membership, did so generally because they accepted it as a commandment from God. They believed that Joseph Smith was restoring an ancient order, an order that had existed in the Old Testament with the original patriarchs, who had practiced rarified temple rituals and exercised God's power in the form of priesthood. The concept of plural marriage, or celestial marriage, was presented to Church members in this context. But that didn't make it easy to accept. Brigham Young famously stated that after he learned what would be required of him, he saw a funeral procession pass and wished he could exchange places with the corpse. The subterfuge and confusion with which Joseph introduced "the principle" in Nauvoo magnified the feelings of jealousy, betrayal, and loneliness in those involved. It was easy for those outside the Church—and also, sometimes, within—to see it as a way for men to sidestep the sexual confines of monogamy and enjoy multiple partners in a sanctioned way.

But many who participated in plural marriage for the almost fifty years it was practiced came to see—eventually if not immediately—divine reasoning in the sacrifices and pain. Perhaps "the principle" was meant to test and try God's chosen people. Perhaps it was intended to allow the people to more easily and quickly populate God's kingdom on earth. Perhaps it was a way for righteous women (who it was suggested there were more of than righteous men) to find safe and stable homes with righteous men. Perhaps it was God's way of protecting women from the hazards of single womanhood and single motherhood, giving them a way to avoid prostitution and the pitfalls of the street. Perhaps it was a way to force men to step up, to work hard and provide for large families and avoid the roguish behavior that landed men in saloons and brothels.

As the practice moved from generation to generation, some women became bold in the way they took advantage of their nontraditional lifestyles. Traditional marriage, with its close proximity to a property contract, legitimized a woman by connecting her with a man, but it also tied her to hearth and home, making it difficult to balance her wifely duties with the pursuit of her individual interests. Further education or skill-building was often impossible; husband and children were a full-time job. For women like Emmeline, the great revolution of polygamous marriages was that they upended the very fundamental equation of how women spent their time. When there were additional women in a household, there were more hands to address the household work. Often, not all wives were expected or needed to perform traditional duties. Wives with natural inclinations toward childrearing or education could focus on the children, freeing up women like Emmeline to spend time on other skills like writing or medicine. Dr. Martha Hughes Cannon, the fourth wife of Angus M. Cannon, famously quipped, "A plural wife is not half as much a slave as a single wife. If her husband has four wives, she has three weeks of freedom every single month. A plural wife has more time to herself, and more independence in every way, than a single one." While private diaries betray no shortage of loneliness and dysfunction, the Latter-day Saint polygamous women of the nineteenth century demonstrated a profusion of education, ambition, independence, and skills that had rarely been found among a community of American women.

These twin experiences—membership in the Relief Society and the practice of polygamy—were the foundation of most Latter-day Saint women's experience in the latter half of the nineteenth century, when the women's rights movement gained momentum in Utah. To outsiders, they seemed contradictory: how could a religion that seemed to subjugate and oppress women through barbaric marriage practices also sponsor an institution whose mission was to support the social, emotional, and spiritual development of women? To those within the lived experience of Mormonism, they were both the reason the women needed to express their voices and also the mechanism through which they could speak. Their nontraditional marriage practice, odious to those not of their faith, was the platform upon which caricatures and images of victimization were heaped. Even if a Latter-day Saint woman was among the 70 to 80 percent not directly tied to a polygamous marriage, the specter of the practice was unavoidable, since it was the most well-known characteristic of Mormonism among Americans. To those who accepted polygamy as God's will, even if they individually struggled with the practice, the external attacks were unacceptable. The Relief Society was the platform through which the Latter-day Saint women themselves could present contradictory evidence to their victimization: they were, as they demonstrated through their work, organized, effective, and independent.

CHAPTER 3

It strikes us that Miss Anthony and the Rev Doctor Anna Shaw are a day or so behind the feast. When woman's suffrage was pending, perhaps their visit to Utah would have been all right, especially from the standpoint of the suffragists, but is any good point served now by their raking over the burnt ashes of the late, bitter battle, more especially as some of that bitterness still remains?

The Provo Dispatch, 15 May 1895

1847–1870
Salt Lake City, Utah

LOOKING BACK

A third factor joined polygamy and the Relief Society to define the Latter-day Saint woman's experience after 1847: they were refugees. After the death of Joseph Smith at the hands of a mob in Nauvoo and the issuing of an "extermination order" against the Mormons in Missouri, where another group of Mormons had settled, Brigham Young took on the enormous job of leading 60,000 people out of the United States. When the Latter-day Saints first left Nauvoo, the land area of Utah was not a part of the United States. Officially, the land was part of the Santa Fe de Nuevo Mexico state of Mexico. The exodus from the country in search of religious liberty would, in theory, take them to a land that was out of the reach of extermination orders or federal oversight. Leaving the United States—fleeing it, in fact, as Moses had fled Egypt—was the goal of the modern-day exodus.

The Mormon pioneers first entered the Salt Lake Valley in the summer of 1847. But, ironically, due to the Mexican-American War and the resulting Treaty of Guadalupe Hidalgo of 1848, their new land was incorporated as a territory of the United States almost as soon as they arrived, and they were once again on American soil. Although the pioneers had just tried to leave the United States behind, achieving statehood for the new Territory of Utah became a primary goal for the people's single-minded leader, Brigham Young. He knew that the people of Utah would actually have more freedom and autonomy as a state, which had protected rights under the Constitution, rather than as a U.S. territory. Latter-day Saint leader Wilford Woodruff explained, "We are now, politically speaking, a dependency or ward of the United States. But in a State capacity we would be freed from such dependency, and would possess the power and independence of a sovereign State, with authority to make and execute our own laws." Utah territorial leaders would apply for statehood a total of seven times between 1850 and 1896.

But as long as the people—any number of people, no matter how small—in the potential new state practiced polygamy, the federal government was not interested in welcoming them into the embrace of the Union. Plural marriage, in the government's view, was a moral stain reflecting on the entire country, akin to heathenism and the exotic harems of non-Christian lands. Protestant, Victorian-era mainstream Americans loathed the Mormons. The second attempt at statehood in 1856 corresponded with the Republican Party's first presidential campaign, whose platform featured eradication of the "twin relics of barbarism," slavery and polygamy. "The doctrine of the Mormons is blasphemous in the extreme," the *Boston Herald* reported. "The effects of polygamy [are] extremely horrible. Woman is degraded, all her finer qualities being sunk to give place to licentiousness.... Most of the Mormons have two wives, but six appears to be a favorite number with the leaders." So statehood was a nonstarter then too.

At the end of the 1860s, once the Civil War had addressed the issue of slavery, tensions between the federal government and the territorial government of Utah finally came to a head, after two decades of wary diplomacy. Each felt they had arrived at an impasse: Congress had made it clear that under no condition could Utah enter the Union while its majority religious population allowed plural marriage. Utah was still primarily a theocracy under Young's leadership, with no sign of abandoning polygamy as an acceptable marriage arrangement. The question of whether the Latter-day Saints could legally be allowed to practice plural marriage was at the intersection of law, morality, and religious freedom. Was the practice of polygamy a religious freedom protected by the First Amendment? Was the federal government granted the constitutional powers to interfere with questions of domestic systems? In a time and place where state and territorial powers often took precedence over federal oversight, was it the responsibility of local government to mediate domestic affairs? These questions, collectively known as the "Mormon Question," proved to be one of the most far-reaching issues in nineteenth-century American politics.

Washington, D.C., made the first move. If repeatedly denying statehood wasn't sanction enough to get the Mormons to abandon polygamy, Congress decided it had to take bolder action. Lawmakers began discussions about imposing legislation that would make polygamy illegal. As early as 1862, anti-bigamy legislation was proposed and considered and even signed into law by Congress. An editorial in the *New York Times* that year expressed how completely "every true friend of morality and civilization" should be committed to eradicating plural marriage: "The duty of the Government to exert its power for the extermination of this great social evil is almost universally recognized, and we may consider that question to have passed beyond the field of discussion." But the Morrill Act of 1862, Wade Bill of 1866, and Cragin Bill of 1868 (all designed to criminalize polygamy) lacked teeth and were largely ignored by the Latter-day Saints in Utah Territory, who believed the bills deprived them of their First Amendment right to freely practice their religion and who were far enough away to escape the government's physical retribution, at least temporarily. From Congress's point of view, however, the right to practice polygamy was separate from religious belief. While the right to believe any doctrine was protected under the First Amendment, the right to engage in practices that defied the law of the land was not.

Then, in the first days of 1870, the U.S. House of Representatives, led by Illinois Republican Shelby Cullom, chair of the House Committee on Territories, introduced the Cullom Bill, which stipulated that "no one living in or practicing bigamy, polygamy, or concubinage, shall be admitted to citizenship of the United States; nor shall any such person hold any office of trust or profit in said Territory, vote at any election therein, or be entitled to the benefits of the homestead or pre-emption laws of the United States." The message was that practicing polygamy would disqualify people from American citizenship. The bill was intended to give force to the previous bills, which were largely unenforced. The Cullom Bill was drafted so forcefully that it could not be ignored.

The Latter-day Saint women of Utah responded to the proposal of the Cullom Bill with one of their first forays onto the national political stage, voicing their objections in a letter to the editor of Salt Lake City's *Deseret News*: "We, the 'Mormon' ladies of Utah, would offer an expression of indignation towards Senator Cragin and his despicable Bill, did we not consider those subjects too preposterously degrading to merit our contempt." The letter was signed: "'Mormon' First Wives, and all other 'Mormon' Wives."

The *New York Times* offered the first recorded suggestion to enfranchise the women of Utah as an antidote to the polygamy problem. An editorial on December 17, 1867, expressed the hope that the Utah Territorial Legislature would give women the right to vote, thereby giving women—the editors assumed—the opportunity to vote against polygamy and polygamous leaders. In the United States Constitution, it is states and territories, not the federal government, that regulate voting affairs within their borders, and so the Utah Territorial Legislature would be within its rights to enfranchise its women. If the project succeeded in Utah then it could be tried elsewhere, but if it failed, then "only the Mormons would suffer."

Both mainstream Church media organs such as the *Deseret News Weekly* and Latter-day Saint dissenter groups such as William Godbe and his "New Movement" supported the radical idea. In the view of the *Deseret News Weekly*, "The plan of giving our ladies the right of suffrage is, in our opinion, a most excellent one. Utah is giving examples to the world on many points, and if the wish is to try the experiment of giving females the right to vote in the Republic, we know of no place where the experiment can be so safely tried as in this Territory. Our ladies can prove to the world that... women can be enfranchised without running wild or becoming unsexed." To the anti-polygamists, it opened a door to democratically ousting LDS Church leaders from the political halls and thus reducing the impact of polygamy on Utah's national image. Those on both sides of the ideological question thought enfranchising Utah women was a good idea. The question then was not whether it should happen. The question was, whose purpose would ultimately be served?

November 1869
Cheyenne, Wyoming

Utah wasn't the only place in the nation where giving women the right to vote was a fraught and prominent topic in the 1860s. As the national suffrage movement gained traction through its conventions and Eastern organizations, Anthony and Stanton pivoted from their original goal of pushing for a constitutional amendment giving women the right to vote. Instead, they began working to achieve women's suffrage in a state-by-state approach. But even getting individual states to adopt women's suffrage into their constitutions was an uphill battle: amending an existing state constitution required a two-thirds vote of both state legislative houses, the governor's approval, and acceptance by the citizens of that state in a special election. Plus, the established Eastern states were roiled by the effects of the Civil War, drawing the attention of the suffrage leadership to the possible inclusion of women into the Fourteenth and Fifteenth Amendments, the two constitutional amendments that emancipated slaves and reconstructed political rights after the war.

The Fourteenth and Fifteenth Amendments provided the backbone of the country's Reconstruction era, establishing fundamental rights for black men following the official end of slavery and clarifying the guidelines of citizenship and citizens' rights. As the amendments were being discussed and drafted, the national suffragists made it clear that the amendments provided a natural opportunity to include women in their language, shutting the door once and for all on the question of whether American women were included in the Constitution's definition of "citizens" and thereby inherently endowed with the right to participate civically. Anthony in particular became strident in her insistence that the Fifteenth Amendment should not be passed if it did not enfranchise white women alongside black men. And Stanton quipped, "If that word 'male' be inserted, it will take us a century at least to get it out." But neither the Fourteenth Amendment (ratified in 1868) nor the Fifteenth Amendment (ratified in 1870) fulfilled their wishes. Voters were officially defined as men. At least for the time being.

At the annual meeting of the national suffrage leadership in 1869, participants broke with each other over whether or not to support the Fifteenth

Amendment. On the one hand, Anthony and Stanton condemned the amendment for not including women and refused to support it. On the other hand, other leaders like Lucy Stone and Julia Ward Howe supported the amendment, believing it would not pass at all if it included women, and feeling that the amendment was at least a step toward female enfranchisement. Lucy Stone declared, "I will be thankful in my soul if *any*body can get out of the terrible pit [of legal disenfranchisement]." The effect was a fissure among the leadership ranks that would last for decades: Anthony and Stanton formed their own National Woman Suffrage Association (NWSA), and Stone and Howe formed the American Woman Suffrage Association (AWSA). The animosity between these two groups weakened the national movement and made even a state-by-state approach to achieving women's suffrage seem insurmountable.

This is where the territories came in—those vast western lands still only loosely tethered to the federal establishment. They were lands where gold was king, where self-preservation and vigilante justice were still acceptable forms of law, where populist movements were challenging the established political party system. While Utah was wrestling with the federal government over polygamy and statehood, proposals to enfranchise women were narrowly defeated in the legislatures of three western territories: Washington in 1854, Nebraska in 1856, and Dakota in 1869. The idea was still too radical even for the adventurous frontier. Finally, it was in Cheyenne, Wyoming, in the fall of 1869 that the idea of women's political emancipation had its first official triumph.

The Territory of Wyoming was itself quite new. Established on July 25, 1868, by an act of Congress, Wyoming was run by a territorial legislature that had two chambers: thirteen House seats and nine Council seats, with representation divided between the territory's five counties. Like all territories under the protection of the federal government, Wyoming was assigned a governor, and Governor John A. Campbell arrived from the East to take the reins.

Gold was the main attraction of the land. Miners came from all over the West to make their fortunes in the South Pass, Wyoming, gold strike of 1867. One such miner was William H. Bright, a former Union army soldier who fought in the Civil War and later settled in Salt Lake City with his much younger wife, Julia. Hearing about the gold rush, Bright joined other miners in traveling to Wyoming in July 1867. There he made a nice fortune for himself and then settled down by opening a saloon in the gold town of South Pass City. He was soon elected as one of his county's representatives to the territorial legislature, and so in October 1869 he traveled to Cheyenne to participate in the legislative session.

Why William Bright, of all people, ended up being the man who first cracked open the door to women's political liberation is a bit of a mystery. He didn't run for his legislative seat on any sort of radical platform. He positioned himself as toeing the standard conservative Democrat line. There was no grassroots movement in Wyoming demanding that women receive the vote that might have pressured him. He showed no inclination to support women in any other dramatic ways. Nevertheless, it was Bright who sponsored Council Bill #70, put before the Wyoming Territorial Legislature for consideration on November 12 and officially passed on November 30, 1869.

Race influenced Bright's actions, as it did for many white Americans at that time in the country's history. He opposed the political rights given to black men in the Fifteenth Amendment, and since there was no chance the nation would now repeal black male suffrage, he reasoned that white women should also vote since, in his mind, they were more capable of contributing civically than former slaves. "His wife was as good as any man and better than convicts and idiots," a Nebraskan suffrage paper reported Bright saying.

The fact that his wife, Julia, was twenty-one years younger than he was may also have influenced his actions. Julia was herself an ardent suffragist, and, like many Wyoming residents, had come from eastern and midwestern states where suffrage debates already had healthy lifespans. The issues were not new, nor were they coming out of nowhere. In fact, Edward Lee, the newly appointed secretary of Wyoming Territory, had recently proposed a suffrage bill in his home state of Connecticut that had narrowly failed. He was clearly motivated to try again in this less established environment.

Reports after the legislative session revealed that some legislators thought of the bill as a joke, or as a Democratic prank on a Republican governor. A writer for *Harper's Weekly* suggested, "Wyoming gave women the right to vote in much the same spirit that New York or Pennsylvania might vote to enfranchise angels or Martians if their legislatures had time for frivolous gaiety." *The Wyoming Tribune*, reporting on the legislative session after it was over, described the lighthearted mood and suggested it had all happened by accident. "Once during the session," the Cheyenne paper reported, "amid the greatest hilarity, and after the presentation of various funny amendments and in the full expectation of a gubernatorial veto, an act was passed enfranchising the women of Wyoming."

Some of the men who voted for the bill did so sincerely and with consideration. A few may have been motivated by true moral dedication to women; some others may have joined Bright in wanting to balance out the Fifteenth Amendment's enfranchisement of former slaves. But many were motivated by the desire to make Wyoming a desirable destination for other Eastern migrants. Prior to 1869, work on the transcontinental railroad and gold fever had ensured a steady stream of new residents into the new territory. At the end of 1869, the writing was on the wall that those two sources would soon dry up. The railroad was completed in Utah earlier that year, and some of the most prosperous gold mines were beginning to go cold. Wyoming needed to compete with the other newly formed western territories for population, on the eve of its first financial bust. A move such as enfranchising women would generate national headlines and create a positive, progressive brand for the territory, hopefully attracting much-needed settlers. An added bonus would be attracting women themselves. With about 9,000 residents in the whole territory, only 1,000 were women. It didn't feel like too much of a hazard for the frontiersmen, who were starved for a bit of female company in their brutal work of settling a barren land.

Despite a conservative Democratic majority in the territorial legislature wanting to avoid particularly progressive moves, Bright's suffrage bill did pass. There were many who expected (and may have wanted) Governor Campbell, a progressive Republican, to veto its passage.

Campbell's own views on suffrage were unknown. It is clear that he hesitated; the equal suffrage bill sat on his desk untouched for four days. Nervous about his uncertainty, a prominent Cheyenne woman named Amalia Post paid a visit to the governor's home along with a group of her local female friends. In an act of civil disobedience that presaged decades of suffragist actions in the future, Post and her friends vowed not to leave the

AMALIA POST

Born January 30, 1826, in Johnson, Vermont
Died January 28, 1897, in Cheyenne, Wyoming

Born in 1826 in Vermont, Amalia Simons had little in her childhood that would suggest she would be a revolutionary. She married Walker T. Nichols in 1855, expecting to act the part of a traditional wife and mother, and the two headed west to Nebraska to seek their fortunes. After deciding Denver would offer better financial opportunities, Nichols left for Denver without telling his wife, and Amalia had to borrow money to return to her own family's home. She eventually traveled to Colorado to rejoin her husband, but Nichols deserted his wife again, this time with another woman. This time, Amalia Nichols got a divorce and started raising chickens and loaning money. She became one of the most prominent business leaders in the region.

In 1864, Amalia married one of her business partners, Morton E. Post, who was fourteen years younger than she was. Together, they moved to Cheyenne, Wyoming Territory. Amalia Post kept herself financially independent by owning property under her own name. Before the passage of Wyoming's suffrage act in 1869, Amalia showed little interest in voting rights, but her experience running her own business and protecting her own property opened her eyes to the need for female political representation. In March 1870, Amalia was the first woman to serve as a jury foreman on the first American jury to include women. In 1871, she represented Wyoming at the NWSA conference in Washington, D.C. That fall, when the Wyoming Territorial Legislature attempted to pass a bill to repeal the suffrage bill passed in 1869, she made a personal appeal to the governor to prevent the bill from passing. After the governor vetoed it, she lobbied legislators against overriding the veto, a decision that came down to a single vote.

Her husband, who had not been entirely supportive of her suffrage efforts, lost all of his profitable business ventures and moved further west to California. Post remained behind in Cheyenne, well able to support herself and confident in her own pursuits.

governor's home until the bill was signed into law. On December 10, 1869, Governor Campbell signed the bill.

> *Be it enacted by the Council and House of Representatives of the Territory of Wyoming:*
>
> *Sec. 1. That every woman of the age of twenty-one years, residing in this territory, may at every election to be holden under the laws thereof, cast her vote. And her rights to the elective franchise and to hold office shall be the same under the election laws of the territory, as those of electors.*
>
> *Sec. 2. This act shall take effect and be in force from after its passage.*

William Bright returned home to South Pass City after the eventful legislative session. Ironically, it was the delegates from Bright's county that had provided the least support for the bill during the legislative session, so Bright wasn't widely greeted as a conquering hero when he returned home. Soon after he was settled back at home, he was happy to receive two fellow saloonkeepers at his door. John Morris and his wife, Esther Hobart Morris, came to congratulate Bright on his great triumph. The Morrises' visit, and their support for women's suffrage, was particularly welcomed in the otherwise hostile neighborhood.

Esther Hobart Morris had, like so many of Wyoming's residents at that time, only recently arrived in the territory from the East. Esther, John, and their three boys moved to South Pass City in 1869 to follow the gold fever. Stepping out of her stagecoach in South Pass City at the age of fifty-five, Esther must have felt as though she had arrived at the ends of the earth. The barren landscape of the mining district, perched at 7,500 feet above sea level, was all rocks and crags. How different it must have felt from her lush New York home, or even fertile Illinois! Unlike the Mormon pioneers who found a divine calling in their desert home and the struggle that would accompany its settlement, the Wyoming newcomers hoped gold and personal wealth would make their hardships worthwhile.

Morris's willingness to support Bright's suffrage bill was surprising considering her lack of previous activism. Those who knew her before 1869 might have lifted an eyebrow at her enthusiasm, since her life up until that point had been quiet and uneventful. But it didn't come out of nowhere. Morris had the fire of women's emancipation lit in her, and she had her reasons to act. Many of the women who supported early Western suffrage efforts had an inciting incident that made it clear to them personally that things had to change regarding the legal condition of women. For Morris, it had been the issue of property. After her first husband, Artemus Slack, died just before Morris's thirtieth birthday, Morris tried to claim property in Illinois that belonged to her husband. Because women at the time were not allowed to own or inherit property, Morris was forced to confront widowhood and single motherhood of a young son without the financial resources she deserved.

Now was her chance to set that right. In Wyoming, a new and rough land where social experiments were more welcomed than in the established East, she could take a risk. And she could support the men who were taking a risk on her. She didn't care if they had voted for the suffrage bill as a joke; she didn't care if they had voted for it to increase the appeal of Wyoming to migrants; she didn't care if it was a hedge against the state's imminent financial bust. Her gratitude was sincere and she meant to show it.

But what happened after her congratulatory visit to William Bright surprised even Morris. Governor Campbell, eager to put his mouth where his pen had gone, decided he needed to have a woman in a position of political power. And soon. What position could he appoint quickly and easily (so the appointment wouldn't cost too much of his political capital) and did not require exceptional education (since women did not attain the same educational levels as men)? Justice of the peace was the perfect place for a woman. No formal legal education was needed to qualify for the position. And, ironically, there was just that very position open in South Pass City, due to the fact that the sitting (male) justice had resigned in protest over the governor's approval of the suffrage bill.

Governor Campbell called upon Esther Hobart Morris in January 1870 to request that she, one of South Pass City's most ardent supporters of his recently passed suffrage bill, apply for and accept the position of justice of the peace.

Morris did not bite at first. "But Governor, you know there are four men to every woman here in South Pass City. How will I ever be able to gain the respect of all of those men enough for them to see me as their lawmaker?"

"Mrs. Morris, you've lived in South Pass long enough to know the type of man you'll be dealing with. The miners and gamblers and speculators often don't know their head from their feet by the time they get to somebody like you. They're either drunk or so down on their luck that they're just there in body. The hand of a strong woman—and the mother of three boys, no less—is exactly what this crew needs to keep them in line. Don't you worry, Mrs. Morris, they'll be showing you respect when you start passing sentences on them!"

What he didn't say was that he thought her experience with her own husband, John Morris—who was well known around town as a drunk who would inevitably end up in his wife's court—was qualification enough for handling the rough crowd.

"But Governor, doesn't it feel rather hasty to put a woman into a political position while we're all still just getting used to women having the right to vote? Maybe we should slow down and just take one thing at a time."

"You leave that up to me, Mrs. Morris. We've passed the bill; now we've got to show people we're serious. We don't have an election in which you women will even have a chance to vote until next fall. What if between now and then people think about it a little too hard and decide the legislature made a mistake? What if they start getting ideas in their head about reversing the decision? I've got some scoundrels in my government already cooking up ways it can be repealed. We've got nine months until our next election. I want some sort of action now to show that we've done this thing, and we're going to stick with it."

"But Governor, I don't have any legal experience. Or education. How will I know what to do?"

"Mrs. Morris, you're being too humble. You're an orphan and a widow, aren't you? That's not a lot the faint of heart bear very well. I've heard you ran a successful hat business back in the day. And that you had your fair share of experience with the law in Illinois, trying to get your husband's property after he died. That's more experience than most of the men around here will ever have."

"But Governor...."

And so, in the rich tradition of women being their own worst enemies when it comes to seizing opportunities for power, Morris was prodded and cajoled. She finally completed an application for the post and submitted a required $500 bond. The Sweetwater County Board of Commissioners approved her application in a vote of two to one.

Governor Campbell received the continued notoriety he desired for the state. On February 14, 1870, Morris was sworn into office. The county clerk telegraphed a press release, announcing the historic event of the first woman justice of the peace, which read: "Wyoming, the youngest and one of the richest Territories in the United States, gave equal rights to women in actions as well as words."

Justice Morris served in her position for eight and a half months, ruling on a total of twenty-six cases during her term, from the living room of her log home. "Boys, behave yourselves," was a common refrain of the justice's. When the term she had stepped in to fill ended and she went up for reelection, she was defeated. She never ran for political office again. While she never regretted her experience, she was not particularly politically active in the broader suffrage movement. "I do not agree with all that I hear about the enslavement of America," she said in a speech to the women of Albany County, Wyoming. "The women of America are not enslaved. There are many laws that ought not to be, but the majority of them are the extreme of liberality."

CHAPTER 4

Utah is a land of marvels. She gives us, first, polygamy, which seems to be an outrage against 'woman's rights,' and then offers the nation a 'female suffrage bill,' at this time in full force within her own borders. Was there ever a greater anomaly known in the history of society?

Phrenological Journal, November 1870

January 1870
Salt Lake City, Utah

LOOKING BACK

News of Wyoming's November 1869 suffrage bill victory traveled to the nearby Territory of Utah, where Utahns were wringing their hands over the attack they had suffered from the federal government's Cullom Bill. The *Deseret News* reported, "The agitation of the [suffrage] question has reached the Rocky Mountains. In our neighboring Territory, Wyoming, the cause has triumphed; in Colorado the ladies are petitioning to have female suffrage legalized there.... We believe in the right of suffrage being enjoyed by all who can exercise it intelligently." The editorial continued by citing arguments that were common outside of Utah as well: that women would add "purity" to the political process, that they would advocate policies for the "betterment of humanity," that giving white women the vote would show "greater propriety" since black men now had the right to vote. Then the editorial addressed the specific Utah challenge. "The degraded condition of the women in this Territory is a very fruitful theme among our friends outside; in this respect as well as in many others they seem unmindful of, or callous to, the real evils around themselves, but very sensitive to imaginary ones at a distance. They are like the fabled worthy who, through admiring the splendor

35

of the stars, became, or feigned to be, totally ignorant of the dirt, squalor and wretchedness of the earth."

Editorials like these inflamed Utahns' appetite for self-defense and self-expression in the face of their Eastern detractors. The various legislative efforts coming from the federal government to abolish the practice of polygamy, and the momentum gained from the Wyoming news, lit a desire among Utah's women to use their emerging voices to defend polygamy. While opponents could not imagine that women would willingly enter into plural marriages, Mormon women reconciled their commitment to the practice of polygamy and their desire to be fully enfranchised citizens. Additionally, they likely felt that it was one thing for them to commiserate with each other over the struggles of plural marriage, and quite another for outsiders to claim to know of their experiences. They wanted to tell their own stories. They soon had an opportunity to make their voices heard.

News of the January 1870 Cullom Bill, which changed the territory's judicial structure in order to prosecute, fine, and imprison any man cohabitating "with more than one woman as husband and wife," spread across the country, sparking debates about its constitutionality and severity. Influential journals as far away as the *Omaha Herald*, it was reported, "oppose the Cullom bill for the abolition of polygamy in Utah, on principle as well as on the grounds of expediency. It is given out that even our 'Gentile' [i.e. non-Latter-day Saint] friends in Utah consider it an extreme measure, and it is our opinion it is unwise as it will certainly prove futile."

Utahns certainly agreed. And to make their point, women in Utah held their first protest meeting on January 6, 1870. The ability to organize and gather in mass wasn't new to them; they had been gathering as members of the Relief Society for many years. But a gathering of this scale to answer a threat from outside their community felt risky and exciting. They repeated the exercise on January 13, 1870, this time in the Old Tabernacle in Salt Lake City.

The Old Tabernacle had been built in 1852 and was designed to seat only 2,500 people. On that day, between five and six thousand women gathered to hear speeches from twelve "leading ladies" of their community. Apparently, no men were present except reporters, who dubbed the gathering "the Great Indignation Meeting." The Great Indignation Meeting stretched the adobe brick building to its maximum capacity. But the large gathering did help the ladies to keep each other warm during that night's especially inclement winter weather.

The energy of the evening was visible in the puffs of steam haloing each woman's words as she gathered and chatted with her fellow agitators in the dark winter air. They huddled in groups, keeping warm and sharing their nervous conversation. They were so very indignant! *Didn't they have the right to represent themselves?* they asked each other. *To have their own voices? To govern themselves rather than be dictated to by those unfamiliar with and uninterested in their community?*

Eliza R. Snow called the meeting to order, standing at the pulpit side by side with Sarah M. Kimball. Both ladies were virtual royalty when it came to the Latter-day Saint women of Utah: both had been present at the founding of the Relief Society in Nauvoo, Illinois, almost thirty years earlier, and Snow had been responsible for reviving the Relief Society in Utah with the help of a book of meeting minutes she had carried across the plains with the Mormon pioneers. She had very literally carried the handbook for the organization to its new home, and was considered the mother of its rebirth in Utah. Sarah Kimball had been one of the originators of the idea of a Relief Society and was one of the most revered women in Utah at the time. She would go on to play a key role in Utah's suffrage quest almost until the end of the century.

After some logistical business, Kimball opened the meeting with her comments. "We are not here to advocate woman's rights, but man's rights," she began. "The bill in question would not only deprive our fathers, husbands and brothers of enjoying the privileges bequeathed to citizens of the United States, but it would also deprive us, as women, of the privilege of selecting our husbands, and against this we most unqualifiedly protest."

Another high-profile Mormon woman, Bathsheba Smith, followed Kimball with her own reflections of leaving the persecutions of the East behind, coming to the barren desert valley and hoping for religious liberty. "We were buoyed up with the happy reflections that we were so distant, and had found an asylum in such an undesirable country, as to strengthen us in the hope that our homes would not be coveted, and that should we, through the blessing of God, succeed in planting our own vine and fig tree, no one could feel heartless enough to withhold from us that religious liberty which we had sought in vain amongst our former neighbors."

SARAH MELISSA GRANGER KIMBALL

Born December 29, 1818, in Phelps, New York
Died December 1, 1898, in Salt Lake City, Utah

Kimball grew up in Phelps, New York, before moving to Kirtland, Ohio, and later Nauvoo, Illinois, as a member of The Church of Jesus Christ of Latter-day Saints. In 1840, she married Hiram Kimball. During her time in Nauvoo, she started a charitable sewing society that eventually became the Female Relief Society of Nauvoo. In 1842, this became the official women's organization of the Church. From the very beginning, Kimball understood the program as inherently connected to women's rights, "the sure foundations of the suffrage cause" (*Woman's Exponent*, 1 December 1891). After driving her own team of oxen west to the Salt Lake Valley in 1851, Sarah continued to grow the organization. She served as Relief Society president of her ward for over forty years, from 1857 until 1898.

Together with Eliza R. Snow, Kimball worked to create Church-wide programs. They oversaw the construction of the two-story Relief Society Hall in 1868. The first floor of the building housed a cooperative store run by women. The second floor of the building housed an assembly hall used for weekly meetings and was dedicated to art and science. From 1880 until her death, Kimball also served as general secretary and later a counselor in the Relief Society in addition to her ward calling. Beyond her service in church, Sarah served as a delegate to the National Woman Suffrage Association and traveled to Eastern suffrage events on several occasions. In 1889, she served as the first president of the Utah Territorial Woman Suffrage Association, cementing her role as one of the most important leaders of women in Utah.

One after another, the leading ladies stirred the audience up into a realization of what was at stake. They harrowed up memories of the massacres against the Mormons in Missouri and the deprivation they experienced while crossing the Great Plains to escape persecution. They defended their choice to participate in polygamy and expressed the claim that "wherever monogamy reigns, adultery, prostitution, free-love and foeticide, directly or indirectly, are its concomitants." They claimed that their way of life—the way of life they felt was at the brink of forced extinction—was entered upon freely and solved many of the social ills that befell women in other societies.

With limited tools available to them for civic engagement, women made the most of the freedom to assemble. Protesting was an avenue for expressing public will in a democracy that, in theory, reflected the will of the people. And though the Constitution imposed a gender requirement for voting, it did not impose gender limitations for assembling. The tool for codifying that public will, expressed through strength in numbers rather than in individual ballots, was the resolution.

A resolution is a written series of statements publicly accepted by a governing body to reflect a general will. The women wielded this tool to document their indignation. The resolutions presented during the course of the evening included, "That we, the Ladies of Salt Lake City, in mass meeting assembled, do manifest our indignation and protest against the Bill before Congress." Also, "That, in our candid opinion, the presentation of the aforesaid bills indicates a manifest degeneracy of the great men of our nation; and their adoption would presage a speedy downfall and ultimate extinction of the glorious pedestal of Freedom, Protection and Equal Rights established by our noble ancestors." In an effort to "unitedly exercise every moral power," they gathered.

It was Eliza R. Snow who first mentioned the right to vote in her comments. As she entered a conversation with the audience in which the women shouted an enthusiastic "No!" to her rhetorical questions, she asked, "Do you know of any place on the face of the earth, where woman has more liberty, and where she enjoys such high and glorious privileges as she does here?" After the audience's response, she continued, "Instead of being lorded over by tyrannical husbands, we, the ladies of Utah, are already in possession of a privilege which many intelligent and high-aiming ladies in the States are earnestly seeking, i.e., the right to vote. Although as yet we have not been admitted to the common ballot box, to us the right of suffrage is extended in matters of far greater importance." Snow was referring to the practice instituted in The Church of Jesus Christ of Latter-day Saints since 1837, in which all members of the Church, including women, voted on matters of Church governance and in support of members' volunteer assignments. While Snow acknowledged that women of Utah were not yet participants in their political community, she felt that the voice given them by their religious community served as an important symbol of women's power. Her speech continued to demonstrate the very power and voice she was claiming: "Were we the stupid, degraded, heartbroken beings that we have been represented, silence might better become us; but, as women of God,—women filling high and responsible positions—performing sacred duties—women who stand not as dictators, but as counselors to their husbands, and who, in the purest, noblest sense of refined womanhood, being truly their helpmates—we not only speak because we have the right, but justice and humanity demand that we should."

Similar meetings were held throughout Utah Territory in the coming weeks, and by the end of January, it was estimated that 25,000 women had taken part in the protests within fifty communities. If, as the 1870 census shows, the total population of Utah at the time was about 86,000, then approximately 30 percent of the territorial residents took part in one of these indignation meetings that month.

The meetings served several purposes for the Latter-day Saint women of Utah, not the least of which was to demonstrate their intelligence, their free will, and their eloquence. The meetings allowed generations of women to enter public life with a dramatic flourish, from the older women who spoke and led the meetings to the impressionable young girls who attended the meetings and took up the mantle themselves decades later. The meetings also served to solidify the trust of the men of Utah, in their multiple roles as husbands, Church leaders, and civic leaders. After these dramatic demonstrations, the men knew they could count on the women to uphold and defend their lifestyle and religious beliefs. With such a display of solidarity with their men (including their polygamous husbands), why not support women's forays into public life even further? Because the women supported the men and the plural unions of which many of them were a part, the men felt safe in supporting women in their fight for political equality.

Emmeline and others of her generation found the indignation meetings transformative. Emmeline had revered these women—leaders such as Eliza Snow and Sarah Kimball—from her youth, and she admired their eloquence and ease in speaking their minds. Emmeline wasn't the only one affected by the indignation meeting and the corollary meetings around the territory in January 1870. On January 27, Representative Abram Hatch, of Wasatch County, made the first motion in the territorial legislature to consider a bill for women's suffrage. The Utah House of Representatives unanimously passed it on February 5. The bill was then sent to the Legislative Council (or senate) for consideration, where it was debated and amendments were proposed. Both the House and the Legislative Council unanimously passed the amended bill on February 10. Finally, Acting Governor Mann signed it into law on February 12, 1870.

Was the passage of the legislation a logical extension of egalitarian beliefs built into the basic doctrines of Mormonism? Was it the result of the women's convincing stance that they were in fact capable of contributing positively to civic life? Or was it part of a hierarchal male effort to uphold their way of life? An effort to engage women's help in the fight against federal anti-polygamy attacks? Were women pawns of the men? Or were they independent actors playing out radically progressive tenets of their faith system? Depending on the observer or the participant, all were true.

The timing of the resolution was fortuitous, since a municipal election was scheduled two days later, on February 14. For the two days between the passage of the resolution and the opening of the ballot box, excitement rippled through Salt Lake City. Everyone knew that Wyoming's territorial legislature had decided to allow women the right to vote three months earlier, making Wyoming the first territory or state to grant equal voting rights to women. But Wyoming didn't have an election scheduled for eight more months. No woman had ever cast a ballot under equal suffrage laws in a U.S. state or territory since the Seneca Falls convention had made the issue a point of national discussion. February 14, 1870, would be the day that changed.

On the morning of Monday, February 14, 1870, a volunteer brass band from a local Latter-day Saint congregation assembled outside the two-story building that was known at the time as City Hall. Built at the corner of 100 South and 120 East in 1864, City Hall was made of bricks of red sandstone that had been delivered from Red Butte Canyon by railway. The building sat in harmonious symmetry, its four ground-floor windows separated by a central door, while the second floor featured five perfectly spaced and consistently shaped windows. The tidy brick box was topped with a white steeple, featuring not a spire but a small round cupola with a balcony surrounding it. This was a building meant to evoke stability and longevity, a proper home for the legislature of a territorial government that had every intent of becoming an official state in the Union.

An entry foyer ran almost the entire depth of the building, with six well-appointed conference rooms on either side where the city mayor had offices (including Emmeline's husband Daniel Wells during his own time as mayor). The staircase leading upstairs to the second floor started in the back of the foyer and made a turn on itself to land out of sight on the second floor. The twenty-person Legislative Council and thirty-three person House of Representatives met in the Rose Room on the second floor, a room embellished with white plaster molding on the walls and ceilings. It was an elegant room for its time and place, and across the landing was another elegant room: Brigham Young's office. As territorial governor and head of the Church, Young used the white, light-filled room to host important guests and visitors from the East.

At promptly eight o'clock on that Monday morning, the doors to the building opened to voters. Elections were held in the first-floor foyer, a ballot box set up on a small desk outside one of the conference rooms. The morning of the election, the legislative staff made the effort to hang the bunting reserved for July 4th Independence Day celebrations on the windows. It was expected that the "leading ladies" of Salt Lake City would be some of the first to arrive that morning: the ladies who had spoken at the indignation meetings the prior month, those whose husbands served in elected positions, or those related to Church leadership. But the exact number of women who would arrive to cast their ballot was not known.

The morning produced opposing sensations in those present and participating. On the one hand, the band and the festive bunting made the event feel highly newsworthy. Reporters gathered outside the pale stone steps leading up to the front door, waiting to see which woman would be first to arrive. They stomped and blew on their hands to keep warm, likely preferring to be home with sweethearts on this Valentine's Day morning. But they knew this was an event not to be missed. On the other hand, there was an air of the commonplace about the whole event. As Eliza R. Snow had referenced in her talk at the indignation meeting, there was a unique equanimity within administrative affairs that was already comfortable in Mormon life. In their religious culture, they took pride in their "by common consent" voting and even, though it seemed counterintuitive to others, their belief that their marital system liberated women from prostitution and other ills that sometimes befell single young women in nineteenth-century America.

It was in this spirit of normalcy that Seraph Young, a grandniece of Brigham Young, approached the City Hall building that winter morning. A single woman, twenty-three years old, Seraph was a schoolteacher, due to stand in front of her pupils by 8:30. She had no time to dawdle. Even though she was young and hadn't been one of the speakers at the indignation meetings, her proximity to her granduncle made her privy to political discussions in the territorial governor's household. She knew the reasons she should vote: to show that Utah women were intelligent and independently minded, to protect their way of life in the face of outside intrusions, and to extend the vision of God's kingdom to the governance of the nation. She was shy as she approached the reporters and the band and the bunting; she had nothing to say to the press. Wasn't she just doing her duty? There were many more eloquent women who would come after her, she was sure. They just didn't have to be at work at 8:30.

She meekly gave her name to a few reporters who pressed close as she walked up the steps. Seraph Young. She didn't know if it would ring throughout history or remain unknown. Indeed, her name might have rung much louder if it weren't for later events that obscured the significance of that first female ballot.

Perhaps the cold overcame the reporters and they left earlier than planned, or perhaps they just got bored of the parade of ladies who approached the City Hall building that morning and counted bodies rather than gathering names. But Seraph Young was the only name they recorded of the twenty-six women who voted that morning. The details of which positions were up for election, who the women voted for, and who won the elections were all eventually lost.

Only years later did the story emerge of what was happening in

Washington, D.C., on those same days in February 1870, and how close the Utah women came to not making history as they did. It was not only the *New York Times* the Utahns had to thank for planting the idea of women's equal suffrage; it was not only the Wyoming legislature for leading the way; it was not only the impact of the indignation meetings; it was not only the Utah Territorial Legislature. It was also William H. Hooper.

Hooper had been elected to the United States Congress in 1859 as a representative of the Utah Territory, and he served in that position, with a four-year interruption, until 1873. But as a convert to The Church of Jesus Christ of Latter-day Saints in Illinois and an early settler of Utah, Hooper also had a close relationship with Brigham Young. As early as 1867, Hooper was informing Young about the chatter in Congress over polygamy and the possibility of harsh federal repercussions for the practice. Hooper was also promoting a remedy: enfranchise the women. He'd heard the idea thrown out facetiously in the halls of Congress amidst discussion of the "Utah problem," and he knew Young well enough to know Young would see it as a wise, strategic consideration. He was right. Young too advocated for the idea Hooper had planted.

And then, as the Utah Territorial Legislature met on February 10, 1870, to approve the equal suffrage bill, Hooper's well-laid strategy almost collapsed. The proposal to enfranchise women passed unanimously in the all-Mormon legislature, but the acting governor of Utah Territory—a federally appointed position—was non-Mormon S. A. Mann. In order for the legislation to actually become law, the acting governor also had to approve it. But Mann was about to leave office, and his interest in his post was waning. Mann remained in Salt Lake City awaiting the arrival of the new territorial governor, John Shaffer, a Civil War veteran appointed by President Ulysses S. Grant to keep careful watch over the troublesome Utahns. But Shaffer was still in Washington, D.C., on February 12. Although still technically in power, Mann was a lame-duck governor. He was eager to please his successor. But his successor was still 2,500 miles away.

Word reached the nation's capital that evening via telegram that Utah's territorial legislature had liberated its women, and, pending the approval of the acting governor Mann's signature, women would vote in Utah. Shaffer knocked on the door of Hooper's home late that night. Hooper, who had also received word of the vote, was not surprised.

SERAPH YOUNG FORD

Born November 6, 1846, at Winter Quarters, Nebraska Territory
Died June 22, 1938, in Montgomery, Maryland

Seraph Young made history by being the first American woman to vote in an election governed by equal suffrage laws. A grandniece of the Latter-day Saint prophet and statesman Brigham Young, she was born at Winter Quarters, Nebraska. She traveled with a pioneer company as an infant and arrived in Utah in 1847. Young was working as a teacher at the University of Deseret's model school, a primary school, when she voted on the morning of February 14, 1870. She arrived at the polling place on her way to work and was recorded by the media to be the first woman to vote.

In 1872, she married Seth L. Ford, a printer and a Civil War veteran who had fought for the Union Army and was disabled from his war wounds. They had three children, two of whom survived to adulthood. The family moved east in the 1870s, probably to be close to family, since Ford was originally from the east, or to get care for him. The couple eventually moved to Maryland to be near their two daughters.

A *Deseret Evening News* article in the early 1900s said that Young had been unable to visit Utah for years because her husband's condition "has required all her time to care for him; her unselfish devotion is well known by all her friends." But there are records of prominent Utah women, such as Emmeline B. Wells, visiting with Young on their trips to eastern suffrage events. Generally, however, Young's adult life was one of financial hardship and obscurity. The *Deseret News* article continues: "A generation ago she was one of the belles of Salt Lake. Like her sisters, now living in California, she was noted for her comely face and a graceful form, attractions inherited from a mother widely noted for her charm and beauty." But later in her life, the newspaper notes, Young was "almost forgotten."

Young is buried in Arlington National Cemetery, as the wife of a war veteran, but her name is misspelled on her gravestone. While details of her life are few, her act of casting a ballot marked a new era of women's independence in Utah and beyond.

"How am I supposed to govern a territory of the United States when its legislature goes off and does something this inane?" Shaffer boomed to a slippered Hooper. As a former sheriff and brigadier general in the army, Shaffer's dedication to the federal government and the rule of law was absolute, which is what made him a strong candidate to be Utah's federal overseer. "I'm sending a telegram to Mann at first light, telling him he'd better not sign that bill into law. He still may be governor of Utah Territory, but I'm the one who will live with the consequences of this silliness and he will listen to me."

"Now, John," soothed Hooper, playing his part perfectly. "I saw that news come across my desk today too, and the thing is all a hoax. Someone's playing with you to get you worked up about your new assignment out West, wanting you to think you won't be able to keep things under control there in Utah once you get there. Undermining your confidence, you know. You don't think the legislature would do something that bold, do you, when they know Washington is so eager to keep its eye on Utah?"

"Well, they may have gotten some ideas from Wyoming, but the situation is entirely different in Utah, I tell you. Not that I like women voting in Wyoming any better, but there are only a thousand women in Wyoming. In Utah, there are fifteen thousand!"

"Seventeen thousand," added Hooper under his breath.

"You're telling me this is just a little welcome joke?" seethed Shaffer.

"Oh, John, it must be. Let me poke around a bit with my sources tomorrow morning and I'll let you know one way or another."

"Well, you know Mann will be waiting to hear from me. He'll know to wait for my okay before he signs anything into law. I'll need to stop him right away if this is serious."

"Of course, John. Go home and go to bed. I'll certainly check into it and let you know soon what I find out."

Hooper made sure that "soon" never came. As of February 12, Governor Mann in Utah had never heard from his successor in Washington. Showing more backbone than perhaps his successor had expected from him, Mann decided to honor the decision of the legislature, even though he personally disagreed with it. Without the direct approval of Washington, Mann went ahead and signed the bill into law. And on February 14, Seraph Young made history.

CHAPTER 5

We are the people of Utah, and for them; we are the women of Utah, and proud to be so recognized; and our object is to sustain truth, spread a knowledge or correct principles and labor to do good.

We have no rivalry with any, no war to wage, no contest to provoke; yet we will endeavor, at all times, to speak freely on every topic of current interest, and on every subject as it arises in which the women of Utah, and the great sisterhood the world over, are specially interested.

From the first issue of the *Woman's Exponent*, 1872

Sunday, May 12, 1895
6:50 in the morning

As the large red omnibus, the Utah Drag, carried its illustrious passengers past the New Tabernacle, Emmeline glanced over her shoulder to remember the old adobe building, now called the Old Tabernacle, that had previously stood nearby. People said the New Tabernacle was an engineering marvel. Emmeline couldn't disagree, but she missed the former barnlike structure with its pitched roof and drafty chinks in the adobe. That indignation meeting in 1870 had signified an awakening for the younger Emmeline. Even though she was already forty-two years old when she attended that remarkable meeting, it had marked a turning point, the "before" and "after" moment of her own life. Up until that point, from her arrival in the Salt Lake Valley in 1848 to that moment in 1870, her life had been largely dedicated to the support of her husbands, first Newel K. Whitney and then, after his death, Daniel Wells, and her five children. At the indignation meeting, that single-minded focus shifted.

As the memory of that winter night flooded back to Emmeline, she reached across the Utah Drag's red leather bench to clasp the hand of another woman who had been granted a seat of honor for that morning's ride: Sarah M. Kimball. Emmeline could tell that Sarah was also far away in thought on this significant morning. Sarah was ten years older than Emmeline, and her seventy-seven-year-old fingers felt bony and small even in Emmeline's tiny hand. While Emmeline dressed more and more in white clothing as she got older, Sarah almost exclusively favored black. The black crepe of her high-necked dress made her austere face seem even more severe than usual. But Emmeline knew that part of her severity came from how hard Sarah was working to blink back tears.

"It's quite a morning, Sister Sarah, isn't it?" Emmeline smiled, squeezing Kimball's hand. "We've come a long way. And we couldn't have done it without you." Her devotion to the older woman was sincere. Sarah had been a giant in Emmeline's eyes since those first days in Nauvoo when Kimball had initiated the Relief Society.

"Indeed, Emmeline." Sarah was one of the only women who didn't call her Aunt Em, reminding Emmeline that despite all of her years and experience, she would never rival Sister Sarah. Kimball's face remained focused. Her square jaw, which had given her such a look of determination in younger years, now accentuated her sunken cheeks. But then her reverie broke, and her face softened as she broke into a smile. "Oh, the women of this state would have made great strides with or without me, Emmeline. *You* are the one who is the face of our movement here in Utah." Kimball laughed. "But that is not a surprise to those of us who saw you cast your first ballot twenty-five years ago! What a little spitfire you were then. You were either going to explode with your ambition and opinions, or make something great of yourself. Fortunately it's been the latter!"

Emmeline blushed, feeling like the teenager in Nauvoo who had first met Kimball at a Relief Society meeting. "You are too kind, Sister Sarah. It is true that I was bursting with energy to make my mark. After all, I had been raising my girls alone while Daniel took on one civic and Church position after another. I was sequestered in my own house, away from my sisterwives and the happy commotion of the main house. I felt like I was going to disappear if someone didn't take notice of me.

"That indignation meeting you spoke at changed me," Emmeline continued. "Do you remember how you and Sister Eliza and all of the others encouraged us to use our voices to stand up to injustices? I had always loved words and creating my poetry, but I had never before thought to use my words to work in behalf of my people's happiness. Of using my words to been seen as a whole person. You did that for me." There was a catch in Emmeline's throat as she finished her speech and looked away from Kimball to blink. The New Tabernacle was now well out of view as the omnibus continued west on South Temple Street. The other ladies chatted away with each other, oblivious to the two matriarchs reminiscing in the front seat.

"Your subsequent writings, Emmeline, prompted us to remember that gaining the vote was not about seizing political power," said Kimball. "It was about being able to define ourselves, rather than be defined. It was a struggle to gain broader experience and usefulness, to acknowledge the dignity and value of the individual." Kimball smiled again as she reminisced. "I'd never seen such determination. You walked right past that brass band and all those crowds as if there weren't an entire festival going on around you!"

Emmeline laughed. "Well, I was disappointed not to be the first woman to vote under new equal suffrage laws. That honor belonged to Seraph. I was certainly not in a mood to stop and listen to the band when I realized I had missed the opening of the ballot box. Seraph didn't have any children yet, so she wasn't beset by lost gloves and lunch pails the way I was that morning. Didn't she just stop by the City Hall on her way to work? Goodness! If my girls hadn't been so disorganized getting out of the house that morning, I might have been the first woman to cast a ballot in the United States, and heaven knows I wouldn't have been nearly so casual about it as Seraph was!"

"You didn't let that missed opportunity stop you from leading us to other great accomplishments. You've been a treasure to us, Emmeline." Emmeline could see that the older woman was tired by the exchange as she leaned back against the side of the wagon. Tightening her jaw to stem her own tears, Emmeline directed her attention back to the horses leading them to the train station.

Emmeline rested against the wooden side of the Utah Drag as well. So much had changed in the city since that winter day in 1870 when they had made history. Where had all this traffic come from, for instance? For one thing, the annual silver convention was also having its meeting in Salt Lake City that day. Twenty-four years ago, silver tycoon Thomas Kearns had discovered a motherlode mine, and that had certainly changed things. And although the Transcontinental Railroad had been completed north of Salt Lake City in 1869, it wasn't until later that the full effects of the railroad were felt by way of a growing population and increased consumer opportunities. Times had certainly changed, and with them Emmeline's belief in women had only grown stronger.

LOOKING BACK

Six months after that first February 1870 vote, Utah held another election, a larger, statewide election, in which several thousand women across the state exercised their new right. Word of the February election spread quickly through the women's expertly organized Relief Society networks, and turnout at the August election was large. William Hooper, Utah's delegate to Congress who had convinced the new Governor Shaffer that the telegram announcing the equal suffrage law was a joke, was in Utah at the time of the August 1870 vote and described it to a local newspaper. "Brief visits to the polling places gave us to understand that a large number of ladies were exercising the lately granted right of the franchise. And though there was considerable good-humored chaffing, the utmost respect was shown by all to the ladies, for whom a separate entrance to the place of voting was provided." Within the year, women voting in Utah had gone from an idea to a mainstream occurrence.

But not everyone felt so at ease with the way things were playing out in these open elections. Weren't the women of Utah, who were still mostly Latter-day Saint, supposed to rise up against their oppressive male husbands and leaders and use the ballot to liberate themselves? Or, at least, weren't they supposed to be a civilizing force in the political realm, voting as a bloc in the best interest of children and education and temperance? In these two first elections, the vote of the women of Utah was hardly distinguishable from the male bloc, even when it came to voting polygamous men in or out of office. Hooper added to his August 1870 description the fact that the women were helping to determine the "leading public question": the question of whether or not to sustain political leaders who upheld polygamy. The results of the August election kept pro-polygamists in their place. To observers in the eastern United States and local anti-polygamists, this wasn't the way things were supposed to go once the women of Utah could vote.

There was one person who didn't concern herself with *how* the predominantly Mormon women of Utah were voting: Susan B. Anthony. She cared only that they were voting. She herself had cast a ballot in her hometown of Rochester, New York, claiming that she was naturally enfranchised as a citizen of the nation. She was fined and spent a night in prison, underscoring her point that being a citizen as defined by the U.S. Constitution wasn't the only condition required for voting, even though the government claimed it was. The fine, however, was never collected. These women of Utah had done what no other American woman had been able to accomplish: legally participate in a political election. And Anthony was actually pleased that the Utah women hadn't overturned any expectations or caused any revolutions with their newly found political voices. One of the fears Anthony constantly tamped down from critics of women's suffrage was that women, when given political power, would destroy the liquor industry and the railroad expansions and shut down brothels and many other male-favored enterprises. The example of Utah showed that these fears were unsubstantiated.

Another fear Anthony had to quell on a regular basis was that voting women would abandon their homes and children, succumbing to manliness or losing their femininity. The Utah example also showed this wouldn't happen. Politics hadn't seemed to corrupt the women of Utah, neither had they taken it over. Anthony felt these strange women in the West could indeed be very useful to her cause.

Of course, she didn't understand how women who seemed to have such sense and intelligence could exist within—and seemingly embrace—a system of polygamy. But, quite honestly, she didn't really care. Although she made sure to publicly declare her "natural Puritanic horror" around plural marriage, she thought marriage—any kind of marriage—was an imprisonment of a woman's soul by definition, and one kind of marriage didn't seem any better or worse than another. On this point, she diverged from Elizabeth Cady Stanton. Though the two were excellent partners in their advocacy work, in private their lives could hardly have been more different. Stanton was a happily married mother of seven children, while Anthony swore off marriage altogether and lived up to that promise her whole life. Still, their differences allowed the two women to bring different viewpoints to their leadership, and they each tolerated what they saw as the other's eccentricities.

Even while Anthony and Stanton sparred with each other over the value of marriage generally, they were united in their willingness to support the Mormon polygamists in the exercise of their political rights. Members of their organization, the National Woman Suffrage Association, hesitantly followed their leaders' direction with regard to plural marriage. In this, they were different from the American Woman Suffrage Association, led by the more conservative Lucy Stone. Anthony and Stone had broken with each other and created their own organizations over the value of the Fifteenth Amendment, but another issue also served to delineate the two organizational platforms: which organization would support the Mormon polygamists in Utah, and which would reject them? Anthony and Stanton's NWSA accepted the polygamists. Stone's AWSA distanced itself from them. For the next two decades, the divided sisterhoods remained in an awkward dance, with one side gingerly embracing Mormon women as allies with the other side pushing them forcefully away.

Because of her curiosity about the Utahns, Anthony was delighted when in mid-1870 she received a letter, most likely from suffragist Charlotte Godbe, of Salt Lake City, inviting her to visit Utah and see for herself what was happening among the women there. In fact, Anthony had been on the brink of writing to Brigham Young—the only public figure she knew in that far-off community—and inviting herself. She and Stanton were already planning and raising funds for a cross-country trip to California to see how the work was progressing there and to attend the California Women's Congress. Wouldn't it be ideal to stop in Utah along the way?

This was how, in July 1871, Susan B. Anthony made her first visit to Utah, accompanied by Elizabeth Cady Stanton.

Salt Lake City in 1871 still felt like a Western outpost to the seasoned Easterners. San Francisco, where they were ultimately headed, had reaped the benefits of its gold rush and seemed almost as modern as Boston or Chicago. Even with the transcontinental railroad bringing in so many outside influences, Salt Lake City had the musty provinciality of a town still trying to grow out of britches and into a proper suit. Its residents keenly felt the disparity, despite the excellent art, theater, and musical productions that were a hallmark of Salt Lake City social life. Impressing Anthony and showing her how such a remarkable thing as women voting could happen in such a place became the single thought of the leading ladies, once her visit was announced.

Anthony and Stanton began their first Salt Lake City visit with lectures at the Liberal Institute, a non-Mormon intellectual club, being sensitive to the need to address both the Mormons and the non-Mormons during their visit. Anthony spoke there on the value of the vote for working-class women. The pair then moved to an evening rally in the Tabernacle, the same building where the main indignation meeting had been held eighteen months earlier. Standing before a thousand women and men in sweltering July heat, Elizabeth Cady Stanton opened the pair's remarks by looking beyond the demand for the vote—which the Utah women now had—and instead turned her attention to what they should do with this new political tool. In this, she revealed her distaste for the community's acceptance of polygamy. Pointedly, she told the predominantly Latter-day Saint audience that "if there were henceforth any slavery among [them]," or if "any social institution degrading to women" existed, "they held the power to rid themselves of it," and it would be their own fault if they did not. In a second lecture a few days later, Stanton turned to "voluntary motherhood, or the practice of birth control." The "radical" nature of her lectures was too much for the Latter-day Saint audience, despite the fact that Stanton herself had seven children and, by her very presence, was acknowledging the viability of polygamous voters. While the Utahns treated her respectfully, Stanton would never be invited back to speak in Salt Lake City.

Anthony, however, stuck to themes emphasizing the need for economic, emotional, and civic self-reliance among women. These were themes that resonated deeply with the Latter-day Saints, both polygamous and monogamous. The Mormon pioneers had entered the Salt Lake Valley in 1847, twenty-three years earlier, and the challenges of settling a new desert home and making the "desert blossom as a rose" were still fresh for many in the audience. Most of the women listening had left their eastern homes, some even their homelands abroad, and had crafted new lives for themselves and their families amid financial turmoil and, in many cases, religious persecution. They knew from experience how important it was for both men and women to be self-reliant.

Emmeline was starstruck. After the indignation meetings, she had subscribed to the *Revolution*, the official paper of Anthony and Stanton's National Woman Suffrage Association. Their writings prompted her to seek out and study the works of other feminist thinkers such as eighteenth-century Britain's Mary Wollstonecraft and nineteenth-century America's Margaret Fuller. And Emmeline didn't enter this journey alone. All around her, women in Utah formed clubs and societies in which to read and debate the literature of feminist theory. The local newspapers also took up the task of debating the women's movement and the feminist theories of the day. The Victorian image of men as the "sturdy oak" and women as the "clinging vine" were explored in articles, popular verse, and sermons, but these started to give way to editorials stressing the need for women to engage in broader learning and engagement. Brigham Young, in a *Deseret News* editorial, had said, "Let our daughters be intellectually educated as highly as possible; let their moral and social nature receive the highest race of vigor and refinement." Emmeline and her like-minded neighbors followed this transformation of thought, and while not yet openly contributing to the public conversations herself, she followed them closely and encouraged others to do the same. Susan B. Anthony's writings and feminist theories were at the forefront of Emmeline's own philosophies when the leader arrived in Salt Lake City in 1871. To hear her hero speak in person, even as a lowly audience member, was a thrill for Emmeline.

When the meeting concluded, thousands of people streamed into the gentle summer night. While the afternoon had been sweltering, especially for the people standing shoulder to shoulder in the Tabernacle, straining to hear every word of the guests' speeches, the evening turned pleasant in typical Utah style. Emmeline decided to linger at the back of the Tabernacle near a small wooden door set within the thick adobe wall, unrushed to return to the loneliness of her little house, since her daughters had begun to leave home and start families of their own and her husband lived elsewhere with other wives. Anthony had woken in Emmeline a sense of belonging that she had not felt for a long time. Emmeline wanted to meet Miss Anthony.

She didn't have to wait long. Soon, the small door opened and a throng of women emerged. Emmeline expected Anthony to be with her host, Charlotte Godbe, and most likely Eliza R. Snow as well, the president of the Relief Society organization at that time. But she hadn't anticipated that so many other Utah ladies would be bold enough to join the national leaders' posse during their short stay. Momentarily overwhelmed, she tried to search for Anthony in the crowd of hats and feathers, or for anyone she knew. Suddenly, a hand grabbed her wrist. Sarah Kimball forced Emmeline to walk in step with her, quickening her pace to reach Anthony ahead.

"Miss Anthony, may I introduce you to one of the rising thinkers in our community, Mrs. Emmeline Wells?"

Emmeline nodded, stunned to be face to face with the woman she had strained to see all evening. Anthony paused and the crowd of ladies paused with her.

"It's a pleasure, Mrs. Wells. Is it Wells, as in Daniel Wells, the mayor of the city?" Emmeline nodded. "Ah, yes, I met him this afternoon. Very welcoming. Well, we can use all of the bright minds we can here in the West. I hope you will use your mind to help extend the success you enjoy here in Utah to your other American sisters."

Already forty-two years old, Emmeline felt at that moment she finally knew what she wanted to be when she grew up.

Although always engaged in writing poetry and serving in local clubs and associations, Emmeline had mostly dedicated her twenty-three years in Utah up until that point to raising her five daughters—two from Newel K. Whitney and three from Daniel Wells. Even though she was a wife of Salt Lake City's mayor, Daniel Wells, Emmeline spent most of her married years living on her own, in her own house, and her husband's financial situation was not always secure. She knew what it meant to be on her own as a woman. To hear Anthony give words to the strength she already felt as a woman and as a mother connected her to the Eastern cause. She wrote later in her diary that she was determined to "train my girls to habits of independence so that they never need to trust blindly but understand for themselves and have sufficient energy of purpose to carry out plans for their own welfare and happiness." To a mother of five daughters whose very survival required self-sufficiency and independence, Anthony's message struck deep.

Perhaps the most significant communal response to the Anthony and Stanton visit to Utah of 1871 was the creation of the *Woman's Exponent*, which published its first issue in June of 1872 and prominently referenced Susan B. Anthony on its first page. The idea for the paper came through Edward Sloan,

CHARLOTTE IVES COBB GODBE KIRBY

Born August 3, 1837, in Boston, Massachusetts
Died January 24, 1908, in Salt Lake City, Utah

Charlotte Ives Cobb left her hometown of Boston, Massachusetts, in 1846 and moved to Nauvoo, Illinois, with the members of The Church of Jesus Christ of Latter-day Saints. Once there, Charlotte's mother became a plural wife of Church leader Brigham Young. They migrated with the Saints to Utah in 1848 and lived in the Lion House, where Charlotte received the best education available at that time.

In the 1860s, Charlotte traveled back to Boston with her mother and met important American Woman Suffrage Association leaders such as Lucy Stone and Lucretia Mott. Back in Salt Lake City, she married William Godbe, becoming his fourth wife. He was involved with the "New Movement," a religious faction that eventually split with the Church. Despite the break with the Church, Charlotte remained committed to the suffrage cause, and the Godbe household was the first to host Elizabeth Cady Stanton and Susan B. Anthony during their 1871 visit to Utah.

Traveling back and forth to the East Coast, Charlotte became the first Utah woman (and the first woman with voting rights) to speak to an audience of national suffragists and to serve on a national suffrage committee. But in 1873, Godbe separated from three of his four wives, keeping only his first wife, leaving Charlotte with financial burdens and in a complicated limbo with other Utah and polygamous suffragists.

She married John Kirby in 1884. Throughout the 1880s and 1890s, Charlotte remained active on the national suffrage scene. While she was often caught between opposing ideologies, from the LDS Church to the New Movement, polygamy and monogamy, the AWSA to the NWSA, she was never fully accepted by any of them. Charlotte sparred publicly with Emmeline B. Wells more than once over who could claim the right to speak for Utah women. Still, Charlotte remained undeterred. She traveled to London, and contributed several editorial articles to the *Woman's Journal* (the publication of the AWSA), as well as the *Revolution* (the publication of the NWSA). She carved out a legacy of her own, outside of the dominant cultures and people around her.

editor of the *Salt Lake Tribune*, who had attended the Anthony and Stanton lectures. His response to the evening was to consider how he could furnish a platform for Utah women to speak for themselves, especially in light of the negative national media that his own paper regularly addressed. Its first editor was Louisa (Lula) Greene, who although only nineteen years old was a gifted writer. The *Woman's Exponent* followed in the illustrious footsteps of the *Revolution*, which many Utah women already subscribed to, and it wasn't the only suffrage newspaper to be founded that year. Abigail Scott Duniway of Oregon, perhaps also responding to an Anthony and Stanton visit to Oregon that same year, began publishing the *New Northwest*. The Oregon paper would run until 1887, one of at least twelve suffrage newspapers in the West at the end of the nineteenth century. The *Woman's Exponent* ran until 1914, and Emmeline Wells edited it for thirty-seven of those forty-two years.

These were not the first women's rights journals in the West. In 1869, Emily Pitts-Stevens of San Francisco launched the *Pioneer*. Although most of the women's newspapers were short-lived—the *Pioneer* stopped publication four years later—the newspapers that cropped up in the West provided women an acceptable space in which to hone their arguments and their civic voices, even if they still could not participate in elections. The newspapers were relatively easy to produce and distribute, and were an ideal intellectual training ground for western women whose vast travel distances didn't allow for frequent in-person gatherings. Additionally, the extensive geographical spaces of the western states could be more easily reached through the tentacles of the press and mail service than by visitations by activists.

Emmeline started writing for the *Woman's Exponent* soon after the beginning of its publication. She had always been a woman of letters, but Anthony's injunction rang in her ears and she took the challenge to extend Utah's success seriously. Finally, Emmeline had a public forum in which to funnel the multitude of ideas, reflections, and opinions that had lodged in her tiny body. Even still, she chose to begin her journalistic career using a pen name: Blanche Beechwood. The name was a combination of her middle name, Blanche, and her maiden name, Woodward. It was also an homage to a beloved symbol of her New England origins, the beech tree.

Women's literary aspirations extended also to those who wanted to advocate against giving women the right to vote. In 1875, just a few years after the founding of the *Woman's Exponent*, Irish immigrant Jennie Froiseth founded the first literary women's club in Salt Lake City. Not a member of the LDS Church, Froiseth struggled to find connections in the established social circles. The Blue Tea, as she called her club, was her effort to cope with the isolating social landscape. Froiseth and some of the other members of the Blue Tea club started a newspaper called the *Anti-Polygamy Standard*, which took on the complicated position of being anti-polygamy but pro-suffrage. In the paper, Froiseth advocated fervently on behalf of women's voting rights, but argued against giving those rights to Utah women as long as polygamy remained actively practiced in the territory. Froiseth was willing to suspend her own rights to first rid her fellow Utahns of polygamy. Serving as a contrasting view to the *Woman's Exponent*, which consistently defended polygamy and believed it went hand in hand with women's emancipation, Froiseth believed the idea of women's suffrage in Utah was "repugnant," but only due to the "anomalyous condition of affairs" created by polygamy.

When Emmeline entered the *Exponent* offices each morning, she became part of a prodigious communication web that extended through ladies' newspapers all around the country. These papers traveled from west to east, east to west, unifying the growing army of women suffragists who fervently shared their reasons and rationales for women to be emancipated from political, economic, social, and educational strictures. The *Woman's Exponent* was mailed to the faraway reaches of New York and Washington, where other editors would write witty and well-crafted responses to the Utah paper's editorials. Emmeline thrived on contributing to this web, this bridge to the outer world. The papers allowed the women to share best practices and their most biting arguments, but, perhaps most importantly, it created a highly organized camaraderie that would prove essential in the early years of the twentieth century to achieving national enfranchisement with the Nineteenth Amendment.

During her editorship of the *Woman's Exponent*, Emmeline wrote hundreds of editorials on the importance of women's emancipation. But she didn't rely solely on her public words; she also wrote thousands of private letters to other local suffrage leaders. And eventually, she got up the courage to write to Susan B. Anthony herself. Their correspondence would continue for thirty-five years, until Anthony's death in 1906.

CHAPTER 6

Is there then nothing worth living for, but to be petted, humored and caressed, by a man? That is all very well as far as it goes, but that man is the only thing in existence worth living for I fail to see. All honor and reverence to good men; but they and their attentions are not the only sources of happiness on earth, and need not fill up every thought of woman. And when men see that women can exist without their being constantly at hand, that they can learn to be self-reliant or depend upon each other for more or less happiness, it will perhaps take a little of the conceit out of them.

Editorial by Blanche Beechwood (Emmeline B. Wells), *Woman's Exponent*, 1 October 1874

Sunday, May 12, 1895
7:00 in the morning

While the large delegation assembled by Ruth May Fox approached the Union Pacific railroad station in the Utah Drag and accompanying carriages, Miss Susan B. Anthony and the Reverend Anna Howard Shaw made their final preparations to disembark the train. They had traveled through the night from Cheyenne, the train arriving in the Salt Lake station at five o'clock that morning. However, all passengers were permitted to remain on the train until 7:30 to allow them a full night's rest and a leisurely disembarkation upon waking. Anthony and Shaw shared a sleeping car, as they had for all of their many overnight train rides. As the junior companion, Shaw always slept in the upper bunk, giving Anthony, who was twenty-seven years older than Shaw, the more comfortable lower bunk. But Reverend Shaw was herself not young, already almost fifty years old, and the constant train travel was taking its toll on her. She was a heavyset woman, and her back frequently reminded her how much she disliked sleeping on trains. But her pleasantly round face framed by wispy white hair rarely betrayed any discomfort once Reverend Shaw became engaged with her audience.

Shaw felt called to preach from an early age, growing up on a struggling farm in Massachusetts, where her family had immigrated to from England when she was four. In 1873, she was voted into the Methodist Church with a license to preach in Michigan, where she had gone to find work after the Civil War. Shaw received a medical degree as well, granted in 1886. As a doctor of both the body and soul, she went to work advocating on behalf of suffrage, with the vision of using the vote to pass temperance legislation. In this position, she proved her worth to Anthony, who made use of Shaw's bridge-building nature at a sensitive time: in 1890, Anthony's National Woman Suffrage Association was maneuvering a merger with its rival group, the American Woman Suffrage Association, after twenty years of division following the ratification of the Fifteenth Amendment.

Shaw's gentle approach to diplomacy made her an essential tool during this turbulent time, and she soon became Anthony's constant companion as the two traveled the country promoting the strength of the new, unified organization: the National American Woman Suffrage Association (NAWSA). Elizabeth Cady Stanton herself was opposed to the merger of the two groups after their years of rivalry, and although Anthony diplomatically made Stanton the president of the newly formed NAWSA, Stanton was too frail to keep up the demanding travel schedule advocacy required. Shaw was now Anthony's right-hand woman.

As a preacher, Reverend Shaw had a twinkle in her eye and a dimple in her cheek that made audiences warm to her message. She wasn't considered a strong administrator or decisive leader, deficiencies that would limit her later when she became president of the NAWSA after Stanton. But her rhetoric blended folksy spiritualism with a pointed mission, which felt comfortable and appealing to Americans eager to blend their political actions with their religious beliefs. "The Millennium will not come as soon as women vote," she quipped, referring to the belief that Jesus will come a second time to the earth to usher in a thousand years of peace. "But it will not come until they do vote." She plumbed Christian scriptures for deeper truths as well: "[We learn] from the teaching and example of Jesus that life itself is a religion, that nothing is more sacred than a human being, that the end of all right institutions, whether the home or the church or an educational establishment, or a government, is the development of the human soul."

Anthony, who had been raised Quaker, was no more religious than nineteenth-century American culture demanded. Stanton described her as agnostic, and Anthony herself declared that work was her worship. "Work and worship are one with me," she said to a magazine reporter. "I can not imagine a God of the universe made happy by my getting down on my knees and calling him 'great.'" So it was very useful to her to have by her side a trained preacher who could speak the language of mainstream Christianity and put aside any concerns about Anthony's orthodoxy.

Shaw had never been to Utah before. Like many Americans, she had heard of the Mormons. Their claim of having a living prophet and a new book of scripture, the Book of Mormon, felt too far out of line with Methodism or any mainstream Christian denomination to allow for a meaningful spiritual connection. But Shaw wasn't inclined to condemn the Mormons, as many religious leaders did. She had, after all, as a female preacher, depended on people's open minds for her own welfare. She was willing to extend the same courtesy to others and express curiosity rather than condemnation when faced with beliefs as different as the Latter-day Saints'. She was also following the example of her mentor, who, since her first visit to Utah twenty-four years earlier, had kept up written communications with many of the Mormon women and had developed a meaningful friendship with Emmeline Wells in particular.

Even still, Shaw couldn't help admitting to herself that she was curious to see the women who had spent much of their adult lives as multiple wives. Would they look or act different to her? By the time she and Anthony disembarked from the train, Shaw was already endeared to the enclave in the tops of the mountains. The train porter had made the rounds with a local paper, the *Salt Lake Herald*, as passengers were waking and dressing, and Shaw was gratified to read the paper's warm welcome. The words about Anthony were expected, but the praise on behalf of Shaw was even more superlative than she had experienced elsewhere:

"Salt Lake will have some distinguished guests during the next few days. Today two celebrated women will be received by a large delegation. . . . Miss Anthony's name is so intimately associated with the movement for women's rights that it is scarcely possible to speak of one without the other. For many years she has devoted her life, time and talents to the elevation of her sex and the endeavor to make women equal with man in all respects before the law. . . . Miss Anthony is a very remarkable woman.

"Rev. Anna Howard Shaw is also an American celebrity. She is a double doctor, being both a medical graduate and a regularly ordained divine. Her ability as a preacher is no less than as a political orator. In the pulpit and on the platform she is equally at home, and her exceptional talents are devoted to the amelioration of her sex.

"The *Herald* voices the feelings of many thousands of Utah's people in welcoming these ladies to Salt Lake and in wishing them a pleasant and profitable visit to the valleys of the Wasatch Mountains."

Reverend Anna Shaw felt that she liked Utah already.

The station clock chimed seven o'clock as the railroad car doors began opening and porters heaved steamer trunks over their heads to bell boys waiting on the station platform. As the first train to arrive in the station each morning, the overnight from Cheyenne was usually greeted by the most ambitious of the local boys, eager to make the first tips of the day by helping the passengers off the train at the stroke of the hour. The whole station seemed to come alive. The massive monument of steel, which had lumbered into the station two hours earlier but had sat resting in the predawn morning, seemed to wake once again as its passengers finished their ablutions and readied themselves to move on. Heads popped out of opened windows, looking to see if family or friends had arrived on the platform. Other passengers bustled down the train steps with shouted commands to the porters and bell boys, directing them to carry luggage to waiting coaches that would take them to hotels. A huddle of ladies deliberately slowed their departure preparations, dawdling to check once again that they had received all of their luggage. The gossip that Anthony and Shaw were sharing the overnight train had traveled through the cars soon after their departure from Cheyenne, and the ladies stalled in hopes of glimpsing the celebrities. For their part, Anthony and Shaw had learned to hang back when disembarking a train, lest the other passengers become frustrated or encumbered by the waiting crowds that inevitably gathered to greet them. This morning in Salt Lake was no exception. Despite the early hour, the Utah Drag and its large delegation pulled up at the station at ten minutes past seven o'clock, and the seventy women all vacated their carriages, but only after Ruth Fox assisted Sarah Kimball and Emmeline from their seats of honor. Following the older matriarchs, the parade of feathered hats and Utah silk dresses rustled its way through the station building to the platform on the other side. The ladies were mindful to let Emmeline and Sarah lead the way.

Emmeline strained to catch a glimpse of her old friend through the activity of the platform. The last of the other passengers cleared out, but as passengers and porters exited the platform, the Utah ladies filled in the gaps to better their chances of seeing Anthony and Shaw descend. Even as the others fidgeted to get closer to the train, Emmeline settled on a spot a respectable distance from the massive machine so as not to crowd her friend's descent. She stood still and waited.

Her patience was soon rewarded. When it seemed that no other passengers were left to disembark, Susan B. Anthony appeared at the door of one of the cars. Shaw came from behind to grip her elbow as the famous woman stepped gingerly down the steep steps. The crowd of ladies hushed, knowing to follow the lead of their tiny but mighty commander, Emmeline. Once Anthony was safely on the pavement with Shaw behind her, Emmeline stepped forward.

"Dear friend!" said Emmeline, extending both of her hands and walking quickly down the platform to where Anthony was standing. Kissing each other on both cheeks, they then embraced. "This is such an auspicious visit. Here you are on your second visit to Utah, to once again congratulate us on a unique achievement! And what a beautiful day for you to arrive! I'm sure you'll find much changed in the twenty-four years since you were last here. I hope it was an easy trip?" Emmeline felt her chatter betray the slight intimidation she felt at having her important friend on her own home turf.

"Yes, of course! We are used to these overnighters, aren't we, Reverend? Mrs. Wells, let me introduce you to the Reverend Anna Howard Shaw, who is making her first visit to your fair city."

As Reverend Shaw stepped from behind Miss Anthony to take Emmeline's hand, a little girl stepped out of the still hushed crowd, holding a bouquet of local Wasatch wildflowers. A nice touch by Ruth in her planning for the morning, to be sure.

"Oh, how lovely!" exclaimed Shaw, and her delighted grin showed off her dimple to perfect effect. "I have already grown to love the Rocky Mountains in springtime. The Colorado and Wyoming mountains were so impressive even from the train. But I'm sure I will be thrilled by the Wasatch as well. Thank you so much."

"And you may remember Mrs. Sarah Kimball from your previous visit, Miss Anthony. Mrs. Kimball has led us Utah women for decades and has been key to the success and efficiency of our organization." Emmeline once again clasped Sarah's small, frail hand.

"Mrs. Kimball, what a pleasure. Of course I remember you. In fact, if I remember correctly, you were the one who told me long ago that Mrs. Wells would be a force to be reckoned with here in Utah!" Anthony said slyly.

"And so she has been, Miss Anthony." Kimball's expression remained severe as she peered over her spectacles, but the tone of her voice belied a tenderness of heart. "Mrs. Wells has kept us all engaged in the work. And I continue to believe she will take our victories beyond Utah and the Rocky Mountains to all of the women of our nation."

"Well, that is what we are here to discuss this weekend, is it not? How to take this remarkable work you have achieved here in Utah and in Colorado and Wyoming and replicate it all over the country? I have high hopes for our gathering today! High hopes. Shall we?"

With that, Anthony broke the spell of the women's reunification, motioning for her hosts to move ahead and bringing the silent onlookers back to animation. She led the party back through the station and out to the waiting carriages, which would have to squeeze in two more on the ride back to the hotel. Although no one dared say it out loud, it was clear there was, at last, one person who commanded those around her with an even greater presence than Emmeline.

At the Templeton Hotel, preparations were in full swing to receive the important guests when they arrived from the station. Dignitaries had arrived on the five o'clock overnight train from Cheyenne many times before, and the hotel staff knew well the timing for picking up passengers at the seven o'clock disembarkation and getting them back to the hotel in time for breakfast. They expected the ladies to arrive just as the clock struck seven thirty.

At Emmeline's request, Ruth May Fox had asked several of the conference's most important participants to remain at the hotel instead of participating in the pickup, so they could greet Anthony and Shaw when the carriages arrived from the station. Emmeline hadn't wanted every important lady in the city trotting back and forth across town on a Sunday morning. She had worked hard over the past couple of months to ensure that this conference would be perceived as consummately planned and executed, not only in its logistical details but in the kinds of people participating and taking leadership roles. Too much enmity had existed between the Mormons and the non-Mormons, the pioneer settlers and the other immigrants, the monogamists and the polygamists, the suffragists and the anti-suffragists. When Anthony had visited Utah twenty-four years ago, they thought it was the end of political turmoil in Utah over women's rights: Utah women voted, the Eastern establishment was subdued, and the Mormons had held their ground on polygamy. But it had really just been the beginning. This Rocky Mountain Suffrage Conference needed to embody a feeling of unity and optimism that hadn't been felt in the territory for a long time.

To achieve this sense of unity, Emmeline worked tirelessly to lobby politicians, diverse religious leaders, and suffragists from all faiths to attend and support the conference. As she orchestrated every detail of the conference, deputizing the execution to Ruth and others, Emmeline envisioned a tableau of solidarity greeting the carriages when they arrived at the Templeton Hotel. She anticipated and welcomed media scrutiny; she knew that after Utah women's bumpy ride over the last twenty-five years, the convention would be the subject of curiosity and debate among the nation's army of suffragists, and she was shrewd enough to know how to control the story.

As the carriages pulled up to the Templeton Hotel at seven thirty on the dot, Emmeline was gratified to see the exact sight she had imagined. Standing in a refined semicircle on South Temple outside the hotel entrance, like household staff waiting to receive the manor house master upon a return home, a dozen of the city's finest leaders waited patiently for the Utah Drag to come to a stop. Behind them, hotel porters stood with hands clasped, attempting to be invisible but ready to offer services when needed. And clustered on the far side of the entrance, opposite to the direction of the omnibus's approach, a posse of reporters was politely kept in their place by a police officer standing resolutely in front of them.

"Mrs. Wells, such a welcome!" exclaimed Anthony when the tableau came into sight. Emmeline immediately chastised herself for not requesting that a band be present at the gathering too.

"Well, we're hardly the same city you experienced twenty-four years ago, Miss Anthony," Emmeline observed. "I think you'll find your welcome here to be uniquely robust, even among your many admiring cities."

"Salt Lake has always been close to my heart, you know that. But I must say, I'm already noticing the electrical lines and impressive buildings that certainly weren't here before. And that!" Anthony exclaimed as she pointed to her left at the granite temple they were about to pass. With its six ornate spires and gold angel statue atop the tallest, the Church's Salt Lake Temple dominated the skyline and commanded attention. "That was still a mere construction site. I heard it had been completed but didn't imagine it to be so magnificent."

"Yes, it was a construction site for a very long time," laughed Emmeline. "In fact, it was completed only two years ago. It's been under construction for almost my entire life in Utah, and I sometimes find it hard to believe that time keeps moving now that we don't have its construction by which to measure our progress.

"You will be most impressed by the City and County Building," Emmeline continued. "I've scheduled our sessions there tomorrow. It was built with something of a rival vision to the temple—it was designed by our local Masons and went through terrible controversy to get funded and constructed—but I think it is such a lovely symbol of the high regard in which we hold our government here. And, after all, it is where we just held our constitutional convention, which, as you know, had such a happy ending."

"Indeed!" Anthony was nodding approvingly. "I will very much look forward to standing in the room where equality triumphed." They knew there was much more to be said regarding those recent events, but for now, a knowing smile between the two sufficed.

Reverend Anna Shaw, meanwhile, was drawn into her own conversation during the old friends' exchange. Mrs. Emily S. Richards had been assigned to be the new visitor's first introduction to Salt Lake City hospitality.

Richards was often tapped to be the face of Utah suffragists, both at home and at gatherings around the country. As the monogamist wife of an influential lawyer and LDS Church general counsel, Franklin S. Richards, Emily was the perfect showpiece of the Utah suffrage movement. Educated, elegant, well-traveled, and well-off financially, Emily had been among the first generation of Utah Territory babies born to parents who had crossed the plains. She grew up with the spirited pioneer belief in suffrage, had been twenty-five years old when the first Utah women voted, and quickly moved to the forefront of the fight for women in the turmoil since. In fact, Sarah Kimball, uncomfortably tucked in on the bench right next to her, had been Emily's elementary schoolteacher.

"I'm very much looking forward to hosting you in my home tomorrow, Reverend Shaw," ventured Richards in her most practiced eloquence. "We expect the very finest of Salt Lake City will be on hand to meet you."

"I'm sure it will be lovely," responded the affable Reverend. "Tell me, will there be any occasion to meet Mrs. Charlotte Godbe at your home? I have heard lovely stories from Miss Anthony of how well Mrs. Godbe hosted her during her previous visit in '71. She has written to me on several occasions, and it seems that she offers strong voice for Utah's women."

Richards's well-tuned poise faltered and she stumbled over her next words. "Oh, well, Miss Shaw, I'm really not sure. I am not particularly close with Mrs. Godbe—actually Mrs. Kirby now—and so I really couldn't say if she plans to attend any of the events this weekend or not."

"Not close with her? How is that possible? Isn't she a leader of the movement here, alongside Mrs. Wells and yourself?" Shaw's response reflected genuine surprise and curiosity rather than condemnation. Her surprise was understandable.

LOOKING BACK

Charlotte Ives Cobb Godbe Kirby came to Salt Lake City as a six-year-old child soon after the first pioneers arrived. Her mother, Augusta Adams

EMILY SOPHIA TANNER RICHARDS

Born May 13, 1850, in Cottonwood Heights, Utah
Died August 19, 1929, in Salt Lake City, Utah

As a member of the first generation of Latter-day Saint children to be born in Utah Territory, Emily S. Richards was taught from a young age that the right to vote was necessary and positive. She was also under the influence of her schoolteacher, Sarah M. Kimball, the founder of the Nauvoo Relief Society. In 1868, Emily married Franklin S. Richards. Her husband and in-laws were themselves influential Church leaders and ardent supporters of women's suffrage.

Richards was mentored by Emmeline B. Wells and Eliza R. Snow while working with them on the Deseret Hospital board. She revealed herself to be an exceptional speaker and organizer, and, as a monogamous wife, she became the public face of Utah suffrage. She and Margaret Caine organized the Utah Woman Suffrage Association on January 10, 1889, and the pair attended their first National Woman Suffrage Association meeting that year in Washington, D.C. Richards then created local suffrage associations in conjunction with local Relief Societies throughout Utah and the intermountain West. By 1891, thanks in part to Richards's efforts, Utah women were welcomed into membership in the International and National Councils of Women (ICW and NCW). She also played a large role at the Chicago World's Columbian Exposition and the World's Congress of Representative Women in 1893.

In 1904 and 1909, Richards participated in the Berlin and Toronto ICW conferences, leaving her mark on an international stage. Beyond working for the right to vote, she was committed to charitable and reform work throughout her life. She lived to see the ratification of the Nineteenth Amendment after a lifetime of dedication to the cause.

Cobb Young, abandoned her prominent Adams family, her husband, and five of their children in Boston to join the Mormons and become one of Brigham Young's wives. She took little Charlotte and an infant baby with her to her new home.

Charlotte was raised as one of Brigham Young's daughters and lived in Young's Lion House with his other polygamous wives and children. She was given the finest education of the time, including piano lessons. But her mother returned often to her New England roots and took young Charlotte with her, resulting in Charlotte hearing and meeting Eastern suffragists of the 1860s, including Lucretia Mott and Lucy Stone. In April 1869, back in Salt Lake City, Charlotte became one of William S. Godbe's four wives. Even at the time of their marriage, Godbe was toying with Spiritualism, a religious movement that attempted to channel the spirits of deceased people who were believed to have the desire and ability to communicate with the living. His practice of Spiritualism led Godbe to publicly criticize the then-current leaders of the LDS Church, as he claimed to have received visitations from Joseph Smith and other early leaders, who instructed Godbe to reform the LDS Church in an effort he called "The New Movement." Godbe was eventually excommunicated and formed his own church, the Church of Zion.

Charlotte did not leave the LDS Church when her husband formed the Church of Zion, and she claimed her membership in the LDS Church to be dear to her. Her familiarity with the Eastern suffragists, her sorority with other polygamous wives, and her dedication to the Church made her, at first, a perfect representative of the maligned Utah women. She corresponded with Susan B. Anthony in 1870 to alert her to the historical events taking place in the voting booths of Utah, and it was she who hosted Anthony during that 1871 visit.

But the turmoil that resulted from Godbe's actions against the LDS Church was hard on his four wives, and in 1873 he separated from all of his wives except his first, leaving Charlotte without financial support. Charlotte began to speak publicly about her "painful domestic experience in polygamy," compromising and undermining the narrative of empowerment and choice that Eliza R. Snow, Sarah Kimball, and others were trying to project in their indignation meetings and protests of congressional bills. Charlotte rejected the principle of plural marriage, exposing its dysfunction, and more and more frequently she wove her account of polygamy's painful underbelly into the speeches she made at eastern suffrage conferences. Charlotte spoke mainly with an ideological, feminist agenda, with little regard for the specific goals of her constituents back home: promote the image of Latter-day Saint women, defend polygamy, and encourage statehood. Her rhetoric was too highbrow for the self-preserving Mormons, too philosophical and distant from the practical needs they wrestled with daily in their frontier existences. And so rather than embracing Charlotte as one of their own, the Latter-day Saint mainstream female leaders ostracized her almost completely.

The vacuum left by Charlotte's sidelining opened up the perfect opportunity for Emmeline B. Wells to step into the role of leader of the Utah suffrage movement. And step up she did. Charlotte may have had a ten-year head start on establishing relationships with national suffrage leaders, but Emmeline had the megaphone of a national publication to amplify her authoritative voice. Charlotte hated Emmeline for it. In fact, Charlotte at one point wrote a series of letters to Wilford Woodruff, President of The Church of Jesus Christ of Latter-day Saints, asking to have her leadership in the Utah suffrage movement formally recognized. Her disdain for Emmeline was amply evidenced. That "*little* woman," meaning Emmeline, "*tried* to be—what I was—a representative woman in *political circles*.... For *ten* years she has *systematically mis*represented me, & *never* has my name appeared in her *little* paper with credit." Her letters listed her impressive speaking opportunities and many Eastern suffragist friends.

Woodruff's response suggests he was bewildered by the "diamond cutting diamond" nature of the ladies' feud. "It would seem, from your statement of labors performed," he replied, "that they should have been appreciated by the ladies of this Territory, and no doubt they were by a great many, but of whom we do not hear from.... I trust that amicable and friendly feelings may be cultivated, so that a harmonious working together may be had and the best of feeling engendered."

In this vision of harmony, the prophet of the Church proved unprophetic. No such harmony was ever to reign between Charlotte Godbe and the leading ladies of Utah.

CHAPTER 7

An ancient philosopher of the orient has said: "The veiled slaves of the harem can never become the mothers of a great race of men, but if you would produce a race of great men you must first have a race of great women, both as to body and mind."

This is the true doctrine. The history of the world has demonstrated its truthfulness in scores of instances. Elevate the standard of womanhood! For there is no surer way by which to elevate the standard of manhood. This is today the most important question involved in the future attainment of the highest plane of human civilization.

Amalia Post, Wyoming's Constitutional Convention, 24 July 1890

Sunday, May 12, 1895
7:30 in the morning

On South Temple Street in front of the Templeton Hotel, Governor Caleb Walton West, the territory's federally appointed governor, stepped forward from the waiting lineup to help Anthony down from the omnibus. After being a Confederate soldier and a judge in his home state of Kentucky, he had been appointed by President Grover Cleveland to keep the barren desert territory out of trouble. Like most of the governors assigned by Washington to watch over the vast western territories, he had no personal connection to the people or the land but was just doing his job. He was glad his term was coming to an end and he could return to his own land in Kentucky instead of being in constant power struggles with the democratically unofficial but theocratically powerful leader down the street, Brigham Young. But he knew that for the sake of his career he needed to behave today. Just to be sure he did, Emmeline thinned her lips and gave him a fierce look from behind Anthony as he took Anthony's elbow and helped her onto the sidewalk. Still, he was the highest federal official in the land for the time being, so Emmeline put aside her distaste for his un-pleasant demeanor in favor of Anthony being greeted by the highest federal delegate. With this formality dispensed, West fell back into the crowd as the others in the line pressed forward to welcome Anthony to Utah. They were faces Anthony recognized from conferences she had attended all over the country—the Utah women who had spoken so eloquently for decades about their right to vote. They were the founders and the presidents of the Utah Woman Suffrage Association, the writers of the *Woman's Exponent*, the orators at conferences. Here they were on their home turf: Dr. Romania Pratt, Mrs. Zina D. H. Young, Mrs. Margaret Caine, Mrs. Electa Bullock, and more. Such happy embraces reminded Anthony of the celebratory na-ture of her visit. These were the kinds of moments Anthony had been work-ing toward for decades. She never imagined she would find this moment in Utah of all places, the seat of so much turmoil in past decades.

Among those who were specially invited to welcome Anthony out-side the Templeton Hotel were a handful of ladies who themselves had just arrived in Utah the night before. Mrs. Mary C. C. Bradford and Mrs. Ellis Meredith Stansbury represented Colorado, the home of the most re-cent suffrage victory. Both were considerably younger than most of the other special guests, and while they knew several of them from the recent suffrage campaign in Colorado, they remained deferential to the older women around them. Although young, they caught the attention of the *Deseret News Weekly*, which described them as "eloquent lady speakers." Describing Bradford as a "newspaper woman and lecturer," the paper noted that she was "a woman of superior education, brilliant in literature and an eloquent speaker, has traveled extensively at home and abroad." Of Stansbury, the paper called her a "celebrity": "She is reported to be bril-liant, witty, forcible, logical and particularly winning in style and manner of address, has been very successful in the lecture field, which means a great deal." Clearly, Colorado had sent its own leading ladies.

Mrs. Emma DeVoe also offered a commanding presence among the group. DeVoe had first heard Susan B. Anthony address the question of women's suffrage when she was eight years old, when Anthony visited her hometown of Roseville, Illinois, in 1856. At the end of her speech, Anthony had asked all those in the audience who were in favor of women's suffrage to rise. Little Emma was the only one to stand. Anthony added a perfect touch of drama and religious destiny to the moment: upon seeing young Emma stand, Anthony declared, "A little child shall lead them," quoting the biblical book of Isaiah. DeVoe had been dedicated to Anthony ever since, becoming one of the National American Woman Suffrage Association's national agents. As an organizer and lecturer, dispatched around the country by Anthony and Stanton, DeVoe offered a connection between the NAWSA and the smaller local suffrage organizations that existed in thousands of cities and towns across the nation. She helped local organizations raise money and decide how to spend it, shepherding much of it back into the national movement's coffers. She lent a tactical hand to localized suffrage campaigns. As a veteran of the territorial and state campaigns in the Dakotas and Colorado, DeVoe had recently received orders to engage in the upcoming campaign in Idaho. Because one of the missions of this Rocky Mountain Suffrage Conference was to rally support and refine tactics for the Idaho campaign, DeVoe's presence was vitally important.

Notably, Idaho itself did not have a delegate present to represent them in this celebratory and unifying assembly. The natural candidate would have been Baptist missionary Rebecca Mitchell, the president of the Women's Christian Temperance Union (WCTU) in Idaho and one of the leading suffragists in the state. Despite the many national conferences Utah women attended and the seemingly endless numbers of letters written, Rebecca Mitchell remained aloof to the Latter-day Saints' overtures. She wasn't the only Idahoan to do so.

LOOKING BACK

As the northern neighbor to the predominantly Mormon Territory of Utah, the Territory of Idaho counted members of The Church of Jesus Christ of Latter-day Saints at 17 percent of its total population in the 1880s, mostly concentrated in the southeastern corner of the territory. This was the largest concentration of members of the Church outside of Utah at the time. Like Utah, Idaho looked forward to achieving statehood. And like Utah, some of the Idaho Mormons practiced plural marriage, although in Idaho fewer than one percent of the Mormons actually practiced polygamy. Because of this, the federal legislation coming out of Washington in the 1870s and 1880s also affected Idaho's ability to successfully apply for statehood. Thus, in Idaho too, the "Mormon question" presented the greatest stumbling block to achieving statehood.

But unlike in Utah, the Idaho Mormons didn't have the advantage of being the majority population or having strong representation in the governing bodies, and other Idahoans were hardly motivated to support or protect the minority group. In 1884, the Idaho Territorial Legislature passed the Anti-Mormon Test Oath, an oath administered to any man who attempted to vote, hold political office, or serve on juries. If the man refused to swear he was not a member of The Church of Jesus Christ of Latter-day Saints, he was prohibited from participating in civic life.

The Anti-Mormon Test Oath seemed to the Latter-day Saints to be unconstitutional, denying their First Amendment rights to the free exercise of religion. But by 1884 when Idaho passed the Oath, the Latter-day Saints had no recourse to argue their case in court. In fact, the case had already been argued, and they had lost. Their belief in their right to practice their religion as they saw fit took the issue all the way to the Supreme Court, where, in 1879, George Reynolds, a Latter-day Saint in Utah Territory, argued that anti-polygamy laws were unconstitutional because they prohibited him from the free exercise of his religion. *Reynolds v. United States* asked the question: Is banning polygamy, even as an expression of religious practice, constitutional? Or does the ban violate the First Amendment right to free exercise of religion?

The court ruled unanimously that, while it could not ban the belief in polygamy, it could ban the practice of it. This was, in part, because the court believed marriage to be the "most important" feature of American social life. In the ruling, the court explained, "Upon it [marriage] society may be said to be built. Marriage, while from its very nature a sacred obligation, is nevertheless, in most civilized nations, a civil contract, and usually regulated by law." Additionally, the court concluded that no person could absolve themselves of illegal activity because of religious commitment. "Can a man excuse his [illegal] practices... because of his religious belief? To permit this would be to make the professed doctrines of religious belief superior to the law of the land, and in effect to permit every citizen to become a law unto himself.

Government could exist only in name under such circumstances." The ruling of *Reynolds v. United States* closed the door on any First Amendment protections for the Latter-day Saints and gave federal authorities the backbone they needed to crack down on illegal polygamous unions.

The Idaho legislature's measures to prohibit the Latter-day Saints from engaging in the governance of the territory eventually won them statehood. To become a state, a territory had to appeal to Congress to pass an Enabling Act, a declaration that the territory could move ahead with drafting a constitution for the new state. The territory was then given the right to elect delegates to represent the people and gather in a constitutional convention to jointly draft the new state's governing document. Idaho held its constitutional convention in 1889 with no participation by Latter-day Saints, but with the eloquent voices of Abigail Scott Duniway, a prominent northwestern suffragist, and Harriet Skelton, then the president of the Idaho Woman's Christian Temperance Union, included in the debates. While the right for women to participate in Idaho's civic life did not ultimately make it into the Idaho state constitution, it was seriously considered.

After the constitution of a territory was successfully drafted, the constitution for the new state was presented to the people for a ratifying vote. The people of the Territory of Idaho voted to support their new constitution, and Idaho officially entered the Union as the forty-third state on July 3, 1890. The requirement that no voter be a member of The Church of Jesus Christ of Latter-day Saints was codified in the state's constitution.

The Mormon question was revisited in Idaho before the woman question. In 1892, after having secured statehood in part by successfully distancing itself from the Mormons and appealing to the federal government's distaste for Mormon practices, the Idaho state legislature repealed the Test Oath. Even though the clause barring Mormons from politics remained in the Idaho constitution for almost a hundred more years, members of the Church did have civic doors informally opened to them once again.

But the scars remained. Many Utah Latter-day Saints, including Emmeline B. Wells, had family and friends living in Idaho who had been affected by the Test Oath. Now, with the persistence of Rebecca Mitchell and others, the woman question was front and center in Idaho. Idaho could very well be the next great triumph of the national suffrage movement. But the

ABIGAIL SCOTT DUNIWAY

Born October 22, 1834, in Tazewell County, Illinois
Died October 11, 1915, in Portland, Oregon

Abigail Scott spent most of her youth in Illinois before moving to Oregon Territory with her family in 1852. She was seventeen years old. When she arrived in Oregon, she became a teacher, even though she herself was largely self-taught. She'd had less than a year of formal education in Illinois but worked to become a proficient writer. She met and married Benjamin C. Duniway in August 1853. Soon after, they lost their farms to fire and legal claims, and in 1862, Benjamin was injured in an accident. Abigail Duniway had to step in to support the family of six children as the main source of income.

Nine years later, they moved to Portland, Oregon, and started a paper, the *New Northwest*. Most of the family was involved in its production. Abigail became a successful writer and editor, and remarked that if she were a man, she would have a title and salary. Her principles of "Free Speech, Free Press, Free People" dictated much of the content. This included discussing the treatment of Chinese, American Indian policies, the Temperance and Prohibition movement, and especially the push for woman's suffrage and bettering the legal status of women. She was a tireless advocate for women's rights in Oregon. She also traveled extensively throughout the Pacific Northwest, expressing personal interest in seeing Washington and Idaho grant woman's suffrage, and aiding other state and territorial campaigns as well as national suffragists.

Duniway's efforts and her *New Northwest* newspaper were in contest with her brother Harvey's newspaper, the *Oregonian*. This contentious feud culminated in 1884, when Harvey's campaign against equal suffrage temporarily triumphed.

In November 1912, Oregon voters approved women's suffrage by 52 percent. On November 30, as a symbol of Duniway's long suffrage legacy, Oregon's Governor West asked her to write and sign Oregon's Equal Suffrage Proclamation, cementing the new law. While she died before seeing the Nineteenth Amendment passed, Duniway's influence throughout the Western suffrage movement was vast.

Idaho suffragists would need the Idaho Mormons' help if they were to succeed this time. Their money, their lended labor, and the example of a successful neighboring state to add peer pressure could be the fuel needed to bring
Idaho to the finish line. And as Emmeline greeted each of the visiting ladies
with Anthony and Stanton, the irony descended thickly upon her: she knew
that over the next few days of the Rocky Mountain Suffrage Conference,
Anthony would ask her audience, the predominantly Mormon women of Utah,
to support the suffrage campaign of the state that had so recently stripped
their own men of their innate rights as citizens. Would they be willing to put
past hurts aside? How far would the Mormon women of Utah be willing to go
to aid the neighbors who had turned their own backs in a time of need?

Anthony and Shaw were famished by the time the crowd made its way
to the hotel's ballroom, which was set for an elaborate breakfast for forty.
While the special guests found their comfortable seats and full plates,
Emmeline scanned the room for one woman in particular she wanted to
greet personally: Mrs. Amalia Post.

Wyoming's 1869 suffrage bill didn't only enfranchise women and allow
them to run for public office, opening the doors to Esther Hobart Morris's
stint as justice of the peace. It had also opened the door to women serving
on juries. Shortly after Seraph Young cast her first ballot in Utah in 1870,
Mrs. Post was one of five women to serve on the first jury open to female
jurors. Additionally, Post served as the foreman of that jury, cementing
her own star in the historical firmament. Unlike Morris, who shied away
from the spotlight and further engagement with the suffrage movement
after her service as justice of the peace, Post remained a significant force
on behalf of Wyoming and the women of the nation. In fact, her advocacy
skills were put to good use very quickly after her jury service, when the
next session of the Wyoming Territorial Legislature toyed with repealing
the equal suffrage the previous session had bestowed.

A bill drafted to revoke the right landed on Governor Campbell's desk
in March 1871, and it lay there, reminiscent of the first bill (designed to
grant the right) that had lain there just eighteen months earlier. Over
the course of the eighteen-month experiment with equal suffrage in

Wyoming, Campbell's initial hesitations about women's political abilities had been settled and he personally had become firmly convinced of their value and aptitude for politics. Still, he had to consider the forces behind the bill of revocation, and he paused before automatically vetoing the bill. Post, in a personal appeal to Campbell, induced him to veto the bill, which he eventually did wholeheartedly. "I came here opposed to woman suffrage," he told Post. "But the eagerness and fidelity with which you and your friends have performed political duties, when called upon to act, has convinced me that you deserve to enjoy those rights."

The vetoed bill then went back to the legislature, where the legislators determined that they would override the governor's veto. Post was also credited with lobbying the legislators so that when the vetoed bill returned to the floor, the legislators would vote against the override. The attempt to override the governor's veto passed the House but failed by one vote in the territorial senate—a vote cast by Senator Foster. In one of the rare cases of American history where a single vote truly made a difference, women's political rights in Wyoming were secured for good.

Emmeline sighted Post across the room. Now sixty-nine, Post was only two years away from death. She had stayed active in the national suffrage scene for the intervening decades, and had come from Cheyenne to be feted as a celebrity by Emmeline and Miss Anthony.

She was tended on either side by two other Wyoming luminaries. Miss Estelle Reel, the State Superintendent of Public Instruction, was the first woman that Wyoming voters ever elected to public office. Described by one newspaper as "one of the best educated and most brilliant women in the state," there was even talk of Reel running for governor of Wyoming in the future. Mrs. Therese A. Jenkins was another Wyoming celebrity: a popular writer and speaker, Jenkins was the only woman to speak at the celebration of Wyoming's statehood in 1890, and she continued her work by supporting the recent suffrage campaigns in Colorado and Kansas.

Jenkins repositioned Post's shawl over the back of her chair, and Reel shook out a napkin, placing it on the older woman's lap as Emmeline approached.

"Mrs. Post," gushed Emmeline, extending her hand and kissing the seated woman on the cheek. Even though the women were similar ages,

ESTELLE REEL

Born 1862 in Pittsfield, Illinois
Died August 2, 1959, in Yakima, Washington

Estelle Reel was educated in Boston, St. Louis, and Chicago. She moved to Wyoming in 1886 and campaigned to be elected as the school superintendent of Laramie County in 1890. As a single woman in her twenties, Reel was criticized for traveling around the county without a chaperone, but she was successfully elected.

In 1894, Reel ran as the Republican nominee for the Wyoming Superintendent of Public Instruction. Although Wyoming had granted equal suffrage to women twenty-five years earlier, no woman had ever held a statewide elected position. Reel was elected to the position, making her the first Wyoming woman to be elected to a state-wide office, and one of the first in the country. In this position, she increased funding for schools through careful budgeting and investments. While she attempted to standardize curriculum and establish free distribution of textbooks, neither of these goals was fulfilled during her term, largely due to lack of funds from the state.

Around 1898, she was promoted to be the National Superintendent of Indian Schools under U.S. President William McKinley, becoming the first woman to be confirmed for a federal office by the U.S. Senate. However, like many of her contemporaries, she viewed Native Americans as inferior beings, and she opted for a "practical" pre-professional curriculum, rather than a liberal arts focus, as she believed they would likely be involved in labor for employment.

In 1910, Reel abandoned public life, resigning her federal position, even though she was pressured to run for governor of Wyoming. She did not believe a woman would be taken seriously as a candidate. Instead, she married Cort Meyer, a rancher and farmer in Washington. She was in her late forties and never sought a public position again.

Post looked frail as she sat at the well-appointed breakfast table in one of the Templeton Hotel parlors. At her elbows, Estelle Reel and Therese Jenkins also looked up to greet Emmeline.

"Mrs. Wells. So lovely to see you again. You know Mrs. Reel and Mrs. Jenkins? Please, won't you sit down?" Post gestured to an open seat at their table.

After warm greetings were exchanged between the four ladies, Post turned to Emmeline. "I believe the last opportunity I had to visit with you was in Washington, D.C., in 1891. Four years ago, am I correct? The annual convention of the National American Woman Suffrage Association?"

"Yes, of course I remember, Mrs. Post," replied Emmeline. "That convention was particularly memorable for me because we drafted a constitution for the new International Women's Press Association. That experience inspired me to start a local Women's Press Club here in Utah when I returned home, which has been quite successful in exposing and training our women here to enter journalistic fields."

Post nodded her head in acknowledgment. "Ah, yes, it is an interesting instinct we have—to work on a national level, but then bring those same ideas home with us and implement them on a local level too. It's rather a symbol of this whole great work we are engaged in, is it not? We work for the welfare of women across the nation, but ultimately the only thing we really know how to do is serve the people we live among."

"I'm not sure I would put it so dryly, Mrs. Post," interjected Jenkins, a talented writer and orator who was younger than both Mrs. Post and Emmeline, but not too shy to speak her mind. "I have recently participated in the campaigns in Colorado and Kansas, and although not a native of either, I feel I did much good for the cause in both places."

"I do not doubt that in the least, Mrs. Jenkins," replied Post, placing a maternal hand on Jenkins's. "Do not misunderstand me. I mean simply that those of us who know our people and our lands best should always be entrusted with the scepter of leadership in those communities. There is value in Miss Anthony and Mrs. DeVoe, for instance, aiding our efforts and serving as a unifying force. But as Mrs. Wells just reminded us, locally led efforts often strike the heart more effectively."

Emmeline knew Post was getting at the sentiment that nagged at many western delegates there that very morning: while Anthony and Shaw were admired for their work, were they a necessary ingredient for success? Would Wyoming, Colorado, and Utah have had the triumphs they did even without their oversight? What did the National American Woman Suffrage Association add that the Utah Territorial Woman Suffrage Association— or the Colorado Woman Suffrage Association or the Idaho Woman Suffrage Association—could not provide?

Emmeline felt defensive of Anthony and the NAWSA. Legitimacy with Anthony and among the NAWSA had been hard-won for her Utah women, and they treasured the approval and embrace of the national organization after feeling ostracized from the broader suffrage movement for so long. The visits of the national representatives had allowed the Utahns to feel like they were part of something bigger than themselves, that they were accepted and even admired in the midst of their tensions with Congress.

"I recently attended the annual NAWSA conference in Atlanta, Mrs. Post," Emmeline began her defense, "and Mrs. Carrie Catt promised all of us that the national organization committee would respect the desires of the state associations, and will never put an organizer in the field without the cooperation of the state associations. We have found that to be true here in Utah. Mrs. Caine and Mrs. Richards started our Utah Territorial Woman Suffrage Association some time ago, and we now have suffrage associations in almost every county of Utah. They function aptly on their own, but we benefit from the national sorority we enjoy.

"I have heard," Emmeline continued, "that Mrs. DeVoe in particular is a strong orator and has a unique ability to stir an audience. I can imagine she will be an asset as she goes into Idaho next. But I have never worked on a campaign outside of Utah myself and must defer to Mrs. Jenkins to speak in further defense of the practice."

"Of course you are right, Mrs. Wells, that Miss Anthony in particular has done a great deal to support your efforts here in Utah," conceded Post warmly. "I mean to take nothing away from you or from Mrs. Jenkins here. But," Post smiled slyly at her small audience while a teasing tone shaded her next words, "after Misses Anthony and Shaw have asked you ladies of Utah to pay for their campaigns in Idaho and California with your own hard-earned money, we might chat again."

CHAPTER 8

Will freedom return to the land of the west,
And in Utah's sweet valleys find welcome and rest?
Shall we woo her in vain, in vain her implore
To visit our hearths and the suffrage restore?
Will she suffer her daughters as serfs to remain,
Or give them their rights and the suffrage again?

"Where Is the Suffrage Gone?," by M. A. Y. Greenhalgh,
from the *Utah Woman Suffrage Songbook*

Sunday, May 12, 1895
11:00 a.m.

After the breakfast rejuvenated the travelers, they reboarded the Utah Drag for a more complete tour of the city. This time, the group consisted almost entirely of women visiting from out of town: Anthony and Shaw in the front, in the places of honor occupied by Emmeline and Kimball earlier that morning; the Colorado delegation of Stansbury and Bradford; the Wyoming delegation of Post, Jenkins, and Reel; and Mrs. Emma DeVoe, the floating NWSA representative now tasked with overseeing the Idaho campaign. Women from Montana, Kansas, Oregon, and more also joined the group, hosted once again by Emmeline and several hand-selected Utah women who Emmeline felt represented the breadth and quality of the Utah delegation.

On one of the omnibus's first stops, the driver halted the horses in front of the Constitution Building on Main Street, which housed the offices of the *Woman's Exponent*. This was the newspaper where Emmeline had worked since shortly after Anthony's first visit to the city in 1871 and that she now edited. Emmeline had thought briefly of having her team of editors and copyists hard at work when this scheduled stop of the tour occurred. She'd envisioned proudly waving Anthony into a newsroom pulsing with the excavations of woman journalists, digging for the latest story and uncovering the most pointed opinions. She had imagined the look on Anthony's face when she encountered a room full of professional women. Yes, some of them were lowly typesetters, looking up to Emmeline and the paper's former editor Lula Greene Richards as mentors and inspirations. But the sheer impact of running an enterprise consisting entirely of women never tired Emmeline. Considering, however, that it was a Sunday morning, Emmeline let her ethics and observance of the Sabbath day be her guide. Emmeline knew how to put on a good show when needed, and a roomful of woman journalists would be a good show, but she also knew where to draw the line with salesmanship. A staged Sunday morning newsroom would be inauthentic. And so, while it was tempting, Emmeline put her vision aside.

The party of ladies stepped into the quiet newsroom, as it had been left on Friday afternoon, ready to take up its duties again on Monday morning. But Anthony caught the vision just the same.

"You mean to tell me this entire room is filled with professional women during the week?" queried Anthony, with the kind of impressed rise in her voice that Emmeline had wished for.

"Indeed! And we employ young girls who are interested in learning the trade. You'll see the presses here in the back." She led the party to a back room crowded with the hulking printing machines. "Here, we produce our eight-page paper every two weeks. Our subscribers are of course mostly here in Utah, but we send our little paper to both coasts. We endeavor to speak freely on every topic of current interest, and on every subject as it arises in which the women of Utah and the great sisterhood the world over are specially interested."

"It is of course dedicated to forwarding the purposes of the Relief Society and of your church, is it not?"

"Yes, the paper provides the voice for our women and for the Relief Society as an institution. It did not start as such, but it has become the official instrument by which we defend ourselves from calumnious attacks and put forth a vision for humanity that draws inspiration from our faith. If we Mormon women are to be better understood, we must develop bonds of expression among ourselves, as well as have a tool to express the way we see the world."

Emmeline felt compelled to detail for her guests just how comprehensive the newspaper's offering could be. It included everything from recipes to household tips to poetry, editorials, and investigations into the most prominent social issues of the day. Its editorials, and especially Emmeline's contributions, drove home the need for women to be financially, emotionally, and educationally independent. Emmeline's editorials were a main reason she had become one of the most famous women in Utah. The previous month, for instance, Emmeline's pen had struck as bitingly as ever when she wrote, "It is pitiful to see how men opposed to woman suffrage try to make the women believe it is because they worship them so, and think them far too good. . . . Let us hope the practical experience that will come with the ballot may convince even them that good may follow and they and their children receive the benefit of what they could not discern in the future progress of the world."

Anthony picked up a copy of the paper lying on a nearby desk. "I've seen this masthead so many times," she reflected as she perused the front page. "'The Rights of the Women of Zion, and the Rights of the Women of All Nations,'" she read. "My dear Emmeline, it is impossible to estimate the advantage this little paper gave to the women of this far western territory. From its first issue it was the champion of our cause, and by exchanging with women's papers of the United States and England, it brings news of women in all parts of the world to Utah, and brings your triumphs to them." It was a formal little speech, but Emmeline was not one to feign humility in the face of a compliment. She beamed at her friend's praise. It almost made her feel that the painful struggles of the past decades had all been worth that moment's recognition.

LOOKING BACK

Emmeline had signed on to the staff of the *Woman's Exponent* soon after the transformative experience of Anthony's 1871 visit to Salt Lake City. In 1875, Emmeline was still using Blanche Beechwood as her pen name, but she had gained enough confidence to assume an associate editorship. The founding editor Louisa Greene's marriage and the subsequent death of her first two infants made it necessary for her to accept assistance in her role, and Emmeline moved into the apprenticeship eagerly. By 1877, she was the publication's main editor. She was forty-nine years old.

When Emmeline became editor of the *Woman's Exponent*, she also assumed something of a dual personality that would mark her writing for the rest of her life. Abandoning Blanche Beechwood, she took up a new pen name, Aunt Em, under which she would author eighty-seven sentimental articles and seventy-one poems for the *Exponent*. Aunt Em's contributions were personal in nature, never political—exercises in emotive expression and flowery language. Editorials written under the name of Emmeline B. Wells, in contrast, were the furthest things from trifles.

In the late 1870s and early 1880s, while Utah and Wyoming women were in a golden age of political freedom, participating in civic life in ways no other American women were doing, Emmeline took it on herself to build bridges with other suffrage leaders around the country and do what she could to advocate for the expansion of the rights she enjoyed. She also recognized the opportunity to represent her church and defend Mormon women to influential people around the nation.

She strategically subscribed to dozens of papers around the nation, taking up correspondence with their editors. The *Woman's Journal*, the paper out of New York that was founded by Henry Blackwell and his wife Lucy Stone as a voice for the American Woman Suffrage Association, and the only suffrage newspaper to exist longer than the *Woman's Exponent*, was a particular target of Emmeline's correspondence. The AWSA, as rival to Anthony's NWSA, was not friendly to the Mormon polygamists, and Emmeline saw it as her special cause to use the written word to convince Stone and Blackwell how wrong they were to disavow the Mormon women. In her correspondence, she offered the women of Utah as exhibits for how successful women's civic participation could be: the sky had not fallen in, children had not been abandoned, men still had dinner on their tables. She offered the Utah experiment as a source of national pride that all those engaged in the cause could look to and desire to emulate.

The golden era of women voting in Utah, however, was short-lived. The federal government's anti-polygamy legislation did not end with the Cullom Bill of 1870, despite the neat trick of Utah's female enfranchisement. The anti-polygamy legislation only intensified in the years following the women's civic liberation. In fact, women's voting rights simply became a pawn through which Washington, D.C., could sanction Utah for its barbarous behavior.

Throughout the 1870s and 1880s, members of the Church consistently battled efforts by Congress to handicap the LDS Church and squeeze Church leaders into abolishing polygamy. A particular target was the enfranchisement of the Utah women—a point of pride, Congress knew, for the Mormon leaders. Would the Mormon male leaders sacrifice polygamy or their voting women first? Congress bet the voting women would be the first to go.

The women of the LDS Church were not idle as these threats mounted. They understood the anti-polygamy and disenfranchisement bills as direct threats to not only their voting rights but also to the survival of the Church and to the ability of their men to lead as they believed. Some of the bills included disenfranchisement and also economic and political sanctions against the Church. For the Latter-day Saint women, fighting for the right to keep their vote was intertwined with the fight to keep worshiping as they wanted. They circulated petitions around the state, upped their output of national editorials and correspondence, and became even more engaged in the national suffrage organizations than before. Emmeline's editorials in the *Woman's Exponent* tackled head-on the subjugation of women outside the limited sphere of local Utah politics: "So long has custom tyrannized over women to keep her in subjection that it will only be by small degrees women themselves can comprehend the advantages arising from the progress of independence of thought and action, a knowledge for themselves." Woman is determined, she continued, "to attain to an equality with man and to train herself to fill any position and place of trust and honor as appropriately and with as much dignity as her brother man." What a woman wants, Emmeline argued, is to be "recognized as a responsible being, capable of judging for and maintaining herself, and standing upon just as broad, brand and elevated a platform as man."

The Utah women's efforts were tentatively supported by the National Woman Suffrage Association and by Anthony herself. In 1878, Emmeline was appointed to the Advisory Board of Anthony's NWSA. Other officers of the organization, such as Sara Andrews Spencer, the NWSA secretary, publicly defended the Latter-day Saint women, drawing ridicule from national media. In 1879, Emmeline and Zina Young Williams made the first of many trips back east to attend a national suffrage convention. At that convention, Spencer addressed the Utah women's polygamy head-on by commenting that polygamy was "preferable to the licensed social evil [i.e., extramarital affairs] which is being advocated by many of our bloated public men." She noted that those not in the Church had hoped the women of Utah would use the vote to "discourage the plurality of wives.... Now that these women do not vote to suit [the anti-polygamists], they want to disenfranchise them."

Despite the cordial embrace by the national leaders of the NWSA, Emmeline, Zina Williams, and the other Utah women who attended national gatherings still felt the eyes of their colleagues on them. "Dear me," Zina Williams wrote in her diary. "What an awful thing to be an Elephant. The ladies all look at me so queer." That weight hung over every bridge-building effort Emmeline and her Mormon colleagues engaged in during this time of uncertainty and precious alliances.

Emmeline and her colleagues also went directly to the lawmakers themselves. During their 1879 visit to Washington, D.C., Emmeline and Zina pled their case before the House Judiciary Committee, individual senators and congressional committee members, and even before the president of the United States himself, Rutherford B. Hayes. Hayes showed "kindly sympathy" to the two Latter-day Saints, and seemed genuinely "pained" when the women explained that anti-polygamy legislation would "make fifty thousand women outcasts and their children illegitimate." A private visit with his wife, Lucy Hayes, prompted Emmeline to record in her journal, "Her sympathy seemed to be with us." But within a year of the visit, both President Hayes and his wife offered their personal support to anti-polygamy legislation and organizations. It was a hard blow for the Mormon women.

Polygamy continued to be the radical experiment no one else could get behind, even while the Utah Mormons progressively bent socially prescribed gender parameters on a number of other fronts. To those on the outside, even those interested in progressive social developments, it was all very interesting that women were first admitted to the legal bar in Utah in 1872, the same year Brigham Young encouraged women to attend eastern medical

ZINA D. H. YOUNG

Born January 31, 1821, in Watertown, New York
Died August 28, 1901, in Salt Lake City, Utah

Zina Huntington joined The Church of Jesus Christ of Latter-day Saints as a teenager in 1835. She married Henry Bailey Jacobs in 1841. In that same year, after multiple proposals, she also became a plural wife to the Prophet Joseph Smith. She was still married to Jacobs and had two children with him, but he was constantly called on missions. After Smith was martyred, she entered into a polygamous marriage with Brigham Young in 1846. Her marriage to Jacobs was then considered annulled, despite the lack of legal proceedings.

Zina Young became a schoolteacher and midwife. She helped raise the children of Young's other wives besides her own. She established the Deseret Hospital in 1882 and served on the board and as president. She was deeply involved in the temperance and women's suffrage movements in Utah, and participated in an NWSA conference in New York as well as the Women's Conference in Buffalo in 1881–1882. Young was a proficient nurse and encouraged other women in the medical field. She became the third General President of the Relief Society in 1888 and served as the vice president of the Utah National Council for Women in 1891. She was also the matron of the Salt Lake Temple from 1893 until her death in 1901.

schools so they could provide a high standard of medical care in the territory. Utah's schools admitted women as students, faculty members, and even
as trustees at an unusual rate. As one visitor to Salt Lake commented, "They
close no career on a woman in Utah by which she can earn a living." These
nondomestic careers were made possible in part by polygamy's shifting of
the traditional gender model, where plural wives were the heads of their own
households and sometimes freed from domestic duties to pursue their own
careers. But as interesting as these other developments continued to be, the
specter of a practice that was so repugnant to Victorian moral values could
never be brushed aside. It lay over the Salt Lake Valley as a heavy thundercloud that neither outsiders could ignore nor the people themselves could
blow away.

Eventually, the thundercloud erupted. The tense dance the Territory
of Utah and the U.S. Congress had engaged in since the Collum Bill of 1870
came to a chaotic end in 1882. In March of that year, Congress passed the
Edmunds Act, which disenfranchised all polygamists—men and women—in
the Territory of Utah. This included Emmeline. While the psychological blow
to the polygamist Utah women who had voted for twelve years was severe,
Emmeline tried to demonstrate graciousness in their setback. In an editorial
from that dark time, she recommitted herself and the women of Utah to re-
gaining the vote for all Utah women and working for the enfranchisement of
all American women. She appealed to the universal political, economic, and
social benefits of voting for all communities, not just her own. "It is not alone
because of unjust taxation and a desire to stand equal with their husbands
and brothers, but it is for the better protection of the home, the foundation
of all good government that women are asking and interceding for political
rights." From 1870 to 1882, Utah women had led the nation with the largest
number of voters in the country. Now, that distinction was stripped from
them, and it was just a presage of things to come.

Characteristically, the Mormon women did not take these blows lying
down. The indignation meetings were resurrected, needed once again to
draw public favor to a group that was increasingly vilified in the national
press and challenged in their own land. As in the earlier indignation meetings, the female speakers at the later mass meetings expressed outrage at
the national government for interfering with what they believed were their

rights of religious freedom. A particularly large meeting on May 6, 1886, was advertised through local newspapers to "the ladies of the Church of Jesus Christ of Latter-day Saints" as an opportunity "to protest against the indignities and insults heaped on their sex . . . and also against the disfranchisement of those who are innocent of breaking any law." At the gathering, fifteen women spoke to the two thousand guests gathered at the Salt Lake Theater. Nine additional talks were published with the proceedings in a pamphlet entitled, "Mormon Women's Protest: An Appeal for Freedom, Justice and Equal Rights."

Mary Isabella Horne opened the 1886 meeting with some of the most forceful public language yet shared by the Mormon women of Utah: "Must we, women of the Church of Jesus Christ of Latter-day Saints, still submit to insults and injury without raising our voices against it? And why are we thus persecuted? Because we choose to unite ourselves to honorable, God-fearing men, who, in virtue, honor, integrity and faithfulness to the marriage vow, stand head and shoulders above Federal officials who ply our brethren with questions regarding their future conduct which is without precedent in the annals of court proceedings. We all feel the insults offered our sisters when brought into court and forced to answer indecent questions by threats of fine and imprisonment. And we do most solemnly protest against further legislative enactments to disfranchise a whole community, who have committed no crime, only for religious belief." Dr. Romania Pratt, a graduate of a Philadelphia medical school and a plural wife, declared, "Hand in hand with [plural marriage] is the elevation of women." Another pioneering physician, Dr. Ellis R. Shipp, concurred with, "We are accused of being down-trodden and oppressed. We deny the charge!"

After the meeting, the women prepared a pamphlet that included transcripts of many of the speeches. They also wrote a resolution to formally declare their position. They distributed both pieces to eastern media and suffrage counterparts in a last-ditch effort to speak beyond their local community, to both the federal leaders in Washington, D.C., and the national suffrage leaders. As before, it was an effort to represent themselves as intelligent, autonomous agents who were not pawns of male religious leaders. The women intended to show the healthy growth that had come to their community through women's civic engagement and to renew their commitment to the national cause even in their besieged state. Again, Emmeline was sent to Washington, this time with Dr. Ellen B. Ferguson, to personally deliver the memorial to Congress and President Grover Cleveland. Emmeline noted, "I walked into the White House... where we sat about an hour and a quarter waiting our turn to speak to the President of the United States. Shortly after twelve o'clock we presented to him our credentials and the Memorial of the women of Utah Territory, and had an opportunity of stating to him some facts and incidents relating to the abuses and outrages perpetrated in the name of law." The president reportedly responded to the women, "I wish you out there could be like the rest of us." The women did not take this as a hopeful sign.

They were right to worry. In 1887, the next blow came. The Edmunds-Tucker Act was signed into law. All Utah women—Mormon and non-Mormon, polygamous and monogamous—were now disenfranchised, along with all polygamous men. Seventeen years after the first female vote, only Utah men—and this time only monogamous Utah men—could vote. The Church, its polygamous members, and now all Utahns were beleaguered by the increasingly harsh sanctions designed to eradicate what federal authorities considered the moral cancer of polygamy. The law inspired new energy surrounding the federal authorities' campaign against polygamous husbands. Polygamous men were imprisoned, forced to select a single legal wife, and children from other wives were placed in legal limbo as neither full heirs nor full bastards. Wives were forced to testify against their husbands, or hide if they refused. Homes could be searched at any time; mock trials condemned men to long sentences and high fines. It was a time of constant movement among the Latter-day Saints, as many women moved frequently, leaving Utah for places as far away as Mexico and Canada, going into hiding to escape jail. The outcast women and children of which Emmeline had prophesied to President Hayes were now a reality.

Whereas Utah had previously had one political goal—achieving statehood—they now added another to its ranks: restoring civic rights to their women. To Emmeline and the other Utah suffragists, only combining the two goals was acceptable. Suffrage must accompany statehood. And both must come soon.

CHAPTER 9

Like a whirlwind approaching, vile laws now are pending,
If passed, all the pillars of freedom will shake;
"Our cause is most just," yet it claims such defending;
"The women of Mormondom" needs must awake.
Thus, we humbly petition Columbia's nation,
To frown on oppression, and harsh legislation.
Our foes trouble little, or nothing to mention,
For "poor Mormon women," or "down-trodden wives."
Were polygamy only the bone of contention,
The "Mormons" might vote all the rest of their lives.
Our foes may not count us smart, sensible folks;
But we see through their purpose—contempt it provokes.
We prize not their pity, whose aim is to plunder
A people who strictly to peace are inclined;
If the "Mormons" lose patience need any one wonder,
Who considers our wrongs, by the crafty designed.
Yet they'll harvest disgrace where they hope for renown,
Who for power or place thrust the innocent down.
We appeal to the people in freedom's dominions—
To the fair-minded millions who love what is right;
Must the "Mormons" be robbed for their faith and opinions—
Crush'd and ground, 'twixt the millstones of greed and of spite?
Is it needful or lawful to wrest freedom from us
For what we believe, or for what we can't promise?
Our honor is priceless, our rights are all precious,
Our affections are sacred, our households are dear;
Our husbands are heroes, in spite of the specious

And wonderful (?) rulings of judges so queer,
Who shift their decisions, around and around,
Till for "Mormons" a verdict of "guilty" is found.
"Give the 'Mormons' Their Rights," by Emily Hill Woodmansee, 1886

Sunday, May 12, 1895
Noon

There was one woman among the gathering of eager hostesses that Sunday afternoon who did not descend the omnibus to visit the offices of the illustrious *Woman's Exponent*. While the other two dozen or so women disembarked from the Utah Drag and crowded into the newsroom to hear Emmeline tout her famous paper to their special guests, Mrs. Jennie Froiseth kept her place on the omnibus's bench. When she did not file down the rickety platform steps, as the others had, she received a few glances, and several companions inquired after her wellness, but none questioned her decision to stay behind. They knew why she chose to sit out a visit to Emmeline's precious paper. It was she, Jennie Froiseth, who had penned its rival.

———— ✿ ————

LOOKING BACK

Froiseth, a well-educated Irish woman whose husband's engagement with the U.S. Army brought the couple to Salt Lake City, felt like the vast mountains exiled her from intellectual associations and stimulating society. During a trip to New York in 1875 to visit family and friends, Froiseth had the opportunity to meet Julia Ward Howe, famed author of the words to "The Battle Hymn of the Republic," who urged Froiseth to follow the lead of many Eastern women in creating a women's club for literature and continuing learning. Froiseth heeded the advice upon returning to Salt Lake City; she founded the Blue Tea, whose "purpose was to organize exclusively for women . . . to promote mental culture." The club met in Froiseth's well-appointed living room at Rose Cottage, her Salt Lake City home on 600 South just west of Main Street.

The society was limited to twenty-five members, due only, Froiseth explained, to the constraints of their meeting area. The wife of the territorial governor was invited to be one of the earliest members, along with other wives of government officials, businessmen, mining operators, and merchants. They were Presbyterians, Methodists, Unitarians, Congregationalists, and Jews. They were not Mormons. No active Mormon was allowed to be a member.

Three years after the founding of the Blue Tea, in 1878, several members lobbied for a larger membership that could embrace more of the non-LDS women who craved weekly discussions and literary study. Jennie was not interested in swelling the ranks, and the other women broke off to form the Ladies' Literary Club. Eventually, the tensions created by the split softened, and the clubs fostered a productive organizational environment for strategizing effective tactics to abolish the women's common enemy: polygamy.

For Victorian-era women who were raised in Europe, like Jennie, or on the East Coast, like many of the clubs' members, living among a people who were consumed with religious devotion and still overcoming wounds of violent persecution must have been an otherworldly experience. On top of the theocratic kingdom-building into which they had landed, the Mormon women seemed not only alien in their practice of—and defense of—plural marriage, but dangerous and antagonistic to the standards of civilization. A battle to preserve the "holy modern home" was not only a battle for the future of the American frontier, but it was also a battle to preserve their understanding of what it meant to be a civilized woman. It was their very identities that were at stake. If they sought to understand or sympathize with the Mormon women's defense of polygamy, they would betray the ideals that held up their homes, their countries of origin, and their ancient faiths. Thus, as Froiseth explained to the *Salt Lake Tribune*, "On moral grounds, there can be no affiliation" between Mormons and non-Mormons.

The Blue Tea and the Ladies' Literary Club provided the raw materials needed to form the Anti-Polygamy Society, whose stated purpose was "to fight to the death that system which so enslaves and degrades our sex, and which robs them of so much happiness." In April 1880, Froiseth drove the founding of a newspaper, the *Anti-Polygamy Standard*, which functioned as the official organ of the Anti-Polygamy Society. It was an eight-page monthly with an annual subscription price of one dollar. Each issue of the *Standard*

JENNIE ANDERSON FROISETH

Born December 6, 1843 (or 1849), in Ballyshannon, Ireland
Died February 7, 1930, in Salt Lake City, Utah

Jane "Jennie" Anderson Froiseth worked to create a space for non-Mormon women in Utah and upheld her beliefs in rights for women. She emigrated from her home in Ireland to New York when she was young. In 1870 she moved to Utah, where she married Bernard Froiseth and had five children. Together, they built the Rose Cottage to host national celebrities and hold important social and political meetings. In 1875, Froiseth founded "Blue Tea," an exclusive, non-Mormon, literary women's club. She often felt there were too few opportunities for "Gentile" women in Utah. This paved the way for the Anti-Polygamy Society in 1878, for which she served as vice president. She also worked as editor of the *Anti-Polygamy Standard.*

Jennie traveled around the nation and spread anti-polygamy sentiment. She saw polygamy as a fundamental block to women's rights. While she was a strong proponent of suffrage, her ideals often clashed in Utah. She publicly opposed the enfranchisement of Utah as long as polygamy was upheld. This included refusing to participate in the Utah chapter of the NWSA. However, once polygamy was officially banned in 1890, she became involved in helping encourage women's participation in politics. She worked with her former rival Emmeline B. Wells and built up the Republican Party in Utah. She also supported the creation of safe spaces for the elderly and orphans, as well as a children's daycare. Froiseth worked for women's equality and elevation in social and political spheres, and strove to provide opportunities for all women in Utah.

carried as its motto the biblical verse "Let every man have his own wife, and let every woman have her own husband" (1 Corinthians 7:2) and a call to action to the "Women of America" written by Harriet Beecher Stowe: "Let every happy wife and mother who reads these lines give her sympathy, prayers and effect to free her sisters from this degrading bondage [of polygamy]. Let the womanhood of the country stand united for them. These are a power combined enlightened sentiment and sympathy, before which every form of injustice and cruelty must finally go down." The *Standard* published articles on the Society's history, the activities of the Blue Tea, advice for homemakers, and the missionary efforts of various Protestant churches in the territory. Primarily, it published numerous exposés of polygamy, such as "How Wives Are Coerced into Giving Consent for their Husbands to Enter Polygamy."

In 1882, Froiseth published *Women of Mormonism*, which republished many of the newspaper's exposés for a larger, national audience. Thousands of copies were sold from three different printings throughout the 1880s. Froiseth took up an East Coast book tour, promoting the stories of domestic unhappiness she had collected and marshalling support for the national anti-polygamy movement. The *Anti-Polygamy Standard* itself was not a financial success, and Froiseth had to close its doors in 1883. Working "in the midst of the enemy's camp," Froiseth wrote, made it impossible for the paper to "struggle against fearful odds."

But Froiseth's stance against the Mormon women of Utah did not mean that she herself did not want the right to participate in public, civic life. As a Utah woman, she enjoyed the right to vote, thanks to the 1870 enfranchisement, the entire time she was leading the Blue Tea and the Anti-Polygamy Society and publishing the *Anti-Polygamy Standard*. But in the Mormon women's vote, Froiseth saw the propagation of the patriarchal dominance of Mormon men. Speaking to the *Salt Lake Tribune*, Froiseth explained that while she was a believer in woman's suffrage as a general principle, she did not believe in it for Utah, because of the "anomalous condition of affairs here, and because when tried before, it resulted so deplorably [because the Mormon women had not voted out polygamous elected officials]." Froiseth believed the Mormon women voted at the command—explicit or tacitly expected—of their husbands, and so the Utah female vote only served to prop up the Mormons' theocratic hegemony. With the vote, a Mormon woman "used her own mind no further than to remember her covenants and obey." Froiseth compounded this argument with the assertion that members of the Church looked to their President of the Church, the "head of their creed," as "the rightful sovereign of the earth," and that members were thus "disloyal" to the United States of America. In this, she echoed a common fear within the national press: that Latter-day Saint political strength was actually a conspiratorial and nefarious tool intended to subjugate American authority. The territory's frustratingly detached stance during the Civil War and as well as armed confrontations with the United States government, such as the 1857 "Utah War," stoked the flames of this argument.

Froiseth's complex position put her at odds with both the Latter-day Saint women she lived among in Utah and with some of the leaders of the National Woman Suffrage Association, of which she was a member. In the 1880s, at the height of Froiseth's anti-polygamy campaign, Emmeline had already established her friendship with Susan B. Anthony, and Anthony, as the leader of the NWSA, firmly supported Emmeline and her Mormon sisters' right to vote. Thus, even though she served in leadership positions for a time, Froiseth was not fully ideologically accepted into the NWSA because she advocated for the removal of suffrage rights for those very women Anthony praised. And of course, Froiseth was not welcomed into the ranks of the Utah voting women because the majority of them were Mormon. Nevertheless, she did not budge. She opposed suffrage for Mormon women—and if they could not be parsed out, all Utah women, herself included—until polygamy was abolished.

With the congressional legislation of 1882 (the Edmunds Act, disenfranchising polygamous women) and 1887 (the Edmunds-Tucker Act, disenfranchising all Utah women and polygamous men), Froiseth found her work rewarded, despite the fact that she herself was disenfranchised in 1887. But the Edmunds-Tucker Act had the ironic effect of making allies out of previous enemies: in 1887, all Utah women—both Mormon and non-Mormon, both polygamous and monogamous—were again on the same side of the suffrage cause: they had to win it back. Emmeline and Emily Richards used the opportunity to extend an olive branch to Froiseth, and in 1887, they approached Froiseth and sought her help to establish a Utah chapter of the

National Woman Suffrage Association. Froiseth refused on principle, but the door had been cracked opened for future collaboration.

That door of reconciliation and cooperation was thrown open in 1890, when LDS Church President Wilford Woodruff finally capitulated to mounting pressures to abandon plural marriage as a religious practice, issuing a Manifesto instructing Church members not to engage in polygamous marriages in the future. Although the Manifesto didn't solve the logistical complications of those in existing polygamous families, it removed the barrier to supporting Utah's female enfranchisement that Froiseth had clung to. Plural marriage as an official public practice by members of the Church was over.

Froiseth voiced the relief of the nation when the "foul blot" was finally eradicated. But for women who had grown up in the system of plural marriage and had come to terms with, and even cultivated, identities of otherness within the broader American culture, the transition did not come easily. Emmeline wrote in her journal that the new situation—the revoking of a way of life she had experienced since her teens—felt "peculiar" to her. Using a word—"peculiar"—to describe the future monogamous culture that others had used to describe her community's polygamous culture, Emmeline expressed confusion over the fact that there would no longer be "opportunity for married men to increase their families." Despite the psychological adjustments required by the community and the vast logistical complications of acknowledging (or not) the families of existing polygamous unions, the official end of plural marriage meant that new doors of collaboration and cooperation were thrown open to the Utah women.

The steps toward alliance were tentative but consistent. One of the most significant opportunities for the diverse women to finally work together came in 1893, at the Columbian World's Fair Exposition, held in Chicago. This World's Fair attracted twenty-seven million people from forty-six countries. It was one of the first major projects the women of Utah took on as a united front. Emmeline spent a month in Chicago at the Exposition with her fellow Utah delegates rehabilitating their image in the broader world. And it worked.

Three interwoven factors allowed the Utah women to come together in "a more universal sisterhood," as Emmeline described it, in time for the World's Fair. First, the 1890 Manifesto rescinding the practice of plural marriage lifted the most dramatic barrier between Mormon and non-Mormon

Utah women, allowing them to join forces in their advocacy, where before polygamy had stood in the way. Secondly, the political punishments for polygamy resulted in turmoil for the whole community. As plural marriages dissolved in divorce, plural wives were left husbandless and often destitute, men hid to avoid federal prosecution, and children of plural marriages were declared illegitimate. To the Mormons and the non-Mormons, the need for women to have recourse and their own independent means was more obvious than ever. Lastly, the issue of statehood continued to loom, and although the territory continued to petition Washington for the opportunity to draft a state constitution and join the Union, the possibility was closer than ever before since plural marriage no longer stood in the way.

Not only was this Exposition the first to involve women in administrative roles, but it was the first to include exhibits featuring women's talents and skills. The Utah women took advantage of the opportunity. In a very deliberate effort of unity between Mormon and non-Mormon Utah women, Alice J. Whalen and Margaret Blaine Salisbury, two non-Latter-day Saint women, were appointed to the national planning Board of Lady Managers, the official women's planning commission for the Exposition. Monogamous Mormon Emily S. Richards was appointed to lead the territorial Board of Lady Managers. Emmeline became the chair of the Salt Lake County Board of Lady Managers. About their ambitions for the fair, Salisbury stated, "The women of Utah are engaged in many branches of industry and we wish to make the best possible showing of their achievements in every line of labor, education, artistic, literary, benevolent, etc. It is important that we show… the conditions of the industrial women, their productions and earnings, whether in the studio, counting house, school room, factory, mill, dairy, or on the farm." Together, the Mormons and non-Mormons put aside their former tensions and put on a terrific show in Chicago.

The Utah women's physical exhibits were the result of years of planning and hundreds of women's efforts organized into highly structured and effective committees. There were exhibits featuring their paintings, drawings, sculptures, and hand-made china showing the refinement and elegance of the frontier society. Patented inventions and homemade furniture were accompanied by agricultural and mining samples to emphasize industry and productivity. Artifacts of native cultures added historical depth to the offering. And the women's musical performances and public speeches were prolific.

But one element of their exhibit outshone all others: the silks. While other states brought their silk handicrafts, the superiority of the Utah silks was "confirmed on all hands." It was reported that Utah's silk "stands easily at the head" of all the states and territories.

Brigham Young had imported the first mulberry trees, the trees needed to feed silkworms, from France in 1855, believing that a silk industry in Utah would be practical and would provide economic support to women who were also occupied with child-rearing. For decades, LDS women participated in hatching, tending, and feeding the worms and transforming their output into thread and then fabric through the Relief Society organizations around the territory. The monumental effort to produce such fine and high-quality material was a source of great pride, and the Utah women's multiple sets of silk curtains on display at the Exposition also included a display of the entire silk-making process. It earned them substantial recognition.

The Exposition experience fostered enhanced solidarity among the Utah women, binding a "vast army of [woman] workers" to the mutual goal of resecuring Utah women's suffrage as part of Utah's future statehood. United, they would now be a formidable force in reclaiming for themselves as a group what they had lost when divided.

Still, Froiseth, out of habit or the tenderness of old wounds, decided that she didn't need to subject herself to the lauding of the *Woman's Exponent*, the paper whose whole mission and message she had tried to counteract. Emmeline was a fine leader and effective figurehead for the suffrage cause in Utah. If the women of Utah were re-enfranchised, now in a post-polygamy era, Froiseth could even see partnering with Emmeline on certain lobbying efforts. But for now, today, on the street outside the *Exponent* office, Froiseth decided to wait in the carriage.

CHAPTER 10

I am sure that you, my dear sisters, who have not only tasted the sweets of liberty, but also the bitterness, the humiliation of the loss of the blessed symbol [of suffrage], will not allow the organic law of your state to be framed on the barbarism that makes women the political slaves of men. . . . Now in the formative period of your constitution is the time to establish justice and equality to all the people. That adjective "male" once admitted into your organic law, will remain there.

"Susan B. Anthony's Letter," *Woman's Exponent*, 1 and 15 August 1894

Sunday, May 12, 1895
1:00 in the afternoon

In addition to visiting the offices of the *Woman's Exponent* and Froiseth's Ladies' Literary Club nearby, Anthony and Shaw's formal tour of Salt Lake City included an introduction for Shaw, who was visiting the city for the first time, to the city's renowned grid system, which allowed a visitor or new resident to become oriented quickly to the streets' layout. A few days after arriving in the Salt Lake Valley in July of 1847, the Mormon pioneers had drawn plans for a city that would start from a central point and fan out in a grid system of ten-acre blocks. The central point was determined to be the place where the pioneers were going to build their temple. The "Base and Meridian," a small pillar, was fixed on August 3, 1847, as the point from which all city streets and buildings were to be named and numbered. Brigham Young reportedly touched his cane to the ground and said, "Here we will build the temple of our God." The point marked both the physical and metaphorical center of the new religion's Zion home: the temple that would eventually stand there represented all that was strange and beautiful and threatening about the Mormons, because of the eternally binding rites they believed took place within it. Thus, North Temple and South Temple, so named because of their orientation to the focal point, became two of the first streets laid out.

The thoroughness of the urban planning in such a slight western town was lauded from the beginning, but as the buildings and modern amenities grew up, the foresight of the early planners became even better known. Visitors to the city requested to make large U-turns in the middle of the streets, having heard about the uniquely wide streets that allowed a horse and buggy to easily turn around. Even the Utah Drag could make a tight turn on South Temple, and the driver performed this trick to the delight of its passengers. The tour included a drive by the Lion House and Beehive House, the two former residences of Brigham Young and his large family, recently turned into Church offices, as well as a pilgrimage to the City Hall, now called the Council Hall building, where Seraph Young had cast her first vote. That building had also been turned into offices—for the police department—and the city government had decamped to the new Salt Lake City and County building, which Emmeline pointed out as the ladies drove by.

"That new gothic structure will be the location of our meetings tomorrow morning. As you know, just a few weeks ago, it was the site of our greatest triumph."

"Oh, do share the details with us, Miss Emmeline!" burst Reverend Shaw, all dimples and energy. "Of course, we read accounts of the constitutional convention's proceedings, following as best we could. But full accounts in the Eastern papers were hard to come by, and it sounded like there were so many twists and turns!"

"I do hope I never have such heart palpitating moments ever again," agreed Emmeline, and she chose the most decisive moments to sketch for her guests.

LOOKING BACK

On March 4, 1895, about six weeks prior to the Utah Drag's Sunday afternoon tour of the city with its special guests on board, the wrestle of the past twenty-five years between Utah and the federal government seemed finally to be approaching its final bout. That day, 107 delegates—all men—chosen from Utah Territory's twenty-five counties, convened to start drafting a constitution for their proposed new state. Nothing was guaranteed; they had simply received permission from the federal government through an Enabling Act passed by Congress of the United States in July of 1894 to propose a constitution for the future State of Utah. The constitution would still need to be voted on by the people of Utah and signed by the president of the United States, Grover Cleveland. But after appealing to Congress six times previously, the Enabling Act seemed a miraculous opportunity the Utahns did not want to squander. The limitations of the 1887 Edmunds-Tucker Act were still in place throughout Utah Territory, but with the official ending of polygamy, Congress was finally ready to consider embracing the quirky place as one of its own.

On day one of the convention to draft the new state constitution, the delegates addressed the elephant in the room head on: their first order of business was to express that "perfect toleration of religious sentiment shall be secured, and that no inhabitant of said State shall ever be molested in person or property on account of his or her mode of religious worship: Provided, That polygamous or plural marriages are forever prohibited."

But a week into the deliberations, the Utah suffragists began to get nervous: not one of the 107 men had yet addressed the issue of whether female suffrage was to be included in the Utah state constitution. Between their indignation meetings and their editorials and their lobbying with their husbands and brothers and sons, the women had assumed suffrage—like plural marriage—would be addressed early on. Had they been wrong?

The irony of their situation was not lost on the women. Twenty-five years earlier, the fate of their civic participation had lain in the hands of an all-male territorial legislature. Those men had made a decision that lifted the Mormon polygamous Utah women to an esteemed but tortured realm: first to vote, but last to be understood. Seventeen years after they first voted, that right to vote, which had catapulted Utah women to the front of the national women's movement, was taken away, again by all men, this time in Washington, D.C. Now, they stood on the brink of statehood and their fate was once again in the hands of men. Without the freedom to vote as they once did, they could not help select the constitution's drafters. The all-male delegation assigned to write the new state's proposed constitution held the women's emancipation in their hands alone. But there was so much history now, so much baggage. Would they see women as intertwined with Utah's future as they had in the past?

In 1870, the vote had practically fallen into the women's laps. Not so this time. From the time they were disenfranchised by the Edmunds-Tucker Act in 1887 until the moment of the state constitutional convention in 1895, they had fought to regain their rights. By the time the delegates met to write the new state constitution, the Utah suffragists had established an overarching Utah Territorial Woman Suffrage Association, nineteen county suffrage associations, and several individual town associations. For Emmeline, the intervening years had brought constant travel around the territory to each of the suffrage associations, as well as back east to national conferences. She kept up active correspondences with national activists in addition to Anthony, including Lucy Stone and her husband Henry B. Blackwell, Belva Lockwood, Elizabeth Cady Stanton, and others. She had withstood internal challenges from her peers, such as Dr. Ellen Ferguson, who had staged a coup to displace Emmeline as the president of the Utah Territorial Woman Suffrage Association. She had managed to keep the Utah women's suffrage organizations united—not an easy feat in the face of many who wanted to take more militant and aggressive approaches than Emmeline was comfortable with. She had, in short, experienced "diamond cutting diamond," as she described this time, as women she admired grated against her and against each other in their disagreements. The experience plunged her into one of her dark moods and left her "very ill with my heart."

In effect, the Utah women had experienced the path to civic engagement backward. As they worked for suffrage rights a second time, they learned the lessons they should have learned originally, but hadn't been forced to. They had voted for seventeen years, from 1870 to 1887, without having gone through the crucible of organizing and struggling for that right. Because the majority of the suffragists' ranks in the 1870s were Latter-day Saints, they had not had to reconcile various demographics and opinions. The anti-polygamists were so outnumbered and out-represented in the territory's male political bastions that compromise and negotiation at home was not something the majority bloc had to confront seriously. Their struggles had been abroad, with Washington, not within their own borders. But now, with real strategy needed to win back the vote at this crucial moment of statehood, even the Mormon women were breaking ranks to put forward different approaches and preferences. According to Dr. Ferguson, Emmeline was too passive, too willing to trust the male delegates. She was too trusting of her Gentile (non-Mormon) friends, too caustic and strong-willed with other women. Others, like Dr. Ferguson and Emily Richards, preferred more confrontational, direct paths to getting the vote enshrined in the new state constitution.

Emmeline's approach prevailed. By the time the constitutional delegates were chosen and the convention was planned, Emmeline had managed to keep the various factions intact. None of the local suffrage associations in the counties or towns rebelled against her Utah Territorial Woman Suffrage Association leadership. No militant approaches were adopted widely. Her relationship-based, grassroots campaign to persuade delegates to reinstate women's rights remained the dominant strategy going into the convention. She expressed the hope in a letter to the Beaver County Woman Suffrage Association that "there will be a feeling of unity" among the territory's female leaders, as they approached the constitutional convention together. In fact, so confident was she of her strategy and of the ability of the women to finally come together that she accepted an invitation to attend a meeting of the National American Woman Suffrage Association in Atlanta, Georgia, in January 1895, just six weeks before the constitutional convention was set to begin. She felt that her work in Utah was done. Along with Marilla John Daniels of Provo and Aurelia Spencer Rogers of Farmington, she left for the East, confident the men—her Utah men—would once again deliver.

In Atlanta, Emmeline experienced none of the slanted glances and grotesque curiosity she had borne at previous national meetings. With the issue of plural marriage now settled among the national suffragists, she was seated next to Susan B. Anthony at the opening session for delegates. At the plenary session, she took ten minutes to report on the hopeful state of Utah's affairs and was deeply moved when, after she spoke, Anthony embraced her. The *Atlanta Evening Journal* reported that evening, "President Anthony came forward and putting her arm around [Emmeline] gave her endorsement of the speaker. As she told of the work being done in Utah she kept her arms around the delegate and the audience was visibly affected at this exhibition of affection." The moment of unity Emmeline had dearly hoped for seemed to be upon the women of Utah and the women of the nation.

When she returned home from the East Coast, Emily Richards alerted Emmeline to the men's lackluster discussions regarding including women's suffrage rights in the new Utah state constitution. At first, Emmeline did not seem anxious. She was confident in her vision of unity—not only among the women, but also in the bonds of loyalty with the men of Utah. Still, she didn't take any chances. Emmeline acted in the face of the men's inaction. With the help of Emily Richards and other devoted suffragists, she put out a call to the most prominent suffrage associations in the state, such as the Suffrage Association of Salt Lake City, the Suffrage Association of Salt Lake County, and the Suffrage Association of Utah County, all run by her colleagues and peers. They had to force the men to confront an issue that had brought so much turmoil to the territory over the past twenty-five years. They could not let the men skirt around it any longer. The various groups drafted eloquent admonitions to the men to return Utah to its former glory as a leader in the "justice and privileges of all citizens." From the Woman's Suffrage Association of Salt Lake County, Dr. Ellen B. Ferguson concluded her letter, "Believing that you are actuated by sentiments of true liberty and justice and because you have solemnly pledged yourselves to the enfranchisement of the women of this Territory, we respectfully request that you insert a clause in the Constitution of the State of Utah, conferring upon women the right of suffrage, and your memorialists will ever pray." The language was supplicatory, honorific, and deferential to the men in whose hands their fate lay.

On March 18, 1895, seventy-five women joined Emily Richards, Sarah M. Kimball, Zina D. H. Young, and Emmeline B. Wells on a visit to the Salt Lake City and County Building, up the central staircase to the second floor and down the hall to the Convention Hall. Upon their entry into the hall, the gentlemen stood and offered their seats to the visitors, prompting the *Salt Lake Tribune* to quip, "During the time . . . that the numerous ladies occupied the seats of members, the convention was an object lesson, showing what the second State Legislature will look like [after women can run for office]." Once there, Emily handed her husband Franklin S. Richards, a delegate to the convention, an impassioned "memorial" from the main Utah Territorial Woman Suffrage Association, of which Emmeline was president. This letter made the language of the regional associations look prosaic in comparison.

> To you, gentlemen of the Utah Constitutional Convention, it is given to make other deep and fundamental principles of our government effective in the administration of law. We do not doubt your ability and willingness to do so. But we come to greet you in behalf of the women of Utah to strengthen your hand and to assure you that we are keenly alive to the importance and far reaching consequences of your labor in our behalf.
>
> And above all we would impress you with the fact that the women of Utah are by no means indifferent spectators of the drama that is now being enacted. We believe that every age has its rising and its setting sun. We believe that the woman movement has come because the sun of our civilization has thrown across our social horizon the dawning of a new and more glorious era in the history of man. We believe that "through the ages an eternal purpose runs," and that in the full enfranchisement of women there will come a larger, truer sovereignty, a national conscientiousness in fuller harmony with the temporal welfare and happiness of man. We believe that both men and women will be benefited morally, sociably, and economically. We believe that now the time clock of American destiny has struck the hour to inaugurate a larger and truer civil life, and the future writers of Utah history will immortalize the names of those men who, in this Constitutional Convention, define the injustice and prejudice of the past, strike off the bonds that have heretofore enthralled woman, and open the doors that will usher her into free and full emancipation.
>
> We, therefore, ask you to provide in the Constitution, that the rights of citizens of the State of Utah to vote and hold office shall not be denied or abridged on account of sex, and that male and female citizens of the State shall equally enjoy all civil, political, and religious rights and privileges.

The document had been written by committee, but as she was the president of the association, the document had Emmeline's signature flourishes all over it: the evocation of natural metaphors like the setting sun, the hyperbolic compliments to men as allies and advocates of women, the devotion to harmony and partnership in civic life. She was endlessly romantic in her writing. In adulthood, Emmeline was publicly recognized as an advocate for women, using language and persuasion as tools for achieving her goals. But as much as Emmeline believed in the advancement of women, women were also merely the scaffolding around which she pursued her true love: a poetic life. The pleasurably addictive act of crafting words drove her work as much as her belief in the self-made woman. Words, in her mind, were the activist's ultimate tool. She was not a protester, a complainer, a destroyer. She was a writer, a persuader, a romantic. Whether she knew the phrase or not, she lived by the adage coined by English author Edward Bulwer-Lytton that the pen was mightier than the sword, and it was her ambition to wield the pen as expertly as any before her. In a poem in the *Woman's Exponent*, Emmeline revealed the spiritual awakening that underpinned her longing:

> Was it under the hemlock boughs or the hardy oak tree with proud ambition burning in my soul, ambition to be great and known to fame, when a gentle whisper came? I used to think it was a fairy, and whispered so strangely I scarcely comprehended, but I know its purport: 'There is no excellence without labor you must work, toil, not sit idly indulging in fruitless day-dreams, but active work must be done if you would attain to any degree of honor, or be useful to yourself or others' . . . These mysterious whisperings were cautions, they awakened higher thoughts and nobler ambitions, I yearned for a field of usefulness.

Thus with a document touched with poetic romanticism, Emmeline and her associates challenged the men to take up their fight for them, since the ladies themselves had only the pen as their sword and not the field of a constitutional convention on which to battle. The *Salt Lake Tribune* picked up on the grandiosity of the memorial's supplications in its report of the incident the next day: "The woman suffragists yesterday promised immortality to delegates for their votes for equal rights. The ladies overlooked the fact that there is a statute against bribery."

Emmeline believed that the decades of relationship-building, of newspapers and letters, of indignation meetings and friendly meetings, of marriages and loves and loyalties and heartbreaks and prison sentences would allow for smooth sailing into the legislative port of safety. But her confidence was unrewarded. She did not count on Brigham H. Roberts.

B. H. Roberts was a delegate to the constitutional convention who fully understood the arguments Emmeline and her team made on behalf of women's suffrage. He knew that the women of Utah had exercised the right responsibly for seventeen years. As a member of the LDS Church and a polygamist, Roberts knew firsthand how the Latter-day Saint women were suffering from their husbands' imprisonment—how they especially needed independence, political voice, and financial opportunities now that plural marriage was disavowed by the Church and federal officials were cracking down on the unorthodox marriages. Even though Roberts had long been opposed to the enfranchisement of women personally, these were not the arguments that Roberts chose to address on the eve of the constitutional convention. His was an entirely different battle, on an entirely different front: Roberts was concerned that if Utah submitted a proposed constitution that included the still-radical notion of women's suffrage, it would be rejected by the United States government and not approved by the president. Roberts even suggested the people of Utah themselves would not vote to adopt a constitution that included women's enfranchisement. After all the Utahns had been through—six previous unsuccessful requests for statehood, all of the anti-polygamy legislation—Roberts didn't think the women were worth the risk. He wanted separate submission.

The concept of separate submission didn't give up on women's enfranchisement altogether. It suggested that the people of the Utah Territory— meaning the politically empowered men—be given the chance to vote on two separate issues: on the new state constitution as a whole, *without* women's suffrage in it, and a separate ballot on women's suffrage alone. Roberts argued that the delegates should submit a state constitution that did not include women's suffrage, get it passed by Congress and the president, and then perhaps add something for the ladies later on when statehood was in the bag. "My appeal to you [i.e. the constitutional delegates] is to do your duty in first securing statehood for the people of Utah, and then let these questions take what course they may after that," Roberts explained. "It is a sacrifice that I believe the women of this Territory are capable of making."

Susan B. Anthony foresaw this trick. Months earlier, when Utah was first granted the right to create a constitution through Congress's Enabling Act, Anthony wrote to Emmeline with a warning: "The adjective 'male,' once admitted into your organic law, will remain there. Don't be cajoled into thinking otherwise!"

But Roberts was so convincing, his language so slippery and eloquent. To a packed audience of constitutional delegates, suffragists, and the general public, Roberts spoke to the constitutional convention about women's most powerful place of influence, "the fireside," and the baseness that would greet them in the political sphere. "You are the queens of the domestic kingdom. If you become embroiled in political agitation... the reverence that is paid you will disappear." Across the days of the convention, Roberts chipped away at the phalanx of support the suffragists had fought hard to build up. On day twenty-six of the convention, Roberts argued, "I offer you three reasons why women should not be given the elective franchise: One, the structure of the family—fixed by the Creator—is such that women are not in a position to act independently. Two, women are already represented in governments by their husbands, fathers and sons, and though this representation is indirect, it has been sufficient. And, thirdly, and most importantly, there is a universal belief that there is a different sphere of man and woman."

To cement his persuasive powers, Roberts turned to poetry, quoting Alfred Lord Tennyson, in a move that cut to the heart of the woman who loved poetry for its emancipating beauty:

> Man with the head and woman with the heart,
> Man to command and woman to obey,
> All else is confusion.

On day thirty of the convention, he turned to storytelling, appealing to a setting of domestic bliss that would be forever dashed: "Suppose a man comes home after struggling for the success of a candidate, and is met at the door by a wife opposed to him in politics, and again he has to go over the fight on tariff or free trade, or else observe a sullen silence because of the impropriety of engaging in such a discussion with his wife. Where then will the brow be cleared of the frown, and the heart lose some of its bitterness, so he may have some milk of human kindness running in his veins? Gentlemen: leave the home as it is. Women: be content to reign over the empire of domestic life, and it will bring more joy to your hearts than all the success you could have in casting your ballots at the polls. Leave man, I say, some asylum, some refuge, from the storms and cares of life."

The arguments were as old as the suffrage movement itself: women would be sullied by their excursion into politics; the peaceful sphere of home would be shattered; feminine dependence on men would be eradicated against the will of God. Never mind that Roberts, as a leader in the LDS Church at the same time, was going against the teachings and advice of his male superiors in the Church leadership hierarchy. Never mind the seventeen-year experiment during which Utah women had proved that the dire predictions would not come to pass. The *Salt Lake Herald* reported on the Roberts oratory: "A stream of language, potent and pleasing, flowed from his lips and caught his listeners until even those who were most bitterly opposed to him were compelled to pay compliment to his power with rapturous applause." Emmeline and the suffragists felt their hope destroyed as insidiously from one of their own as they had from the legislators in Washington years earlier.

At home each evening, Emmeline entertained streams of women who came to her home to commiserate. Her journal, which is unusually spotty during this time with entries only once a week or so, records that the women prayed together, strategized together, and expressed their concern to each other. "Today, all is confusion," Emmeline recorded in her journal during this time. "I feel such distress." It was a time during which one "could not keep one's head level." For Emmeline personally, the time was more disjointed by measles in her daughter Annie's home, the anniversary of her enchanting daughter Emmie's death seventeen years earlier, and harsh winter storms that continued to delay the coming of spring.

Since Emmeline, as a woman, couldn't fight back in the convention itself, she responded with the best tool she had: the pages of the *Woman's Exponent*. There, she vocalized her disdain for Roberts's evocations of queenship. "It is pitiful to see how men opposed to woman suffrage try to make the women believe it is because they worship them so, and think them far too good.... One would really think to hear those eloquent orators talk, that laws were all framed purposely to protect women in their rights, and men stood ready to defend them with their lives." Even though privately she was sick at heart, her public voice maintained its characteristic bite.

The women employed another strategic advantage: they called upon the support of a significant male ally, Joseph F. Smith. Smith, a nephew of Church founder Joseph Smith, was a member of the Church's First Presidency, its highest governing body. He was also an ardent suffragist. Even though the line between politics and religion was clearer than it had been during the early days of the territory under Brigham Young's governorship, the fact that most of the convention's delegates were members of the Church—and many of them leaders within its hierarchy—implied the Church had a not-so-subtle influence on what went on in Convention Hall. The leading ladies of the suffrage association were still mostly members of the Church—Emmeline, Sarah Kimball, Zina D. H. Young, Emily Richards—but the post-polygamy and post-Chicago World's Fair goodwill spirit meant that there were many suffragists who were not LDS. But even the non-Mormons, such as Margaret Blaine Salisbury, Alice J. Whalen, and Emma McVicker, understood the power of the religious endorsement even if they didn't condone it, and so the women called on Joseph F. Smith.

In return, Smith spoke on behalf of suffrage that spring, in speeches that were public, but outside of the official court of the constitutional convention. To an LDS Relief Society conference, for example, he railed on women who "rest content and seek no changes, however much for the better a change might be.... Women may be found who seem to glory in their enthralled condition, and who caress and fondle the very chains and manacles which fetter and enslave them! Let those who love this helpless dependent condition and prefer to remain in it and enjoy it; but for conscience and for mercy's sake let them not stand in the way of those of their sisters who would be, and of right out to be *free*." When done castigating women who did not support the cause, he turned his attention to the men. "Shall the male citizen have a voice in civil government simply because he is a male, and a female citizen be denied the same privilege simply because she is a female?... Why shall one enjoy civil rights and the other be denied them? Shall a man indignantly resent 'taxation without representation,' and a woman not do likewise, or tamely submit to that which must be as great a wrong to her as it can be to him, simply because she is a woman and he a man?"

Smith delivered to the ladies an extra bonus at this time by moving beyond simply the right to civic participation and into the broader principle of equal pay for men and women in the workplace. "Do not women eat bread as well as men? Shall men be favored as breadwinners, and women be handicapped in their effort to win bread? Shall a man be paid higher wages than is paid to a woman for doing no better than she does the very same work? Shall the avenues for employment be multiplied to men and diminished to women by the mere dictum or selfishness of men?.... God never did design that a woman should receive less for the product of her labor, whether of hand or brain, skilled or menial than a man should receive for the same labor no better executed than hers. Nor did he design that women should be required to bear equal burdens with men without sharing equally the benefit thereof."

From the day Elizabeth Cady Stanton and Lucy Stone drank their tea in upstate New York in 1848 and dreamed up their Declaration of Sentiments, the women's movement was always about more than just voting. Voting was a tool, a blunt hammer by which generations of women hoped to shape other inequitable aspects of society, like the pay gap and access to education and property. While the Utah suffragists needed to keep their eyes on the singular issue of securing voting rights in their new state, Smith didn't let them forget everything else that was at stake. Outside the Convention Hall, he kept his eyes on the grander vision.

The engagement of the press and of the Church leader didn't go unnoticed. The women had raised the stakes, and Roberts was now on the defense. On day thirty-two of the convention, a thousand spectators showed up to the Salt Lake City and County Building to hear Roberts conclude his oration. People were packed so tightly into the little room that many, including the women who came to see if their hopes would go up in flames, had to stand on tables in the back of the room. "I want to tell you, in frankness," Roberts intoned, "that from the great mass of women in this Territory there comes no spontaneous, heart-felt demand for woman's suffrage. I know what whips and spurs have been used to drag women into these suffrage meetings in my own county. The demand is not spontaneous and widespread, notwithstanding your petitions. When you bring in a petition signed by 500, the list looks long, but remember it does not contain the 40,000 names of Utah's women, or scarcely a fraction of them."

But on this claim of public apathy, Emmeline and her team were also one step ahead of Roberts. In their late-night meetings, the women had strategically decided to tap into the oldest and most powerful political tool yet available to women: the petition. Mobilizing the vast network of city and county suffrage associations and the LDS Relief Societies that had been transformed into suffrage associations across the state in the previous years, the suffragists collected signatures during the weeks that Roberts was weaving his spell. By early April, the suffragists' hopes started to rise. The papers were coming in from all over the territory, covered with women's names from suffrage associations near and far. Emmeline and the women collected them, waiting for the perfect time to present their case for popular endorsement. But those in favor of separate submission also mobilized and collected their own signatures. It seemed that the convention would play host to a final showdown before it was through.

As the lists of petition signatures grew, and as Roberts continued his arguments day after day, the suffragists had yet another weapon on their side. In fact, they had two. Their names were Franklin S. Richards and Orson F. Whitney. Franklin (Emily's husband) and Whitney were, like Roberts, also high leaders in the LDS Church, and they came down on (and spoke eloquently for) the exact opposite side from their brother in the Church. Like skilled fencers, they parlayed Roberts's arguments with stirring oratory of their own, debunking fears and staid arguments. "I do not believe that woman was made merely for a wife, a mother, a cook, and a housekeeper," invoked Whitney. "These callings, however honorable—and no one doubts that they are so—are not the sum of her capabilities. All the arguments against woman suffrage, however plausible, however sincere, are simply pleas for non-progression."

Whitney countered Roberts's image of a disturbed domestic scene with one of his own. With a glint in his eye and a charming smile, Whitney addressed Roberts. "You say that women should be satisfied that, at the polls, they are represented by their husbands. I tried to convince my wife this was the correct philosophy just the other night. I had stepped into the theater and witnessed a play in progress, and later, reaching home I endeavored to persuade Mrs. W that she had witnessed the performance as well, that I had 'represented' her there. It did not work."

Richards for his part took one of Roberts's key arguments (and one of the most common arguments of the anti-suffrage movement generally) and turned it on its head: instead of being sullied by politics, women's civic engagement would serve to purify the political realm. Richards elaborated by leaning into the assumed synonyms of "women" and "purity," not by fighting against it:

> Only recently women have been permitted to enter the universities, professions and business walks of life; and while this has been beneficial to the women, and has made them more independent and self-respecting, it has at the same time tended to purify business and add to public life an element of brightness and cheerfulness. We all know something of the influence of the woman nature in a mining camp. When composed of men exclusively it soon recedes backwards into rudeness, profanity and vulgarity. Let woman come upon the scene and a transformation soon takes place. Men become human, loving, self-respecting and courteous. The better and higher impulses of life are encouraged, and the mining camp puts on the air of respectable and orderly society. Is any man so dull as not to perceive that what is accomplished here in a little mining community would be of inestimable value when put into operation in the State and in the nation at large? Government is simply national housekeeping, and we all know that woman has peculiar gifts for housekeeping. She is the original housekeeper and home maker. Out of her very life, and in her deepest sympathies she made the home, she guarded the little inmates of the home; through her the little bunch of chattels was gathered about the home; and if she is given a chance she will do a noble and God-given part in purifying and perfecting the national household.

Emmeline wasn't so sure she and her fellow suffragists were particularly interested in cleaning up the national messes made by men, but still she gushed in gratitude to Franklin at the end of each day of debate. "Generous, chivalrous, brave and yet tender and true," she wrote rapturously. Her eyes became moist when Whitney, facing the argument that including women's enfranchisement in the proposed state constitution would lose Utah their statehood altogether, retorted, "There are some things higher and dearer even than statehood." Here was a suffragist's hero. And they cheered when Richards concluded one particularly rousing speech with galactic metaphors. "Equal suffrage will prove the brightest and purest ray of Utah's glorious star;

it will shine forever in the immortal galaxy, as a beacon light on the tops of the mountains beckoning our sister states and territories upward and onward to the higher plane of civilization, and the fuller measure of civil and religious liberty."

All of the flamboyant oratory was prelude to the real zenith of confrontation, which came when the petitions were finally presented to the constitutional delegates. On day forty-six of the convention, Roberts presented to the delegates a collection of 15,366 signatures collected to show support for separate submission. He offered the petitions to his peers as evidence of the will of the people. "I do not care what the number may be upon the other side," he claimed. "I take it that this Convention cannot blindly ignore the petition of so many American citizens asking, not that woman's suffrage shall be kept out of the Constitution, but that they should be able to vote on the constitution separate from the suffrage question." Coming to his aid, delegate William F. James added, "These signatures do not say we do not want woman's suffrage. They say we do not want it choked down our throats without the opportunity to vote on it fairly."

At this, Susan B. Anthony's warning—"The adjective 'male,' once admitted into your organic law, will remain there. Don't be cajoled into thinking otherwise!"—reverberated through the heart of every woman in the room.

The proceedings took a very strange, but, to the women, advantageous turn when delegate Anthony W. Ivins (another one of Roberts's Church leadership peers) held up one of the separate submission petitions to his fellow delegates. Standing dramatically at the front of the room, he waved high the paper covered with signatures. "I have in my hand here one of the actual petition documents. As I read the instructions on the top of the document, there is no indication that signatures fixed to it would advocate for separate submission. The intent of the petition is not made known to the signers." The room erupted. Both the male delegates and the female onlookers immediately grasped Ivins's implications. The convention president had to slam down his gavel. "Gentlemen, keep your seats!"

Ivins continued, "In fact, participants are not told at all what they are signing for. It says rather, 'Get this filled with signatures and mail it to your delegate at the Constitutional Convention. Don't delay.' There was no other communication with it. Furthermore, I also hold in my hand a letter from one of my constituents in that very precinct which says that the people that signed that petition did not know what they were doing!"

"Do those who are opposed to woman's suffrage have not the right to try to defeat it if they can?" boomed Roberts above the din.

"Certainly they do," replied Ivins. "But I want to say that the records show it is largely children who were recorded on these petitions asking for a separate submission. Mr. Roberts, are *they* the majority who are opposed?"

Pandemonium reigned as cheers and jeers filled the room. Roberts was finally silenced, exposed. His spell was broken by his own deceptions. It was time for the suffragists to take advantage of the chaos and slip in with their own trump card. They presented to the delegates the official count of the pro-suffragist (and scandal-free, adult-signed) petitions: 24,801 signatures for including women's enfranchisement in the constitution. The president of the convention immediately moved for a vote to be taken: thirty-two of the delegates voted in favor of separate submission. Sixty-nine voted against. Suffrage would be included in the new state's constitution.

In her journal that night, Emmeline wrote of the day, "A little bitterness was manifest from Roberts & [Charles S.] Varian and also James, but altogether it was smooth sailing." She reported that the suffragists tactfully "kept very quiet and made no demonstrations," although the desire to celebrate prevailed. She concluded matter-of-factly: "I sent a telegram to Susan B. Anthony to let her know. " In response, Anthony wrote back immediately. "Hurrah for Utah, No. 3 State—that establishes a genuine 'Republican form of Government.'"

CHAPTER 11

Must woman give her fairest years
As wife and mother and then find
Herself a silent figure-head—
No voice, no vote 'mong human kind?
May woman toil with hand and brain,
Yet in their profits hold no right—
Shall others gather what she sowed
And conscience blush not at the sight?
Nay, sons and brothers, well ye know
Should wives and daughters vote with you,
The candidate to win the race
Must be the right kind through and through.
The brain that reels with drink and smoke
Is not so clear as your own wives,'
The step that totters to its place
Is not the step to lead our lives.
Then true and noble men, ye need
A mighty balance in your power,
A woman's vote goes to the good
She is your friend through ev'ry hour.

"The Reason Why," by Augusta Joyce Crocheron, from the
Utah Woman Suffrage Songbook

Sunday, May 12, 1895
1:45 in the afternoon

Reverend Anna Shaw was breathless as Emmeline concluded her
dramatic recounting of the convention's close call. "Such perseverance!

Such moral courage!" she marveled dramatically as she fell back upon the wagon siding.

"And how fortuitous that we should be able to visit this new state-to-be just at this moment of triumph," Anthony said as the omnibus pulled up on West Temple alongside the back of the elongated dome of the Salt Lake Tabernacle. She stood resolutely and peered out from under the carriage roof. "Let us congratulate these women of Utah properly." The first public session of the Rocky Mountain Suffrage conference was due to start on the hour, and already the crowds were spilling out of the building into the surrounding grounds.

Known as a monument to craftsman building techniques and acoustical engineering, the Tabernacle was completed in 1875, after Anthony's first visit to the territory. As Emmeline helped Anthony disembark the Utah Drag, she pointed out the building's copper green roof beams, curved over the oval building. Multiple doors provided entrances all around the perimeter, flowing into a massive space that seated over three thousand in wooden pews and extensive balcony. The centerpiece of the interior was the impressive organ, whose pipes rose up into a seemingly endless blue ceiling. The stage had been set for about a dozen speakers and dignitaries, giving each of them plenty of room to be seated in individual armchairs. Emmeline accompanied Anthony up the steps to the dais, where they approached the plush velvet seats. There, looking over the gathered crowd, even Emmeline was surprised. Over eight thousand people sat or stood shoulder to shoulder, both on the main level and throughout the balcony. "The large attendance was a fitting tribute to the two distinguished visitors," the *Salt Lake Herald* reported the next day, referring to Anthony and Shaw, "and was a recognition from the public of the marked abilities of the one as a minister and the other as a guiding light and leader in the affairs of women."

Emmeline had asked Ruth to make sure small placards with individual names written on them were placed on the cushion of each seat. With six seats on each side of a central podium, Emmeline had arranged for Anthony to sit to the right of the podium, with Emmeline at her side, followed by Sarah Kimball, Mrs. Bathsheba Smith, Mrs. Emma McVicker, and Mrs. Zina D. H. Young. On the left side of the podium, Emmeline placed

Shaw closest to the center, with Mrs. Emily Richards next to her, followed by Mrs. Jane Richards (Emily's mother-in-law), Dr. Romania Pratt, Mrs. Josephine Hardy, and Mrs. Electa Bullock. Along with Ruth, these were the women Emmeline had relied on to plan and execute this conference, and Emmeline knew that public recognition and special opportunities like this were an important currency in rewarding volunteers for countless hours of work. The massive audience hushed as the ladies took their seats. Ruth ushered the special guests from Colorado and Wyoming, along with Mrs. Emma DeVoe, to reserved seats in the front row beneath the dais, where they joined several men already seated, including LDS Church leaders Elder Henry P. Richards (Emily's brother-in-law) and Bishop Orson F. Whitney, and Unitarian Church leaders Reverend Stanley Hunter and Reverend David Utter, along with several other denominations' leaders, representing the presence of the "Gentiles" as well as the Mormons. The eyes of thousands of patient onlookers strained to see the women as they entered the building and found their seats.

Emmeline had thought long and hard about how to open this meeting. She had been attending suffrage conferences in the East for over two decades, and she had always wanted to do things differently when it was Utah's turn to host. Typically, a conference would start with a song: a patriotic song along the lines of "Battle Hymn of the Republic" or "Columbia," often with the words rewritten and published in specialized suffrage songbooks. These songs served as an important reminder to critics that the women were gathered to support their country and to contribute to it, not imperil it. The Utah Woman Suffrage Association had compiled its own book of suffrage songs five years earlier, which too included patriotic tunes—often with the words changed to reflect the suffrage demands—and Emmeline had selected some of those to be sung as well over the days of the conference. But as a woman of faith, she felt that the role of the Almighty was rarely sufficiently acknowledged in these conferences. They were in Utah now, and after discussions with Ruth May Fox and her organizing committee, they had landed on an important but subtle decision: they would open the conference with the hymn "O My Father."

Although the music of the hymn was composed by a man, James

McGranahan, the words to "O My Father" had been written by Eliza R. Snow, one of the leading women of the previous generation of Latter-day Saints. Snow had written the poem in 1845 in Nauvoo, Illinois, after hearing the Prophet Joseph Smith teach about the existence of a Heavenly Mother as well as a Heavenly Father. The third verse reasons that if there is a Father in Heaven, there is a Mother too.

In the heavens are parents single? No, the thought makes reason stare!
Truth is reason, truth eternal Tells me I've a mother there.

This radical doctrine made the hymn a favorite of Latter-day Saint women, and they pointed to it as an example to the outside world of how their faith supported and enabled women, rather than oppressing them as the practice of polygamy suggested. But besides the doctrine it represented, the hymn allowed for Snow's presence to be felt at this celebration of Utah's triumphs on behalf of women, even though she had died in 1887. Eliza R. Snow had been the most prominent public woman in the Mormons' early days in the Salt Lake Valley, and many of the women on the stand of the Tabernacle had been personally mentored by her. But Snow had not been an unequivocal friend of the suffrage movement. While she was crucial to the establishment of the Relief Society and a vocal proponent of women's individual strengths and abilities, Snow was a generation older even than Sarah Kimball, and her commitment to the men in her life—and to preserving their power—was absolute. "Order is heaven's first law," she explained, "and it is utterly impossible for order to exist without . . . gradation." She may have codified the idea of a Heavenly Mother, but neither she nor the men she supported ever elaborated on the relationship between Heavenly Mother and Heavenly Father, allowing that relationship to take on a theoretically broad range of possible power equations. Was Heavenly Mother subject to Heavenly Father? His true equal? One of many Heavenly Mothers? Those questions were never addressed.

More than once, Emmeline had been warned and censured by Snow for her devotion to the causes of mankind rather than exclusively focusing on those of God. Snow distrusted "that class known as 'strong-minded,' who are strenuously and unflinchingly advocating 'woman's rights,' and some of them at least, claim 'woman's sovereignty,' vainly flattering themselves with the idea that with ingress to the ballot box and access to financial offices, they shall accomplish the elevation of woman-kind." She continued, "Not that we are opposed to woman suffrage. . . . But to think of a war of sexes which the woman's right movement would inevitably inaugurate, . . . creates an involuntary shudder!" Snow believed that the Latter-day Saint women's elevation came not through "clamoring for our rights" which, she believed, "were only making matters worse." Rather, she proposed that "it is only by obedience, honoring God in all the institutions he has revealed to us, that we can come out from under that curse [of Eve's fall]." For her, female power was a God-given means by which women could magnify their potential as His daughters, even if contained to the providential sphere. At least Snow's providential sphere was larger than the one most widely accepted by nineteenth-century American society.

The silver lining of Snow's oversight was that Emmeline learned how to navigate around those who disagreed with her approach in respectful and gracious ways. Snow's name was connected with every project and movement the Latter-day Saint women undertook from Nauvoo through the first decades of their Utah settlement, and her official sanction was crucial to the success of any effort. And despite her different perspective on where female power came from and the purpose of that power, Snow's enlarged providential sphere always included the right for women to vote.

Perhaps it was in this spirit of graciousness that Emmeline had chosen "O My Father" for the opening hymn. The majority of the assembled audience needed no reminder of the text, but Ruth had arranged for copies of the lyrics to be available to all of the visiting guests from out of state so that they could comprehend the full meaning of the poem. From her position in her velvet chair, Emmeline especially enjoyed the gusto with which the congregation sang, "Truth eternal tells me I've a mother there!"

The decision to include two men in the next portion of the program—Elder Henry P. Richards to say the opening prayer and Stake President Angus Cannon to introduce Reverend Anna Howard Shaw—was a deliberate move by Emmeline and her committee to recognize and reward the men by whose hands the women of Utah, and, in the future, the women of the nation, would be liberated. It had been an all-male territorial legislature in Wyoming and in Utah that had passed local suffrage laws. It had

been an all-male constitutional convention that had included equal suffrage laws in the Wyoming and Colorado state constitutions. The entire
effort, by necessity, had depended on the goodwill of men to grant women
entrance into the hallowed halls of political engagement. Rather than be
embittered by the necessity to rely on men, the most successful suffragists
had embraced men as strategic allies.

Elder Richards approached the pulpit after the song's echoes died
away to say an opening prayer. Although the prayer was offered in the traditional Latter-day Saint style, Elder Richards was generous in his recognition that they were about to hear from a servant of the Divine in the form
of Reverend Anna Howard Shaw and that they were gathered there for a
divine purpose: "To extend the emancipation of women across the land,
from this chosen valley to the farthest reaches of this chosen nation."
President Cannon then took his turn, introducing Reverend Anna Howard
Shaw as the first woman to ever preach in this house of worship. This was
greeted by cheers from the audience, which Shaw acknowledged with a
smile and a gentle wave from her velvet chair on the dais. Asking Cannon
to introduce Shaw had been a reward for his support of their cause so far,
but also a move to ensure his future support for women in politics generally. Emmeline had heard rumors that Cannon's wife, Martha Hughes
Cannon, an accomplished doctor and Emmeline's protégé at the *Woman's
Exponent*, was planning to run for political office once Utah's statehood
was official. But it was known that Cannon himself had his eye on a state
senate seat. A husband and wife running against each other? The complex-
ities of women and men in civic engagement were certainly rearing themselves immediately! This would be the very first election open to women,
and already the critics would point to women's civic engagement as a tool
for wreaking havoc in families. Concerned about how these rumors would
play out, Emmeline deftly asked Angus Cannon to participate in their conference in hopes that he would change his mind and support his wife when
she made her intentions public.

Applause greeted Shaw again as she moved from her velvet chair
to the pulpit and arranged her papers on the stand. She was an experienced public speaker, understanding the energy with which she needed to
project her words in order to reach the farthest crevices of a hall. But as

she greeted the audience in the Tabernacle, she felt her own words bouncing back to her, reverberating off the entire domed roof and the wooden pillars that held up the balcony. Nowhere else had her voice projected so far so easily.

"My friends, on behalf of the National American Woman Suffrage Association, our president Miss Anthony and I thank you for the warm welcome you have shown to us in your city today. Our journey so far has been rewarding. Our receptions in St. Louis and Denver were remarkable. In Denver, the large opera house was packed, and a reception, in which the newspapers estimated that 1,500 persons took part, was afterwards given at the Palace Hotel. From Denver we went to Cheyenne, where we addressed the citizens, men and women. For once there were present at our meeting quite as many men as women, and not only ordinary but extraordinary men: the Governor, Senators, Representatives, Judges of the Supreme Court, city officials, and never so many majors and colonels, and it showed that where women have a vote, men think their meetings are worth going to.

"Yesterday, as the train carried me through the vast and mighty mountains, climbing a craggy precipice on one side and descending carefully on the other, I could realize something of the courageous manhood and womanhood which it cost to subdue these rugged precincts and bring the valleys to their present conditions. For the people of Utah, and Colorado and Wyoming and Idaho, such indomitable courage and fortitude must simply have been inspired by an unshakable hope in a future and a happier state. It is my privilege to be associating with such people today in this remarkable forum.

"We are here today both to celebrate the triumphs of our movement to this date, and also to look forward to how we can replicate them again and again in every state of this great nation. It is to the independent states that we look for this movement's progress. It is to women and men such as yourselves—you who are in your communities working with your neighbors and your legislators and your religious leaders—to whom we entrust the sacred work. It is in this state-by-state approach that we have had the greatest success. We intend to work state by state across this entire land to ensure that all American women have their civic rights enshrined in their states' constitutions!"

A clamor of shouting and applause rang out at this statement of determination.

"Of course this state-by-state approach wasn't always our plan. Before my time, when our beloved Elizabeth Cady Stanton first conceived of gathering millions of American women under this noble cause, her goal was to have women included in the protections and provisions of the Fourteenth Amendment. The period after our Civil War was a crucial time for establishing the rights of our persecuted Negro brothers, but Mrs. Stanton and Miss Anthony didn't want the women who had supported their soldiers for the years of the war to be left behind. We lost that fight. The Fourteenth Amendment introduced the idea that eligible voting citizens must be males of at least twenty-one years of age. As that amendment introduced the word 'male' into the United States Constitution for the first time since its drafting, Miss Stanton lamented that it would take us another century to abolish that word from the Constitution once again. So far it has been only twenty-seven years. We have plenty of time to prove her wrong.

"We then set our sights on the Fifteenth Amendment, which affirmed that the right to vote shall not be abridged on account of race. With that amendment, we craved to have the phrase 'or sex' be added to its phrasing: 'The right of citizens of the United States to vote shall not be denied or abridged by the United States or by any State on account of race, color, or previous condition of servitude ... or sex.'

"But that was not to be. Debate over whether or not to support the Fifteenth Amendment led to dark times for many of our movement's national leaders. How to put one group of people ahead of another in attaining rights? How to step back from demanding one's rights for oneself in order to let another attain those same rights? Mrs. Stanton and Miss Anthony treasured the support of our colored friends since the start of our movement; the most esteemed Frederick Douglass championed our earliest conventions and attended our gatherings, after all. But they felt political freedom should be equally extended to both disenfranchised groups—both women and Negro men at the same time, not one before the other. They opposed the passage of the Amendment unless it was appended to enfranchise women as well as the Negro man. In taking this position, they broke with their old ally and his community. Miss Lucy Stone and Miss Julia Ward Howe disagreed with Miss Anthony and Mrs. Stanton. Miss Stone and Miss Howe felt so strongly about supporting the Negro man's right to vote as stated in the Fifteenth Amendment that they founded the American Woman Suffrage Association, as an alternative to Miss Anthony and Mrs. Stanton's National Woman Suffrage Association. The breaches and wounds caused by those times took decades to heal and still remain tender."

Shaw paused as she remembered the hostility and tension of that time. Maturing in the movement during this time of antagonism had been hard for Shaw, especially as a woman whose faith taught her to forgive and love. She didn't understand how her heroes felt they had to choose one over the other—the woman or the black man—and when recounting this time, she was always grateful that she had not yet been in a position of leadership within the movement but still a lowly foot soldier. The audience in the Tabernacle remained hushed as she paused. They knew this history well too. Because of Anthony's reach in the West and the friendships she had developed there over the years, the Westerners felt loyal to her. They were also uncertain about her decision to favor one kind of person over another, but not uncertain enough to shed their loyalty to Anthony or her cause.

"And yet,"

Shaw brightened as she roused the audience from its dark reminiscing,

"we found a way back to each other, as women do. Five years ago, we worked with our sisters to find more commonalities than differences, and we reunited by creating the National American Woman Suffrage Association. It is that united umbrella that embraces us all here today. Women in the West and in the East, recommitted to a vision for our country that includes all women free and enfranchised. And those dark times led to our most strategic decision of all: If we couldn't affect the Constitution of the United States, we would instead work on state constitutions. The beauty of our union lies in its individual territories to govern themselves, in delicate balance with Washington, and we now rely on you as citizens of individual lands to fight our battle on local grounds.

"As we gather here today, three states have joined the Union with equal suffrage laws included in their state constitutions. Wyoming came in first, as we know. Five years ago in 1890 when Wyoming Territory became the State of Wyoming, the rights of Wyoming women were codified in their state constitution. Wyoming might have been the forty-fourth state to enter our nation, but it was the first to enter with its women free and enfranchised."

At this, applause broke out from the audience. From her chair on the stage, Emmeline beckoned to Amalia Post, seated on the first row of the audience with the other distinguished guests, urging her to rise and accept the applause as a symbol of Wyoming's leadership. With her escorts' help, Amalia arose and turned gingerly to offer a slight wave to the audience. The generous applause continued until the elderly woman sat down again.

"Then there is Colorado."

A small titter went up from a group of Coloradans in the balcony, excited to hear their story told to the assembly.

"Colorado has been a state in the Union since 1876, but its state constitution did not at first include an equal rights clause. Colorado's path was different and distinct from Wyoming's. As a state, a constitutional amendment was required to change its state constitution, but the determined advocates there succeeded in traveling that arduous path. After receiving support in the legislature, a referendum required the citizens to vote on the inclusion of a new woman's suffrage amendment to the Colorado constitution, and it passed. In 1893, Colorado too became a state with its women fully enfranchised."

In response to Shaw's conclusion of the Colorado story, Mary C. C. Bradford and Lyle Meredith Stansbury rose to acknowledge the assembly on behalf of their state. Applause from the audience, strongest in the gallery with the Coloradan concentration, celebrated this triumph that had only occurred two years prior.

"Here today, at this special convocation of leaders and valiant foot soldiers from throughout the West, we celebrate another miraculous milestone: Just last month, in April, the delegates of the Utah State Constitutional Convention voted to include women in the brand new Utah State Constitution!"

At this final announcement, the greatest cheer of all erupted through-out the Tabernacle, as the majority of the eight thousand attendees clapped and waved handkerchiefs in honor of their home state. Emmeline allowed herself the luxury of leaning slightly forward in her chair, tilting her head both right and left to catch the eyes of the women on either side of her who had stayed clear-eyed through the murky days after their dis-enfranchisement. Aunt Zina, Sister Sarah, Bathsheba, Emma McVicker, Dr. Pratt. A knowing glance passed from one to the other, the secret token of a society of struggle that bound them now and forever. No act of govern-ment or God could now take away what they had accomplished together: Utah was about to enter the United States as the third state to have its women free and enfranchised.

"We expected it of the men of Utah,"

continued Anna when the audience became settled again, summariz-ing a story everyone in the audience knew and most had recently lived through.

"It was they who, in 1870, entrusted the women of Utah to stand alongside them at the polls, just three months after Wyoming's legisla-ture passed its own equal suffrage law. It was they, again, as the mem-bers of the delegation assigned to create a constitution for this nascent state, who decided that Utah's women could not be left behind. No, not even if it meant Utah's statehood would be denied. Every star added to that blue field of our nation's flag gives an advantage to every human being. We are just beginning to learn that we are all children of one Father and members of one family; and when one member suffers or is benefitted, all the members suffer or rejoice. So when Utah comes into the Union with everyone free, it is not only that state which is benefit-ted, but we and all the world. As the stars at night come out one by one, so will they come out one by one on our flag, till the whole blue field is a blaze of glory.

"No man of this territory could have stood by the side of his mother and heard her tell of all that the pioneers endured, and then have refused to grant her the same right of liberty he wanted for him-self, without being unworthy of such a mother. Utah is one of the crown jewels of our Union on the crest of the Rockies, above all the others.

Utah is dear to the heart of every woman who loves liberty in these United States!"

The audience rose as a wave to greet her emphatic conclusion, small American flags waving the forty-four stars on a blue field that Shaw had just praised. Utah's own star was not yet included in the firmament, as the new state's constitution had yet to be voted on in Utah and ratified in Washington, but the anticipation of a forty-fifth star joining the others helped fuel the excited crowd.

As Reverend Shaw returned to her seat on the stage behind her, Emmeline rose from her own chair to embrace Utah's newest favorite visiting celebrity. Shaw returned the affection, and the women clasped hands while the audience continued to cheer. Emmeline was grateful for such an auspicious beginning to the weekend's proceedings, and she felt the morning's butterflies finally fly away. Shaw's familiarity with and respect for her audience had already made her visit a success. Harmony with fellow Americans was a rare and treasured feeling for the Utahns, many of whom had living memory of escaping American persecution. It also felt like a treasure to Emmeline herself, who had fought for decades to be respected as an emancipated woman among her skeptical national peers.

Considering Reverend Shaw's closing salute to the men of Utah, Emmeline congratulated herself on her selection of the next speaker: Orson F. Whitney. Whitney was one of those men Shaw had just referenced upon whose shoulders the emancipation of Utah's women had rested. He became an instant favorite of the ladies for his wit, common sense, and linguistic flourishes, as well as for his vanquishing of B. H. Roberts's rhetorical arguments at the constitutional convention the month before.

As with Henry Richards and Angus Cannon, Whitney's participation on the program signaled Emmeline's desire to reward the men who had carried the women to victory. But she also knew there was a limit to how much she should pander to the men. The men had carried the women far enough. She had had to rely on the men to be her advocates and allies during the constitutional debates, when the question of suffrage in the new state's constitution was at stake. But those days were over now.

Her ability to extend the speaking invitations to this conference felt to Emmeline like an important opportunity to re-exert her power as a self-determined woman. Invitations to speak were her special currency, hers to award and give out as she saw fit, a symbolic gesture of her equal footing with men. She had been the guest of men long enough; they were now guests in her domain.

Whitney began with a twinkle in his eye.

"Some of our fellow Utahns recently tried to persuade us that the sensitivity and delicacy of women would keep them away from the polls. That the refined wife and mother would not so much put her foot in the filthy stream of politics."

A murmur rose among the audience. They knew exactly who he was speaking of in his arched manner.

"Our esteemed colleague Mr. Brigham H. Roberts tried to convince us as delegates assigned to create a constitution for our new state that acquiring statehood was more important than guaranteeing our women a liberated state. He argued that equal suffrage is still a delicate enough issue among the halls of Washington that Utah's future statehood could be in jeopardy if we included woman suffrage in our constitution. We applied for statehood—and had been denied—six times before. Why risk the prize, when we were so close to achieving our goal, over the issues of women?

"He almost had some of us convinced. Considering this great land was the first place a woman cast a ballot under equal suffrage laws in the United States and territories, it is embarrassing and shameful how close we came as the delegates assigned to write our constitution to leaving our women behind. To prizing statehood over the basic justice offered to all humanity. It is embarrassing how much conversation and debate had to take place to knock Mr. Roberts off of his soapbox and regain a vision of true justice. No. To Mr. Roberts, I said, 'There are some things higher and dearer than statehood.'"

Whitney was on a roll. He lifted his hand as the audience started to cheer, silencing them so he could continue in fervor.

"It is woman's destiny to have a voice in the affairs of government. She was designed for it. She has a right to it. This great social upheaval, this woman's movement that is making itself heard and felt, means something more than that certain women are ambitious to vote and hold office. I regard it as one of the great levers by which the Almighty is lifting up this fallen world, lifting it nearer to the throne of its Creator."

CHAPTER 12

Equal suffrage is not an end; it is a beginning. It is the commencement of responsibilities and opportunities so vast that time itself is hardly long enough to work out the problems set before us. For years our resolutions have begun with the familiar preamble, "We, as women." The enfranchised woman has passed to a higher plane. It is not we as women, nor we as men who will make this world better, but all of us, working together as human beings.

Ellis Meredith Stansbury, *Rocky Mountain News*

Sunday, May 12, 1895
9 o'clock in the evening

The appetite of the Rocky Mountain Suffrage Conference audience for speeches and celebrations by the visiting guests seemed insatiable. In the evening, after the afternoon session in the Tabernacle, Anthony and Shaw addressed another group of three thousand in the Salt Lake Theater, where they restated congratulatory observations and spun clever anecdotes about the obvious need for women to participate in civic life. From waking up in the train to the last handshake with local admirers, Anthony and Shaw were exhausted. Anthony was comfortably settled at the home of Mrs. W. J. Beatie and Shaw at the home of Joan McVicker. Neither woman had protested to turning in early.

But Emmeline wasn't ready to call it a day just yet. The conference's kickoff events had gone smoothly, but she was too excited and too filled with anticipation for the rest of the conference to feel at all tired. Tomorrow would be just as important—perhaps more important—as the assembled group discussed how to extend the successes of Wyoming, Colorado, and Utah to additional states and, eventually, the whole nation.

That evening, Emmeline sat by herself in front of a small fire in her parlor, a white wool shawl loosely draped over her lap. Though the weather had been glorious for the guests' tour of the city and the opening sessions of the conference, the spring Utah night had turned chill. She finished nibbling on a simple meal of bread and cheese that her daughter Annie had prepared for her after her full day, and put the plate aside. Annie was quietly tidying the kitchen, giving her mother some much needed time for unwinding at the end of the day congested with hosting. Emmeline fingered the tassels on the shawl, bows and ribbons in the ornate style she preferred. She leaned her head back on her chair and her eyes landed on a small photograph of Daniel Wells on her mantelpiece.

Daniel would have been proud of her today. He had been dead for five years already, and not a day went by that Emmeline didn't wrestle with herself over his legacy and impact on her life. Had he been emotionally distant, financially unstable, and callously unromantic? Or had he been a supportive ally and tender lover? The truth was that he had been both. When Daniel died in 1891, Emmeline had been widowed three times, but she had been Daniel's wife for thirty-nine years. Even though her first two marriages—to James Harris at fifteen and Newel K. Whitney at twenty-two—had been impactful both spiritually and emotionally, it was Daniel who had defined Emmeline's adulthood. Actually, it was Daniel . . . and Louisa and Martha and Lydia and Susan and Hannah. As the sixth wife, Emmeline had entered a self-contained community that was fueled by industry, cooperation, compassion, jealousy, and loneliness.

But she hadn't entered it fully. She was the only one of Daniel's wives who had not been sealed to him for eternity, a marriage rite within the Church that linked a husband and wife beyond this life. Instead, she was married to Daniel only for this life. When she had appealed to Daniel to marry her, as a twenty-two-year-old widow who had recently arrived in the Salt Lake Valley, he agreed out of deference to Emmeline's previous husband, Newel K. Whitney. Whitney had been Daniel's mentor, and in a move reminiscent of Boaz's acceptance of Ruth in the Old Testament, Daniel agreed to take care of Emmeline out of consideration to his friend's special place in his heart and their gospel brotherhood.

As she enjoyed the warmth of the fire and the comfortable parlor, Emmeline reflected that she hadn't always enjoyed such a peaceful space to call her own. In fact, she'd only lived in this house, between 400 and 500 East Streets in Salt Lake City, for less than two years. This was the third home since her marriage to Daniel, and it defined her and contained a piece of her heart. But it was her second home in Salt Lake City, a little white house on State Street, that was most beloved of all her homes.

After her marriage to Daniel in 1852, Emmeline had joined the other sister wives in the Wells home, an old adobe house made up of two separate buildings on South Temple Street. But with a sixth wife, there soon wasn't enough room in the Wells's stately colonial "big house" for Emmeline and her children, so Daniel furnished a small two-story home on State Street and 300 South. This little white house contained for Emmeline a fullness of joy as she raised her children and cultivated an impressive garden, as well as the bitterness of loneliness as she struggled to fit her way into Daniel's busy life. Furnished with a housekeeper by Daniel, Emmeline was free to tend to her daughters and indulge in her love of reading and writing, while still being included in the larger family events with her sister wives at the big house such as nightly dinners and birthdays. While some may have suspected her move away from the rest of the family was because Emmeline did not get along with the other wives, it was in fact a practicality due to a growing Wells family. Emmeline couldn't escape the fact that she was different from the other wives, and her children different from the other children. If one wife needed to move due to space constraints, Emmeline was the one who had to go.

Susan and Lydia Ann, two of her sister wives, were especially dear to Emmeline. These were women with whom she felt "closer than sisters," enjoying the "closest intimacy" and expressing in her journal a constant admiration for them and the thirty-seven children the five other women were raising together in the big house. But the benign neglect practiced by Daniel for his sixth and physically separated wife eventually grew old for Emmeline, as her romantic soul pined for true male connection.

As she reflected on the portrait of the man who had shaped so much of her adulthood as her spiritual and legal protector, she had enough distance to recognize that he had also impacted much of her emotional fulfillment as well, but not as a companion. If it hadn't been for his distance, she might never have thrown herself with such determination into her work at the *Woman's Exponent* or into the "woman question." This work satiated a deep hunger she had to connect with others, a hunger that was left unfulfilled in her relationship with Daniel. Looking back years later on her wedding to Daniel, Emmeline wrote, "How much pleasure I anticipated and how changed alas are all things since that time, how few of the thoughts I had then have ever been realized, and how much sorrow I have known in place of the joy I looked forward to." Her loneliness in her marriage had been profound, and in writing and advocating for women, she had found a way to be heard and understood.

Poetry had been her heart's consolation. In it, she poured out her longings in sentiments both shared with Daniel and kept private. In a letter written but never sent, she wrote to him from her little white house:

> *Wilt thou not condescend to come*
> *Once more and spend an hour with me.*
> *Or has thou quite forsaken one,*
> *Who sues to thee for sympathy.*
> *So lone and dreary is my lot*
> *Thy presence brightens all things near,*
> *Say wilt thou not come once again,*
> *And future hopes and prospects cheer.*
> *Or do I ask this boon from one*
> *Who feels no interest for me;*
> *Alas if so how dark and drear*
> *Must be my future destiny.*

Privately in her journal, variations of the sentiment appear as a constant and recurring theme: "O my heart aches so. 'Tis killing me by inches. O will not God be merciful to me and give me power to overcome this terrible feeling of neglect which is preying upon me more than ever before." "What can I do to gain favor in his sight," she asked herself. "My home is a pleasant one, my children are in every way perfect as mortals can be, I always meet him pleasantly though my heart is breaking."

And yet it was precisely those perfect mortals—her daughters—that made the little white house such a haven. Raising there Belle and Mel, her two daughters from Newel K. Whitney, and Emmie, Annie, and Louie, her three daughters with Daniel, had infused the home with happy memories.

It was to the white house Emmeline returned home after hearing Susan B. Anthony speak at the Old Tabernacle for the first time. It was at the white house where she had first explored the stirrings of independent womanhood in the quiet of her lonely room. It was the white house whose repairs and upkeep were financed by Emmeline's paycheck from the *Woman's Exponent*.

Eventually, however, the self-made woman's paycheck wasn't enough. The reality of her reliance on her absent husband set in when, in 1883, Daniel's finances required selling her home of thirty years. Even as a self-made woman, she was still at the mercy of factors outside of her control. It broke her heart to leave her "dear old homestead where my children were born and reared." With her daughters grown and gone, she decamped to the adobe structure across the street from the big house, barely still standing, a "rookery for owls," as she called it. While she was at first jealous of her sister wives' continued comfort, the "big house" was also sold the following year. In fact, after being sold, it was torn down to make room for the Templeton Hotel, the very building where she had entertained Anthony and Shaw earlier that day. Whenever Emmeline entered the Templeton Hotel, she couldn't help but remember that earlier symbol of her ostracism, but also her independence, that had once stood in its place.

Her isolating marriage didn't just prompt Emmeline to seek human connection. It also gave her daily, real-world proof of how vital it was for a woman to be able to support herself and perceive herself as an independent agent. While she poured her heart out in her journals about how she longed to be loved and embraced by her husband, in public she preached women's fortitude and their need for economic, political, and educational independence. Woman's "highest motive," she wrote in the *Exponent* in 1877, "is that she may be recognized as a responsible being, capable of judging for and maintaining herself, and standing upon just as broad, grand and elevated a platform as man." Perhaps both giving herself a pep talk and reflecting her own vision of herself, she said, "Self-made woman is a powerful term. . . . It bespeaks self-help, self-denial, patient hopefulness and persistent determination." She was, by necessity and by sheer will, a self-made woman.

A knock came on Emmeline's front door. She heard her daughter Annie move from the kitchen through the hall to answer it. Sweet Annie. Annie, who had left her own five young children with her husband, John, to tend Emmeline during this busy weekend. Annie, who had lived with her own domestic drama and shared husband complications in another way: she had withstood the tremendous scandal of her husband having an affair with her own sister Louie. Once Louie became pregnant, in this post-polygamous society where that might once have been solved by taking her as a plural wife, John divorced Annie to marry her sister. Then, however, Louie died in childbirth and, in a remarkable act of forgiveness, Annie remarried John and continued to bear his children. Emmeline had weathered the conflict between her two daughters with a torn heart. But she knew it was Annie, of all five of her daughters, who would take her place as a voice for women in the future. The girl had all the raw ingredients of a self-made woman: ambition, skill, and the refining crucible of isolating trials.

"Is Mrs. Wells at home?"

Emmeline heard Annie greet the women at the door and usher them into the parlor. She rose from her comfortable seat by the fire with some effort.

"Mrs. Bradford! Mrs. Stansbury!" Emmeline extended her small hands in greeting and grasped her friends enthusiastically. The two Colorado celebrities rustled into the drawing room, unfastening their shawls and hats as Annie gathered them in her arms. "I'm delighted you came. Please take a seat. I'm sorry we didn't have more of an opportunity to visit during the day. I'm sure you know from my letters how absolutely thrilled I am to have you here this weekend."

"That's very gracious, dear Mrs. Wells," said Mrs. Bradford, who at only thirty-nine was very aware of being in the presence of a much older woman. "I hope we are not inconveniencing you. Please, take your seat. May we join you?"

"By all means." Emmeline beckoned for the two Colorado delegates to join her. "You're comfortably settled tonight, I hope?"

"Oh, yes. Mrs. Caine's home is very spacious, and we are well cared for. Thank you for arranging such comfortable accommodations." Mary Bradford continued the conversation while her even younger colleague, Ellis Meredith Stansbury, remained quiet beside her, nestled on a small damask couch across from Emmeline while the last embers of the fire burned in the hearth. "I hope you don't think us impertinent for coming by tonight."

"Not at all! My home is always open to visitors, especially to thinking women such as yourselves. I can't tell you how much it means to me to have Colorado's contributions to this auspicious conference. What a blessed feeling to put our differences behind us and have sister territories and states come together for the betterment of women everywhere."

"Yes, it has been a long road, hasn't it?" Bradford responded. "As you may know, I only moved to Colorado from New York after marrying, and so my time there has been relatively short compared to many of the women who have carried the cause in the decades before me. But it is so gratifying to see Colorado women's recent victory become a standard to which other states can look. Mrs. Stansbury has been engaged in Colorado's efforts longer than I have, having been raised by the printer and managing editor of the *Rocky Mountain News*."

"Ah, yes, Mrs. Stansbury," said Emmeline, turning to the younger of the two women. "I have read your mother's work. The first professional journalist in Colorado, if I'm not mistaken. What a formidable household in which to have been raised. You were very literally born into the movement!"

"Indeed," Stansbury responded, more confidently than her previous silence would have suggested. "It was a marvelous upbringing. We are all very dedicated to the cause. Perhaps you might also know," ventured the young Stansbury, "that my father-in-law, Captain Howard Stansbury, is credited with having made the first survey in Utah, circumnavigating the Great Salt Lake in 1849."

"I would not have made the connection, Mrs. Stansbury," responded Emmeline in surprise. "That was just after I myself arrived here in the valley, quite a long time ago to be sure! And what did your father-in-law Mr. Stansbury think of our ocean in the desert?"

ELIZABETH ANNE WELLS CANNON

Born December 7, 1859, in Salt Lake City, Utah
Died September 2, 1942, in Salt Lake City, Utah

Elizabeth Anne "Annie" Wells Cannon was the daughter of Emmeline B. Wells and Daniel H. Wells. She attended the Deseret University before working for fifteen years as a reporter and assistant editor at her mother's publication, the *Woman's Exponent*. In 1879, she married John Q. Cannon. Together they had twelve children.

Annie was deeply committed to public service, following in her mother's foot-steps as an intrepid contributor to her community. She served as a director on the Library Board and a member of the board of directors for the American Relief Association. In 1883, she published *The History and Objectives of the Relief Society* and coauthored the Relief Society Handbook. In 1913, she successfully ran for the Utah House of Representatives and served one term before leaving office in 1915.

During the Spanish-American War of 1898, Cannon joined her mother in working with the Utah Red Cross by organizing care packages and food to be sent to American soldiers in the conflict. During World War I, Cannon acted as head of local Utah Red Cross chapters, overseeing the appropriate use of Red Cross funds, determining the kind of materials that would be sent out, and presiding over local Red Cross events.

After World War I, she was selected by Herbert Hoover to represent Utah in the European Relief Drive. In 1918, she became the associate vice president of the American Flag Association. She was also a member of the Daughters of Utah Pioneers, American Woman's Association, Utah Woman's Press Club, and the Order of Bookfellows. She was featured on the cover of the December 1930 issue of the *Relief Society Magazine*.

"Oh, he was most disappointed, Mrs. Wells."

Both Bradford and Emmeline let loose in a warm laugh at the young woman's serious declaration, while Stansbury herself fumbled, chiding her precocious tongue's potential for offense.

"I do apologize, Mrs. Wells. Do forgive me. I have only heard his stories these many years in retrospect, when his descriptions of his four-week journey among the barren shores have been well stoked to maximize his listeners' sympathies."

"Please do not concern yourself, Mrs. Stansbury," reassured Emmeline as propriety reestablished itself among the ladies. "It is true, having spent my own youth so near a true ocean, that the salt water of our lake here doesn't spawn the same invigorating freshness or verdant flora that comes in the vicinity of the Atlantic or Pacific. But I believe you both will be joining us for an excursion to Saltair on Tuesday afternoon? You may see then, Mrs. Stansbury, a different kind of beauty than your father-in-law expected of salty shores.

"And now," said Emmeline, turning to a subject at which her guests felt more at ease, "what will you do, now that Colorado women are liberated through your recent referendum?"

"I've actually joined the staff of the *Rocky Mountain News*, Mrs. Wells," remarked a recovered Mrs. Stansbury. "I've been given my own column, 'A Woman's World,' and just recently I was invited to become part of the editorial staff. I have been assigned coverage of the Colorado legislature and, if I'm not mistaken," she added with a coy smile that was intended to convey humility but really just revealed triumph, "I'm the first woman journalist in the Union to report on a legislature."

"Heavens! What a cause for celebration. We should be sure to inform the group of your position tomorrow. Had you already taken on that position when we met in Chicago a couple of years ago?" asked Emmeline.

"How kind of you to remember meeting me there, Mrs. Wells," beamed Stansbury. "Yes, I believe I had just. I was greatly impacted by the presence of your Utah delegation at the World's Fair in Chicago. Such an elegant presentation of artwork, and such a display of civic conviction."

"Yes, it was a kind of coming-out party for us Utah women, to be sure," laughed Emmeline. "I'm sure your mother remembers how Utah was perceived previously. She may have even written once or twice about our peculiar practices in her journalism. I'm not sure she thought very highly of coordinating with us on our efforts to forward the cause." Stansbury looked embarrassed as Emmeline brought up the tension that had existed between Utah and its neighbors over plural marriage.

"Please don't concern yourself, Mrs. Stansbury," said Emmeline, noticing Stansbury' discomfort. "That is past and done with now. We are several years into our process of returning to more widely accepted marriage practices, and I for one am interested in moving forward, not looking to past offenses." This was diplomatically put.

"I'm very much looking forward to hearing you speak tomorrow, Mrs. Bradford," said Emmeline, addressing the older of the two women once again. "It is an honor for us to have here the first female candidate for a state office."

"Well, I hope it's not too disappointing to our audience tomorrow that I didn't become the first female *elected* to a state office! I suppose my defeat will always be an asterisk on my pioneering efforts. But running for the Superintendent of Instruction in Colorado was, I hope, an important step in paving the way for whichever woman that ultimate honor falls to."

"Mrs. Bradford, if I were you," said Emmeline leaning forward, "I would see no degradation in running in primaries, participating in conventions, speaking in public, and appearing at polls. These are things you did with the sorority of the nation behind you. Actually," Emmeline smiled slightly and leaned back, "I am considering throwing in my hat now myself, and your example gives me hope that I might do some good."

"Oh, Mrs. Wells, you must run for office!" Young Stansbury became surprisingly animated at the idea. "Most certainly. Everything will change here in Utah, you will see, just as it has in Colorado. You cannot imagine how exciting it was to see Mrs. Bradford campaigning for her civilizing ideas, putting herself forward as the right one to drive the impurities out of Colorado's politics. You must do the same here, Mrs. Wells, as soon as Utah's statehood is official. You have been the voice and face of women here in Utah for so long, I feel certain you would be successful."

"You are too kind, Mrs. Stansbury," demurred Emmeline, although privately she was delighted by the assumption that she would be Utah's

MARY C. C. BRADFORD

Born August 10, 1856, in New York, New York
Died January 15, 1938, in Denver, Colorado

Mary C. Craig was born into a wealthy and well-known New York City family, attended school in New York City, and received a thorough education that included French and German. She began writing at an early age, having a short story published when she was only twelve. She married Lieutenant Edward Taylor Bradford in 1876 at the age of nineteen in a fairy-tale wedding extravaganza. The couple left the glamorous life behind in 1878 when they moved to Leadville, Colorado, to pursue mining. Bradford contributed to the family income by teaching school.

When an 1893 referendum passed to include equal suffrage in the Colorado state constitution, Bradford and several other women ran in the next election for public office. Bradford ran for state superintendent, nominated by the Democratic Party, becoming the first woman ever nominated for an elected office in the United States. She lost to another woman, Anjanette J. Peavey, but this nomination and other public roles prepared her for her later elected positions.

After her husband died in 1901, Bradford was elected as the county superintendent of Adams County in 1903 and later as the superintendent of schools of Denver from 1909 to 1912. Under her leadership, schools became more standardized and efficient. Bradford worked on the Educational Council of Colorado and the Colorado Teacher's Association. In 1918, she became the president of the National Education Association, the second woman to serve in that role. Outside of the educational sphere, she also worked as associate editor of the *Modern World* in 1907 and was the first female delegate to the Democratic National Party in 1908. She was involved as a charter member of the Woman's Club of Denver and the president of the Colorado Federation of Women's Clubs.

Bradford spent much of her life as an advocate for education as a county, city, and state superintendent, giving her platforms to enact progress both for education and for women.

choice as its first female elected official. "There are many younger and fresher than I am. And of course our presence on the campaign trail will not stop any men for running for office, so I suppose the ballots shall be fuller than ever. But we shall not dwell on Mrs. Bradford's defeat tomorrow. We are here to look forward. Which brings to mind, what can you tell me of Mrs. DeVoe? I know you both had the happy occasion to work with her on your Colorado campaign. Miss Anthony tells me she will be sending Mrs. DeVoe to Idaho now, to aid in our neighbor's campaign, and that we should support her in every possible way. Those of us who have achieved freedom for ourselves must now turn our attention to others, should we not?"

"We do know Mrs. DeVoe well," answered Mrs. Bradford. "She will be joined in Idaho by Mrs. Carrie Chapman Catt. I believe they intend to join forces with Mrs. Rebecca Mitchell and the Women's Christian Temperance Union. Do you see yourself traveling to Idaho yourself, Mrs. Wells? Is not your daughter there? And a significant population of your church members? I'm sure Mrs. DeVoe and Mrs. Catt would appreciate the insight into the attitudes of the Mormon voters there."

"Oh, Mrs. Bradford, you must be ignorant of how much a liability my Church membership would be in Idaho." Emmeline forced a laugh. "We do not fare much better there than we have in the wider world. Which is why Miss Anthony's supplication to us here in Utah to aid the Idaho campaign is an exercise in taking the high road. My daughter Mel does live in Idaho, and she would benefit from any liberation that might occur there, but it is only recently that Mormon men have been welcomed into the polls. Our members in Idaho waged their own internal version of what we here in Utah contended with in Washington."

"Oh, I'm sorry I was not aware of this," hesitated Mrs. Bradford.

"It is no matter." Emmeline added an easy lilt to her voice to make sure her guests continued to feel comfortable despite the tender subject. "In my faith, we are tasked with following the example of Jesus in forgiving seventy times seven times. I have not yet attempted to forgive the legislators of Idaho even seven times, not to mention seventy times more. The change must come in my heart, and exercising our energies and pocketbooks is as good a way as any to invest in a former antagonist.

As I said," she waved her hand, belying the seriousness of her sentiment, "the past is done with, and we are looking forward at this conference, are we not?"

The conversation turned to lighter fare and pleasantries, Bradford and Stansbury having become shy of the conversational landmines they seemed unable to avoid. But later, after they had left, Emmeline could not help but brood on the next day's vital question: were the Latter-day Saints of Utah—the men and the women—ready to lend their aid, alongside their other neighboring states, to enfranchising the women of Idaho? Of course, there was nothing Emmeline wanted more than to have her Melvina enjoy the civic liberation that came with enfranchisement, but could Anthony—could she, Emmeline—convince the Mormon Utahns to lend their money, time, and energy to Idahoans who had so recently degraded their own worth as citizens?

CHAPTER 13

Rise, Columbia's daughters, rise;
Heaven has surely heard your cries,
Yet to the world we must appeal.
Arise, ye mothers of the race,
Enjoy your heaven-appointed place,
Demand the rights the world accords
Freely to "creation's lords,"
Now let woman's watchword be—
"Equal Rights and Liberty."

From "Equal Rights," sung to the tune of "Hail, Columbia,"
from the *Utah Woman Suffrage Songbook*

Monday, May 13, 1895
9:30 in the morning

"But, Aunt Em, we're not due to start for an hour, and already the room is packed to the brim." It was still early in the day, but already Ruth Fox looked exhausted, biting and twisting her lip with worry. "I did as you asked and only invited our leadership committees to this session, but I guess the word spread, and now the reporters alone are claiming most of the seats. I suppose they are interested in our conversations about what to do next with Idaho and California. Or maybe they just want an up-close view of Miss Anthony. I don't know. I am out of ideas. I have told them there will be ample time to brief them later. But it is not deterring them. What do you suggest?"

Ruth leaned against the railing of the grand staircase that ran through the middle of the Salt Lake City and County Building, bisecting the hallway with equal parts on the right and the left of her. This was the Gothic building Emmeline had pointed out to Anthony the day before. Now that they were inside, it was clear that the space would not be sufficient to hold the crowd.

Emmeline glanced down the northern corridor to the doorway to the left side of the spacious hallway. The entrance to the Convention Hall, the room where the Utah Territorial Constitutional Convention had recently met, was indeed alive with ladies and reporters and curious onlookers jostling each other to get in. It reminded Emmeline of eager fish in the pond near her childhood home, fighting over who would enjoy a small piece of bread she threw to them. While Emmeline took pleasure in the public's demand for the morning's events, she also knew the crowd could easily get out of hand and the goodwill of the previous day could quickly be lost.

"I am determined to hold this session of the conference here, Ruth." Emmeline felt Ruth was whining. Did she have to solve every problem? Her frustration with her young protégé was evident in the clip of her words. "You understand the significance of meeting in this room today, do you not? Just a few weeks ago, our territorial delegates voted to include suffrage as an inalienable right in the new Utah state constitution. That room is sacred to our cause!"

"Yes, of course, Aunt Em." Ruth prided herself on being exceptionally patient with her mentor, even during her patronizing moods. Being able to vent to Emmeline's daughter Annie whenever her mother got on her high horse had helped Ruth get through the past several months' planning. "I myself stood on a table in the back of that room to hear the final vote in April," she reminded Emmeline boldly. "But I'm concerned about our guests' comfort. And reaching the largest audience possible. Should we consider removing ourselves to the Tabernacle again today? Or perhaps the Assembly Hall?"

"Only after we meet in this hallowed space will I consider moving to the Assembly Hall." Emmeline stood firm. "We can all stand to be a little uncomfortable this morning, in honor of last month's events held in that very room. I will count on you to regulate the crowd this morning so as not to be disruptive. Give seating priority to our leadership committees. If there is room left, the reporters and public visitors can stand. If the crowd continues tomorrow, I will consider moving our proceedings to a larger space."

Ruth had the only answer she was going to get, so she brushed aside the wisps of hair that had come undone in her morning's bustle and hurried down the hall to manage the rising tempers as the space grew smaller and smaller and the air hotter.

For her part, Emmeline felt a jolt of pleasure over how the local papers would describe the size of these larger-than-expected crowds. Thousands more than anticipated last night! An overflowing room this morning! With the national silver conference also being held in Salt Lake City that day, featuring a fancy financier from Philadelphia arguing for a national silver standard instead of a gold standard, Emmeline had been concerned the suffrage conference would receive scant coverage in the local newspapers. At least she didn't have to worry about that anymore.

By 10:30 a.m., Ruth had determined who could stay in the room and who needed to listen from the hallway. She ensured both doors leading into the room were left wide open, and the building's live acoustics allowed for much of what was said to reverberate down the hall. The room was festooned with flowers that were "as pure as fair woman promises to make the politics of Utah when she is accorded the right to cast a ballot," as the *Salt Lake Tribune* described later that day.

Watching Ruth manage the crowds on the second morning of the Rocky Mountain Suffrage Conference, Emmeline couldn't help but think what a long—and short—month it had been since that triumphant day in April. Just a few weeks before, the male delegates assigned to create a constitution for the new State of Utah had agreed that women's suffrage would be included in the new state's laws. Once the vote was confirmed, there was a sense of inevitability about it. Of course Utah's men did the right thing for their women. How had she ever doubted them? The right had always been theirs in spirit; it was a mere matter of codifying it.

On the other hand, the days following the vote revealed to Emmeline just how anxious and uncertain she really had felt. She revealed petty jealousies in her journal, directed toward the very ladies with whom she'd just executed the success—"Emily [Richard's] birthday [today] and I suppose will be royally kept as she seems to be fortunate in money matters"—and expressed anxiety over the next task ahead: the planning of the suffrage convention. How fortunate that Anthony and Shaw's visit followed so closely on the heels of Utah's triumph, but regarding the organization of it, "One is puzzled to know how it is all to be done." Thank goodness for Ruth and Zina Young and Sarah Kimball and that young doctor who had once interned at the *Woman's Exponent*, Martha Hughes Cannon. With their help, the conference was so far maintaining the feeling of unity and optimism Emmeline so desired. In fact, the papers had called the previous day's proceedings a "gala day in the lives of Utah's public-spirited women," and her perusal of the coverage in the morning's papers showed it generally to be complimentary and comprehensive.

The format of the Monday morning meeting was similar to that of the day before in that Anthony and Shaw would speak in reminiscing and congratulatory tones, looking back on the challenges and triumphs of their movement so far. However, Emmeline knew that today was the day the group would have to turn from patting itself on the back and celebrating recent triumphs to mapping out a strategy for how to make sure those triumphs continued. How could they ensure that scenes such as the one that had just played out in this very room were repeated in Idaho and Washington and California? As much as Emmeline enjoyed the unique moment of solidarity the conference provided, it was in her nature to continue looking for the next big challenge. And the next challenge was Idaho.

The convention room, so recently dominated by the male delegates, was now thick in yellow garlands. The garlands, draped across the banisters that cordoned off the platform set aside for leadership chairs, featured yellow flowers that were the symbol of the national suffrage movement: yellow roses, daffodils, carnations, and various wildflowers that were in season across the desert valley. The women in their hats and rustling silks gave the room an entirely different air than it had had in April. Many of the banners, ribbons, and ornamentation that had been installed for the constitutional convention weeks before were still in place. Emmeline especially approved of the portraits positioned to the left of the speakers' stand: one of President Abraham Lincoln and another of Elizabeth Cady Stanton (who, though she had never returned to Utah, had been thoroughly exonerated for her comments on birth control twenty-five years earlier).

"Mrs. Bradford! Mrs. Stansbury!" Emmeline spotted her Colorado guests from the night before and elbowed her way toward the front of the room where they were examining the name placards on the platform chairs. "Please, let me help you find your seats. Ah, here you are, right between Mrs. McVicker and Mrs. Ferry of Park City. They will both be most agreeable neighbors this morning. You must have Mrs. McVicker tell you her thoughts on the kindergarten movement, educating even our youngest children. And Mrs. Ferry can update you on the politics of silver here in Utah, which I know is near to your hearts in Colorado." Her special guests dispatched to their seats, Emmeline turned her efforts to settling others of her leadership team. Governor West was due to open the morning's meeting; she wanted to check one more time that he would behave himself honorably, if dispassionately, as he had outside of the Templeton Hotel.

"Governor West, ah, yes, you are seated right here, next to Mrs. Kimball." Emmeline patted a chair next to the one already occupied by her dear friend. Governor West had hoped to get off a little more easily than that, but it was not to be. As the governor nervously bowed, Emmeline knew from Sarah Kimball's slanted glare that she would keep him in his place. Emmeline took a seat in a triumvirate right behind the podium: Anthony in the middle, Reverend Shaw on one side, and herself on the other. The other honored guests' chairs were arranged in a semicircle behind the leading three.

Exactly at 10:30, Ruth caught Emmeline's eye from the open doors leading to the hallway and gave her a nod. All were seated, or at least settled somewhere they could hear. Emmeline in turn nodded to Anthony. Anthony stood to open the meeting. She was dressed in her customary soft black satin, with simple lace decorating the neck and sleeves. The red crepe shawl, which was her trademark accessory, fell gently across her shoulders. But there was no gentleness in her face. Her square jaw and aquiline nose commanded the room before she made a sound, drawing the audience's eyes away from their neighbors, with whom some were still chatting, and entirely to her still gaze. When she did speak, her practiced orator's voice filled the packed room, low and rich, straightforward and serious, in contrast to Reverend Shaw's entertaining storytelling the day before. She expressed her gratitude to those in attendance and then ceded the pulpit to Reverend Shaw for a prayer.

The contrast between the two women was never so stark as when one followed immediately after the other in her remarks. Anthony drew her shawl tightly around her as she returned to her seat, adding to her severity especially since it was already warm in the room. Dr. Shaw, in contrast, was all charm and softness as she approached the pulpit to pray. Dr. Shaw thanked the Almighty that the men of Utah had come to realize that justice is justice, and that there was no distinction of sex in doing what is right. Also, that the men had begun to realize the importance of extending to women the principles of the golden rule. She was further thankful that Utah was soon to be a state—a free state.

After the prayer, Governor West offered perfunctory but polite remarks about how it was proper Miss Anthony and Reverend Shaw were visiting Utah at such an auspicious time. He knew Kimball's eyes willed him to be polite as she stared at the back of his head from her seat on the platform. Miss Anthony, the governor noted, had been in this city twenty-five years earlier and was well known then and now. In fact, he concluded, she needed very little if anything in the way of introduction. Not particularly inspiring comments, but he had behaved himself.

Anthony returned to the podium on the platform. This time, she took a minute to study her hands, which held the edges of the podium. She had no notes, just a look of fierce concentration in her eyes.

"This is the second time recently that I have had the distinction of being introduced by a governor. The first time was just a few days ago in Cheyenne, Wyoming, where Governor Richards graciously performed the same honor for me there. I wish to ask each of you today: Why is it that these two mountain states have led the nation in regards to acknowledging women's unalienable rights? What is it about your lands, your people, that has allowed the vision of liberty to take root and flourish? Your two states have recognized that women are part of 'the people,' of the governed, of the government. But nowhere has the victory been easy or guaranteed. It is not something which men have simply given to us. It has rested on decades of labor and agitation by women such as yourselves. Your states have each done it for different reasons, complicated reasons. Our campaigns are never neat and tidy. But they have been successful.

"Wyoming territory enfranchised women in 1869. As a joke? As an effort to make a 'big noise' to advertise the land to immigrants heading west? Out of a desire to do what is best for women and for our nation and recognize civic engagement as an unalienable right? It was a combination of all of those factors. When statehood became a possibility for Wyoming in 1889, the voting women there elected convention delegates who expressed favor for a permanent woman suffrage provision in the new state constitution. As a result, in 1890, Wyoming entered the Union as a state with its women free and enfranchised, the first state in the nation to include such a provision in its constitution.

"Colorado offered yet another model for success. Woman's equal suffrage was discussed periodically by the territorial legislature in the 1860s, and noble women there lobbied hard for Colorado to include the provision in the new state's constitution. But when that constitutional convention met to write Colorado's state constitution in 1876, the delegates made the opposite decision from what the Utah delegates recently decided: they chose not to include suffrage in the state constitution but pursue the path of separate submission instead. Predictably, it required a massive effort and two separate referendums by the Colorado people to finally include suffrage in the Colorado state constitution. I won't soon forget the journeys from town to town, sometimes on donkeys, who were the only ones who could manage the mountain terrain, in one of our first organized campaigns directed at modifying an existing state constitution. Thanks to the growing labor movement in Colorado, resulting in third-party Populist allegiances with our movement, as well as the rising prominence of the prohibition movement and the Woman's Christian Temperance Union, Coloradans successfully passed a historic referendum in 1893 that added a woman's suffrage provision to the existing state constitution.

"Similarly, we stand here in Utah today at the end of a complicated path. In 1870, like Wyoming, your territory also enfranchised its women, marking a victory for our women nationwide. The elimination of that right in 1887 was an affront to all of us working for the emancipation of women, although not all saw it in that light. Some were relieved to see the Mormon women no longer participating civically. But the men of Utah stepped up. Even though women were not permitted to select delegates to the constitutional convention who they knew would champion their cause, those male delegates still chose to put their women first. They did justice to all people, including the true and noble women who have suffered and labored even as men have suffered and labored. And now, as a new state, Utah will also come knocking on the doors of Congress with the rights of women expressed in its organic act, its women free and enfranchised, offering another star to our firmament of freedom.

"Here we stand today, at this pivotal moment in history, with these three leaders behind us: Wyoming, Colorado, and Utah. We now have three bricks laid down in a row, the start of our path to liberation. In addition, we have municipal voting rights in Kansas, and in twenty-three states women have the privilege of voting on school board matters. We have had struggles in Nebraska, Oregon, Washington, Michigan, and South Dakota. It is glorious, but until every woman in this nation has the opportunity to fully participate in political life and shape the society those politics dictate, it is not enough. It is through the ballot that the women of this country will truly be free."

Anthony finished her brief tour of recent history, campaigns the listening women had either followed closely or participated in with their whole energy of heart, and those in the room waited for the change in her tone. They knew Anthony didn't mean to spend the morning resting on past laurels.

"I propose today that this work continue to flood this western region. I propose that we take hold of the frontier spirit that has contributed to every one of these successes. I propose that we take hold of each other, having put our differences aside. We no longer have plural marriage to divide us. We no longer have the National Woman Suffrage Association and the American Woman Suffrage Association. We have the growing cause of prohibition to give our movement even greater urgency. We have the promise of a new century and an enlightened spirit descending on this nation.

"I propose that we lend all of our efforts and labor to securing Idaho and California as the next states loyal to our cause. This does not come as a surprise, I presume. Following her impressive work in Colorado building coalitions among various alliances, we have dispatched our young colleague Carrie Chapman Catt to support the campaign in

Idaho. They already have a strong foundation, thanks to the work of Abigail Duniway's writings and visits, the prohibition work of Baptist missionary Rebecca Mitchell, and the large cohort of Mormons who have kept a keen eye on the progress here in Utah. In addition, we are sending Emma DeVoe, one of our most effective speakers and coalition builders, to Idaho following her tours in South Dakota and Montana, where she has succeeded in building strong support that will bear fruit in its time. She will form a state association as part of the National American Woman Suffrage Association, raise pledges for the association's work, and host a state convention to cement support for our work there.

"As for California, I will be overseeing that campaign myself. The movement started on the coast with such strength and suggested such promise, but it has faltered there in recent decades without a unified leadership and focused strategy. We cannot find our way when our leadership and our alliances are fractured. Reverend Shaw and I will make our way farther west at the conclusion of our stay here, to oversee a conference in that state that has entertained equal suffrage notions for decades but has never succeeded in building the momentum needed to secure our rights. Now, there is an amendment to the California constitution currently being considered, which will be voted on next year. I intend to throw the entirety of my personal labor into that campaign, but it will be the continued writing, agitation, and funding from free women, such as many of you are, that will secure our victory. We have confidence that next year at this time, we will be celebrating California as the next great addition to the success of our movement."

The passion of her conviction whipped her last lines into a crescendo, and with her final phrase even those standing outside in the hall with their ears swiveled toward the open door broke into applause. This is what the audience wanted: a call to action, a battle plan, a strategy for moving their work forward. As women who agitated and educated and canvassed for years in their home states and now benefited themselves from the enlarging power of the ballot, where were they to put their energies now? Anthony, as ever, provided an answer, a vision. The movement didn't stop with them, as Utah women, as Colorado women, as Wyoming women. Didn't they have a responsibility to all women? The Latter-day Saint women had been guided for a decade by the masthead of the *Woman's*

Exponent: "The Rights of the Women of Zion, and the Rights of the Women of All Nations." Similarly, very few of the other women's periodicals of the time were limited to one particular locale or people. A successful suffrage strategy might require going territory by territory, state by state, and they might not always have seen eye to eye, but weren't their hearts now knit together as laborers in a cause greater than themselves?

Anthony seemed to hear the silent sentiments.

"We may think these next victories will fall into our laps. We've drunk the wine of victory, and women in this very room can testify to the ennobling power of shaping their own destiny through the ballot. The opponents of our cause have their theories of the evils that accompany women at the polls: women will abandon their homes for public life; women will simply vote with their husbands, but elections will become twice as expensive. The theory of one person is as good as that of another until it has been put to the test, but after that both sides must lay aside all theory and stand or fall upon the facts. And the facts are this: the homes have not been broken up. Human hearts are and always will be the same, and so long as God has established in this world a greater force than all other forces combined—which we call the divine gravity of love—just so long human hearts will continue to be drawn together, homes will be founded, families will be reared. And never so good a home, never so good a family, as those founded in justice and educated upon right principles. Consequently, the industrial emancipation of women has been of benefit to the home, to women and to men.

"The claim is made that we are building a barrier between men and women; that we are antagonistic because men are men and we are women. This is not true. We believe there never was a time when men and women were such good friends as now, when they esteemed each other as they do now. We have coeducation in our schools; boys and girls work side by side and study and recite together. When coeducation was first tried men thought they would easily carry off the honors, but soon they learned their mistake. That experience gave to men a better opinion of woman's intellectual ability. There is nothing in liberty which can harm either man or woman.

"What we would like better than anything else is for Congress to appoint a committee of investigation, which should investigate the result of woman's equal suffrage in the states where it has already been granted. So sure are we its report would be favorable that we are perfectly willing to stake our future on it.

"But until that report is produced, we cannot take for granted any victory. You here have suffered for these victories the injustices of men, of other women, of your family members and your friends. You've learned lessons that could only be gained in the crucible of this work. We invite you now to build on those lessons, share them with your sisters in this work, in Idaho and California and beyond. Lend them your fortitude, for they will need it in the coming months."

Anthony paused, her audience still rapt and focused despite the growing heat in the crowded room. Although she never abandoned her trademark red scarf, she let it fall completely to her wrists as she shifted her stance at the podium.

"I am pleased that we have with us here today two leaders from the recent triumph in Colorado. Mrs. Mary Bradford and Mrs. Ellis Stansbury are veterans of our cause there. Mrs. Bradford is an eloquent and magnetic speaker; Mrs. Stansbury one of our finest writers. Together, they were indispensable to the Colorado victory. They cut as wide a swath through Colorado politics as their petticoats would manage. And they come here today as representatives of the second state in this nation to enfranchise women, to Utah, which will be the third state in this nation to enfranchise women. They will be sharing with us some of the hard-won lessons of their experiences, so that we may learn from their success, correct errors, and develop a similarly winning strategy in our next targets. May this chain of influence and inspiration continue on to the fourth and fifth states, and far beyond. Mrs. Bradford, enlighten us please."

Mary Bradford rose from her chair on the platform as Anthony gestured to her and stepped away from the podium. As Bradford approached, Anthony grasped her hand and pulled her close to kiss her cheek. Bradford settled herself at the podium to polite applause.

"Ladies and gentlemen," she began in her famously unusual voice. Bradford had perfect command of French and German as well as English, which was known to be exact and eloquent. "Just fancy coming as a representative of a state where women vote to a territory where women don't yet quite vote and be presented as a defeated candidate. It is perfectly dreadful. Nevertheless, I was the first woman ever nominated for a state office in Colorado, and though I was beaten, they cannot take that honor from me."

The crowd applauded her again, sincerely congratulating her for her candidacy, but not quite sure if they should take her calling out of Utah as a "territory where women don't yet quite vote" as a slight or not.

"With Miss Anthony and Miss Shaw on the program, were it not for the fact that I am from Colorado, it would be quite unnecessary for me to say anything to you; but still I have an advantage, I can vote, I have voted, and I mean to vote as long as I live. And I love to vote."

Did Bradford remember that the Utah women had in fact voted too for seventeen years? That many in the room had had that right she loved so much stripped away from them? She was digging herself into a bit of a hole with her audience.

"In the equal suffrage victory of Colorado, the cause of political justice and human freedom has been advanced further than by any other event in the last twenty-five years of American political history," she continued. "Let me thank God for the recognition of equal suffrage now here in Utah. These victories will yet prevail from clime to clime, from shore to shore, and from Canada to Mexico, wherever the flag of the United States waves it will be dear to our hearts, for it is also a suffrage flag."

The applause from the audience at this pause was more approving this time. Where would she go from here?

"I wish to speak for a moment about Mr. Roberts, one of the delegates to the recent constitutional convention here in Utah." Bradford appealed to the common enemy of almost everyone in attendance, B. H. Roberts, since the wounds of his efforts at the convention just a few weeks earlier had hardly begun to heal.

"Mr. Roberts said at the convention words something to this effect: he said he thought there would be no objection to women going to the ballot box quietly, but the primaries and conventions and things of that sort would be so extremely degrading to women. I am here to say today that, as a candidate, I have taken part in primaries. I have taken part in two conventions. I have stumped across the state of Colorado twice, and I don't feel a bit degraded."

At this, the room finally erupted with cheers. Bradford took a moment to look back at Emmeline, remembering their conversation of the night before and the vote of confidence she had gained from the veteran's words of encouragement. Emmeline offered back a slight smile.

"Mr. Roberts should have studied Colorado more closely before making his assertions. The women in Colorado take a great interest in politics—many of us a far greater interest than the men; in fact, you know there are only half as many women in Colorado as men, yet 60 percent of the votes last year were cast by women. I think that is a pretty good record for the sex who, as he claimed, would not vote even if they could. But he needn't have even looked to Colorado to see how robustly women would claim their right. Indeed, right here in this very land, many of you in this room exercised the right for seventeen years and did so responsibly, civilly, and effectively. If only Mr. Roberts had looked to his own women's history, he might not so easily have discounted our desire to have a voice."

Finally, Bradford had the audience on her side. The Utahns knew not every visitor would have been so generous to even mention their early voting experience. Despite the national recognition the Utah women had received during those seventeen years, so many of the representatives of other states and territories viewed those early voting years as illegitimate and tainted because of the specter of polygamy. It hadn't helped that other Utah women—Jennie Froiseth, for instance—had themselves believed the vote perpetuated the religious bondage and domestic slavery of the Mormon women. So many had discounted the Utahns—shunned them, even. But now, in this moment of reconciliation and unification, with a call to look forward to greater victory, this outsider was following Susan B. Anthony's lead by acknowledging the Utah women pioneers. It was a small but important gesture. Bradford had her audience's full attention.

Bradford continued with detailed descriptions of how she, Stansbury, and others led the Colorado movement by building alliances with a wide array of labor activists, Populist sympathizers, silver standard enthusiasts, and political constituents of all stripes. They took pride in staying above partisan politics, instead pushing suffrage on the grounds of rights and justice rather than a particular political platform. "Our presence has driven many of the impurities from the politics of Colorado," she explained, "whether it was the brusque partisanship of the mining camps or the refined politics of the more pretentious and more aristocratic arena. In Denver, we are putting ethics into politics, and while there are obstacles, woman does not recognize them as insurmountable as long as she knows she is in the right. We are committed to expunging partisan bias from municipal politics."

The Coloradan suffragists' wide array of allies was a key to their success. It had been particularly tempting to secure themselves to the Prohibitionists, since many of the Colorado suffragists were also engaged in the Women's Christian Temperance Union and personally sympathized with prohibition. But on principle, the Colorado suffrage movement officially stayed out of the temperance debate. This was especially difficult in light of the numerous saloons and breweries that contributed to Colorado's cultural identity and economy, and comprised a vast lobbying effort against the enfranchisement bill. But between Bradford's extensive travel and speaking, Stansbury's biting editorials, Carrie Chapman Catt's strong leadership as a representative of the National American Woman Suffrage Association, the presence of ringers like Emma DeVoe, and the tireless work of vast numbers of Colorado women throughout the state, "rights and justice" had prevailed.

The momentum of the meeting kept the crowd rapt for the next hour as Mrs. Ellis Stansbury also spoke and gave her perspective on the Colorado victory. "I am very glad that Aunt Susan has told you that it is my business to write rather than to talk. I am afraid in our state we would think it was cruel to ask me to speak after the speakers that you have listened to here this morning, and yet it seems that we from Colorado ought to thank you for the help that Utah has given us," she began.

She spoke about the power of her paper, the *Rocky Mountain News*, and her editorials to stir up an understanding of what was at stake. Then, Reverend Shaw concluded with an elaborate explanation of the financial workings of the NAWSA and advised that the auxiliary societies raise funds for their own support and contribute also to the national council.

ELLIS MEREDITH STANSBURY

Born in 1865 in Montana Territory
Died in November 1955 in Washington, D. C.

Born in Montana to highly educated parents, Ellis Meredith was steeped in journalism from a young age. Even as a young woman, Meredith started writing a daily column entitled "Woman's World" for her father's newspaper, *Rocky Mountain News*, which she continued from 1889 to 1903. Settled in Colorado, Meredith became the first woman to report on the 1892 Democratic Convention from Chicago.

In 1889, she married Howard S. Stansbury. A year later, she worked with her mother to revive the Colorado Non-Partisan Equal Suffrage Association, which helped put suffrage on the Colorado ballot for a referendum vote in 1893. That year, Meredith traveled to the World's Fair to ask the NAWSA for help, telling Anthony, "If Colorado goes for woman suffrage, you may count on a landslide in that direction throughout the west." She became an important link between the NAWSA and the suffrage movement in Colorado, working to garner support from newspapers, political parties, and unions. The motion passed by more than 6,000 votes, making Colorado the first state to vote for suffrage to be added to an existing state constitution.

During her long career, Meredith wrote articles for the *New York Sun* and the *Atlantic Monthly*, defending suffrage against those who disparaged it as destructive and immoral. In 1901, she divorced her husband. She continued to fight against those opposed to female suffrage, and in 1904, she testified before the U.S. House Judiciary Committee in favor of passing a suffrage amendment.

Meredith wrote and published five novels within the span of three years (1901–1904). She served on the Denver City Charter Commission as vice-chairman of the State Democratic Party and as the Denver Election Commission president from 1911 to 1915. In 1913, she married Henry H. Clements, and the two moved to the East Coast, where she became involved in political organizations in Washington, D.C. After voting for twenty-four years in Colorado, she was now unable to vote in her new eastern home. With legal impediments to the right she had already successfully worked for, she became a powerful force in helping pass the Nineteenth Amendment.

"In this respect," she encouraged, "Utah should be the banner state. We call upon Utah, Colorado, and Wyoming now to turn your gaze outward, to the woman who does not yet enjoy the opportunity to shape the decisions that affect her most. Do not be miserly in your enjoyment of these rights. You have built tremendous structures in your local associations that represent the very best of woman's political ambition and ability. A man once said to me that he was afraid to see women in politics, because politics were so dirty, and he said men were the ones that made them so dirty. Well, I responded, if they are so dirty, why not let women cleanse them. She can use a mop better than anyone else!

"We also organize, petition, and raise funds with the unique expediency of our sex. If representatives of the three stars currently in our suffrage banner commit to supporting Idaho and California, the flag will soon not look quite so empty. The national association has already asked Mrs. Catt and Mrs. DeVoe to lead the effort in Idaho, working closely there with Rebecca Mitchell, who has laid important groundwork. These funds will help support national representatives, like Mrs. Catt and Mrs. DeVoe, in going to Idaho to implement the same aggressive tactics that had been used in Colorado. The funds would also help support Miss Anthony, who will personally oversee the California campaign and spend considerable time there herself."

The audience followed the logic of the morning's presentations: Anthony had given them the calling of aiding Idaho and California, and she had inspired them to use the hard-won skills to ensure future and faster victories. Bradford and Stansbury offered the beginnings of a strategy, or at least a strategy that had worked in Colorado. Shaw had laid out what the campaigns would cost and how the audience could contribute. Wouldn't the same strategy work in Idaho and California that had worked in Colorado? Why not?

CHAPTER 14

There are . . . three classes of women opposed to suffrage. 1. Women who are so overworked that they have no time to think of it. They are joined to their wash-tubs; let them alone. But the children of these overworked women are coming on. 2. Women who have usurped all the rights in the matrimonial category, their husbands' as well as their own. The husbands of such women are always loudly opposed to suffrage. The "sassiest" man in any community is the hen-pecked husband away from home. 3. Young girls matrimonially inclined, who fear the avowal of a belief in suffrage would injure their chances. I can assure such girls that a woman who wishes to vote gets more offers than one who does not. Their motto should be "Liberty first, and union afterwards." The man whose wife is a clinging vine is apt to be like the oaks in the forest that are found wrapped in vines—dead at the top.

Abigail Scott Duniway, speaking at the NAWSA meeting in Atlanta in February 1895

Monday, May 13, 1895
4 o'clock in the afternoon

"But will a multipronged, nonpartisan approach actually work in Idaho, Mrs. DeVoe? What are your thoughts on the matter?"

Mrs. Emma DeVoe stood among half a dozen ladies who leaned in as eagerly as propriety would allow to hear the great lady share her wisdom on the most pressing question of the day. A lively reception buzzed around them. They hadn't exactly cornered her, but she was very literally pressed against a drawing room wall, crushing the yellow bunting that had been hung along the room's wainscoting. In fact, the entire home seemed festooned in yellow, not only on the walls but in the yellow dresses of the young ladies who assisted in serving tea cakes and lemonade to the most notable names of the city.

After the conference's morning session in the Salt Lake City and County Building adjourned, the gathering had moved several blocks away to an elegant reception at the home of Emily and Franklin S. Richards. Some had come via the Utah Drag, which had been recommissioned for the afternoon. Others had taken a lengthy walk through downtown Salt Lake City, through City Creek Park and past LDS Church leader and original territorial governor Brigham Young's grave, and up into the neighborhood known as the Avenues. The pedestrians were animated by the discussions of the morning and were eager to continue discussions they had started in the hallway, but many were also motivated to see the elegant Avenues home of the man who many considered one of their saviors at the constitutional convention in the face of Roberts's threat. A total of three hundred invitations had been sent out prior to the conference, reaching nearly all those prominent in political and social circles in the area. That afternoon, there was nothing more coveted in the entire city than an invitation to the Richardses' reception.

As Emmeline noted in her diary on not a few occasions, Emily Richards had excellent taste. It was taste made possible by her husband's successful legal career. And from the fact that since the Richardses were a monogamous Mormon couple, Church leadership had sent Franklin to represent the institution favorably as its general counsel in Washington, D.C., on many occasions. The Richardses' time in Washington had polished Emily so she sparkled as a token of urbanity rarely seen in the western desert.

In spite of her intimidating exterior, Emily's generosity to her fellow Utah suffragists made her a useful and effective ally, especially on days like this when they wanted to show that Utah was not beyond the reach of fashion consciousness. Her three-story Victorian home on A Street featured pointed gables, bay windows, and a lovely front porch, reached by ascending a set of exterior steps. On the porch, a receiving line enjoyed the mild spring air: the revered Mr. Richards himself, next Emily, then Susan B. Anthony, Rev. Anna Shaw, Mrs. Bradford and Mrs. Stansbury, Governor West, Hon. George Q. Cannon, President of The Church of Jesus Christ of Latter-day Saints Wilford Woodruff, and, of course, Emmeline. Each one shook the hand of every honored guest. The evening paper reported that "the guests of honor declared it one of the most pleasant affairs of the kind they had ever attended and were profuse in their praise of the hospitality of the people."

Though Emma DeVoe didn't have the national name recognition of Anthony or Stanton, in the western region of the country her influence and effectiveness were legendary. DeVoe spent her career on the road, from South Dakota to Montana to Washington State, and had arrived at the conference later than the national luminaries. Annie Wells Cannon, Emmeline's daughter, was herself in the circle pressing DeVoe while her father-in-law, George Q. Cannon, and her mother were in the receiving line. It had been Annie that had formulated the question that was on everyone's minds.

"My sister Melvina lives with her family in Murray, Idaho," Annie continued, "and is quite familiar with the various political discussions in those parts. She says the prohibition forces are gaining strength in Idaho, especially with the state's increased economic dependence on farmers rather than bachelor miners. She thinks the way to win the vote there is to go all in with the WCTU, rather than stay neutral. What are your thoughts on the matter?"

"Yes, she is right," began DeVoe tentatively. "And wrong too, of course. These things are never simple."

Although DeVoe had led an unsuccessful suffrage campaign in her home state of South Dakota, national leaders like Anthony and Carrie Chapman Catt recognized DeVoe's ladylike appearance and eloquent speaking abilities, two of the top criteria they looked for in those who might rise to national prominence within the movement. She'd cut her teeth in Colorado, aiding Bradford and Stansbury and their team, and redeeming herself from the South Dakota loss. Now, the national leaders planned to send DeVoe into Idaho. But she was clever enough to recognize that the Colorado playbook wouldn't necessarily work in Idaho.

"Prohibition as a principle does indeed have more support in Idaho than it did in Colorado, and the WCTU is exceptionally well organized there. The current WCTU president in Idaho, Mrs. Rebecca Mitchell, is a Baptist missionary and a tenacious tornado of a woman. She has done everything short of standing at the door with a shotgun to close all the

EMMA DEVOE

Born August 22, 1848, in Roseville, Illinois
Died September 3, 1927, in Tacoma, Washington

Emma Smith DeVoe was only eight years old when she attended a lecture given by Susan B. Anthony. This touched her so deeply that she became committed to the cause of suffrage from then on. After moving to Dakota Territory in 1881 as a newly-wed, DeVoe began her career as assistant state organizer for the South Dakota Equal Suffrage Association, picking up paid work as an organizer and lecturer for the suffrage cause when her husband's business ventures faltered. As an experienced organizer, she was chosen by the National Woman Suffrage Association leadership to lead campaigns in Dakota Territory, Idaho, and Oregon. Her travel to various locations and work on territory or state campaigns often chaffed local suffragists, who felt they knew their communities best. But DeVoe embodied the logistical and financial power brought to local campaigns by the NWSA.

DeVoe and her husband moved to Tacoma, Washington, in 1906. There, she revitalized the Washington Equal Suffrage Association and became its president. She worked to raise support for a women's suffrage bill by connecting with labor unions and men's groups. She polled voters and met individually with women throughout the city. She also revolutionized the campaign process by creating posters, holding women's days, and selling cookbooks that furthered the cause. It was important for her to use methods such as cookbooks to combat the fear that granting women suffrage would alienate them from their established spheres.

In 1909, the NWSA held a convention in Seattle. DeVoe had the idea to do a "Suffrage Special" train, with women delivering speeches from the rear platform as it pulled into various stations around the state. The vote took place in 1910, and the bill passed with 64 percent of the vote, making Washington the fifth state to join the Union as a suffrage state. DeVoe continued to dedicate herself to the national campaign and the passage of the Nineteenth Amendment.

saloons within her reach. Her companion in the cause, Mrs. Adelia Scott, offers a welcome contrast to Mrs. Mitchell: elegant, refined, pretty. Many like your sister, Mrs. Cannon, have told me we need only to hitch our wagons to Mrs. Mitchell and Mrs. Scott's prohibition crusade and we will easily ride to victory.

"On the other hand," continued Mrs. DeVoe, "you may be aware that in the past, the Idaho legislature has considered bills that join suffrage with prohibition in a single piece of legislation. Such unsuccessful efforts have proven that Idaho men prefer to consider the issues separately. They're uncomfortable with the conflagration of enfranchisement and prohibition as twin cherries on a single stem, assuming both lead to a more moral and upright community. So we may throw salt on old wounds if we throw our hat in with the WCTU. If that is the case, it would be better to replicate our Colorado strategy and attempt to build a broad base of support apart from any other political issue."

"Do you intend to build support among the Mormons, too, Mrs. DeVoe?"

"Hush, Annie," scolded Margaret Caine, a similar figure to Emily Richards in that she was a monogamous Mormon whose husband, John T. Caine, had served in Washington, D. C., as Utah Territory's representative to the House of Representatives. Caine had also been unanimously elected as the first president of the Utah Territorial Woman Suffrage Association when she and Emily Richards spearheaded it together in 1888. (As a polygamous wife, Emmeline had stepped away from a public role in the association's founding.)

"Well, isn't that what you are wondering, Mrs. Caine? Doubtless you have some family member in Idaho who was prohibited from exercising his constitutional rights by the Anti-Mormon Test Oath, do you not? Will that loved one so quickly turn to support the legislature that until very recently discounted his personage?"

Mrs. DeVoe looked uncomfortably from the younger Annie to the mature Mrs. Caine, putting her trust in the older woman to appease the young lady who had clearly not fallen far from her mother's tree.

"Mrs. Cannon," intoned Mrs. Caine, calmly but not patronizingly, "I— and many of my family in Idaho—carry three identities, as do you: I am a woman, I am an American, and I am a member of the Church. Three powerful claims, to be sure. Three treasured claims. To be all three requires a constant balancing of priority: which of those three identifications should I select to honor most at any one time? Which one's claims should I answer before the others? Should I sever myself from diverse associations simply because I wear a different suit of personal attributes than another? I will remind you that other Americans tried hard to distance themselves from those of us who also bear the nation's and the Church's name. But through our tenacious commitment to statehood, we have demonstrated that our twin loyalties both to church and state are possible. Similarly, other suffragists held us at arm's length, not sure they desired to stand in the same circle as us. The bonds of womanhood were not enough for them; they could see only our religion. Again, through our commitment to the great cause of equal suffrage, we have demonstrated that we can hold sacred both 'Mormon' and 'woman.' Now, the women of Idaho need our support. They are women, and the men who may vote for their liberty are American. Let us not enact upon the Idahoans the same tyranny of parsimonious stereotyping that was heaped upon us."

"It is a wise and Christian argument, Mrs. Caine," sighed Annie, who had listened to Caine's speech not as sharp chastisement but as a welcomed poultice of reason to her discontented passion. "I am grateful for your logic. I should not wish to diminish the men of Idaho to a villainous caricature, to be sure. Heaven knows we have suffered under enough of that here, as you say. I should wish to be an agent of binding, not dividing. I suppose you and my mother have seen enough to know that revenge is never the answer to past slights, but I do admit it still allures me with its shiny but false promises of satisfaction."

"You are wiser than your age demands you should be, Annie." Caine's voice softened. "I have no doubt you will be an example to us all someday. But, Mrs. DeVoe," said Caine, returning to the original focus of the conversation, "please do share how you might best proceed in Idaho."

DeVoe realized she had been holding her breath for the length of Mrs. Caine's monologue, and she now exhaled nervously.

"My motto is, 'Always be good-natured and cheerful,' so I will start with that attitude." The exaggerated cheerfulness of her voice was the only thing betraying the fact that her famously ladylike demeanor had been ruffled by the conversation. "If we can't demonstrate the peaceful and civilizing nature of women, we can't expect men to support our desire to elevate the political landscape with our participation. We must at every turn underscore men's and women's natural differences so as to draw attention to our peaceable natures. We have no interest in replacing men or claiming what they have. We are different creatures, in temperament and nature as well as in capabilities. We do not come to disrupt and tear down, but to civilize and build up."

Margaret Caine and Annie felt echoes of their own sentiments in DeVoe's words, but they also marveled at how different groups of women could be motivated by different factors. They supposed that economic independence, the ideal of self-made womanhood, and freedom from the unwanted oversight of the national government wouldn't register on DeVoe's top motivators, even though those had been front and center for them.

"The ground has been made fertile by Abigail Scott Duniway, whose name I assume you are familiar with?" The ladies nodded. As a prolific journalist and editor, Duniway's reach extended throughout the Pacific Northwest and into Idaho and Utah, although she resided in Oregon. Her newspaper, the *New Northwest*, was perhaps the closest competitor to the *Woman's Exponent*, although each was founded for different reasons and served different audiences. The *New Northwest* was founded in 1871; the *Exponent* in 1872. Before the paper's closure in 1887, Duniway wrote hundreds of editorials for the *New Northwest*, as Emmeline too used her paper as a personal megaphone. Although Oregon's legislature had defeated a suffrage bill in 1884 and had not revisited the issue since, Duniway was a legendary—and sometimes meddling—figure on the western suffrage scene. Making the ground "fertile" was a diplomatic way for DeVoe to suggest Duniway was a force to be reckoned with, especially when it came to national representatives sent by Anthony to lead local campaigns Duniway thought she should be spearheading herself.

"Mrs. Duniway has been canvassing Idaho for several years. She will be my first contact when I get there, and I will evaluate how I can aid the local organizations already established. Then we will engage in carrying out the 'still hunt' tactics our leading mothers have advocated in past campaigns: quietly and nonconfrontationally shaping the opinions of key community influencers."

Annie recognized her next question was rash, but she ventured anyway, feeling protected by the immunity of youth and quite certain she had already lost Mrs. DeVoe's esteem.

"Don't you ever, Mrs. DeVoe, find that you might just rather do something grand instead?" Annie became breathless as her voice crescendoed. "Some dramatic gesture to grab the gentlemen's attention? Do you ever lose patience with the 'still hunt'?"

Mrs. Caine exploded in a belly laugh that belied her Washington sophistication. The others around her at first tittered nervously—how could this brash girl be so disrespectful?—but then joined in with Mrs. Caine. Poor little Mrs. DeVoe, so sincere and intent, seemed quite baffled by the younger woman's question.

"I suppose you'd invite Mrs. DeVoe to host her very own indignation meeting in Idaho, Mrs. Cannon? Do you have some clever slogans for her to shout?" laughed Mrs. Caine. "Or perhaps you'd like her to chain herself to the doors of the Idaho state capitol building until the men capitulate?"

Annie did not back down.

"I don't know if I'd recommend those tactics exactly, but something in that spirit. Do we not need a grand gesture that might break the stale nature of the debates in these territories and states where the issue has rattled around the legislatures for decades? Did not our grandmothers begin this effort almost fifty years ago? That's longer than I've been alive, and as the next generation to be taking up the banner, I declare that I do not have that saintly patience."

"'Stale debates'?" Mrs. DeVoe did not catch the rebellious glint in Annie's voice, or if she did, she was offended by it. Who were these brash Utah women, bantering about such unladylike questions and unproductive tactics? "Young lady, you do not know how posters and slogans and mass meetings degrade us as champions of civility."

"Mrs. DeVoe, I apologize sincerely for Mrs. Cannon's audacity." Mrs. Caine became serious, recognizing that this second offense of their cornered guest might break for good the spell of goodwill that was graciously blessing the weekend's proceedings. "But you must understand she has had the luxury of growing up here in Utah, with most of the men around her supporting our cause and *wanting* us to be able to vote. Her own father, our city's mayor Daniel Wells, hosted Miss Anthony here in 1871 when she first visited and joined with our legislators in celebrating our first exercising of that right. And her mother is Emmeline Wells, who I am sure you know from her forceful writings. Men were not the ones we needed to convince of the benefits of the female vote, Mrs. DeVoe. We were bound here—men and women together—by an external foe. Our efforts to rid ourselves of that external foe could be described as grand gestures. Indeed, most of us here, including little Annie, did participate in the indignation meetings. And when our men finally had the opportunity to liberate us, as they did at last month's constitutional convention, they did so. With only minimal dissention," she hastened to add. "So you must forgive Mrs. Cannon for her outbursts. We are simply unschooled here in the ways of the still hunt."

Mrs. DeVoe appeared slightly placated, but still flustered. "That is very pleasant that you have enjoyed such beneficence from your men. I should hope you still recognize what a debt of gratitude you owe them."

"Oh, most certainly, Mrs. DeVoe. I do not mean to suggest I am not grateful," responded a tempered Annie. She was grateful to Mrs. Caine for putting into words what she could not.

"You must show your gratitude by elevating questions of morality and justice in the public square. Your benevolent men did not give you the vote so you could act as a ruffian."

"Yes, certainly, Mrs. DeVoe. Thank you for your guidance."

"Pardon me."

DeVoe had had enough. As the genteel lady curtsied and let her petticoats swish her away into the ocean of other guests, Emmeline approached the little group.

"What have you done to poor Mrs. DeVoe? She looks quite put out," observed Emmeline as she slipped in beside her daughter.

"Oh, dear Emmeline, your daughter only questioned the tactics of the equal suffrage movement of the past fifty years." Mrs. Cain's laugh returned as she updated her old friend. "You should have seen her face! I'm not sure she's encountered such a lack of genteel behavior since she joined the movement. Annie suggested that perhaps continuing to promise men we will behave nicely might not be the most effective strategy going forward."

Emmeline wrapped her arm around her daughter's waist. "What is it that Sister Sarah Kimball always says? 'Agitation and education are our best weapons of warfare.' Sitting by the road and waiting for the prey to find us is certainly not the Utah way, is it? Poor Mrs. DeVoe." Emmeline gave the group a teasing smile. "She's surrounded here by ladies who have already voted and will vote again, while she has not yet enjoyed that privilege for herself. I admire Mrs. DeVoe, but I believe Annie is right. If more agitation and education are not at the heart of the Idaho and California campaigns, it could be decades before the rest of the nation joins our honored ranks."

She didn't know how prescient she was.

CHAPTER 15

What does it mean to be an enfranchised woman? It is easier to tell what it doesn't mean. . . . It does not mean attending a few political meetings and reading a few bits of campaign literature; it does not even mean going to the polls and voting as conscientiously as one knows how. All of that is but a small portion of it. The vital part of being enfranchised is not to be found in its political aspects at all, but in its effect in teaching us our relationship with the life around us. The real significance lies in getting in touch with what newspaper people call "the human interest" of daily life, and finding one's own place in the great scheme of the universe.

"What It Means to Be an Enfranchised Woman," by Ellis Meredith Stansbury

Tuesday, May 14, 1895
6:30 in the morning

How strange it is, thought Emmeline the next morning as she woke early once again in her quiet home, *to be surrounded by so many people all day long, and yet be utterly absorbed in silence now.* From her bed on the second story of her house, Emmeline could look out of the bay windows of her bedroom to an unobstructed view of the Wasatch mountains.

By the time Daniel died in 1891, his finances had recovered enough to allow Emmeline to move out of the adobe structure and build this new home for herself, where the eastern morning rays invited sunshine and a sense of optimism into her small but comfortable bedroom. Watching the dust mites touched by the streaming sun, Emmeline marveled that last night after the reception, she had entertained no fewer than thirty-six people in her parlor. Ruth, Sarah, and Zina were to be expected. But then there had been Bathsheba Smith, Martha Hughes Cannon, Emma McVicker, Margaret Salisbury, Isabella Horne, Romania Pratt . . . and several of their husbands and other men, too: Angus Cannon, Orson Whitney. Was she destined to have everyone for an evening but no one for a lifetime? Would no one stay?

Emmeline rarely employed poetry as a tool of political activism. That she left to her editorial writing. But this morning, waking to the spring sunrise and feeling a glow of harmony with the conference's two days behind her, she sat up and took hold of the pen and paper she kept by her bedside.

> *Woman, awake! as mother, daughter, friend,*
> *Thine energies and earnest efforts lend,*
> *To help thy country in her hour of need—*
> *Prove thine integrity in word and deed!*
> *For woman's star is lighting up the dawn,*
> *And rosy gleams presage the coming morn.*
> *Yes, woman hath a mission to perform,*
> *Embodying the germs of true reform;*
> *For her a nobler era, a broader sphere;*
> *Then banish obstacles, and doubt, and fear;*
> *The inspiration of a clearer light,*
> *Will strengthen her and nerve her for the right.*

She would add more stanzas later when the day wasn't calling. But for the moment, it captured the energy she felt from the weekend's celebrations thus far. So much had already been accomplished, so much doubt and fear already waded through, but the hard-won lessons would be useless if not called upon to banish obstacles for other women in the future. In just a few short years, she had gone from an enemy of the United States, as an indecent plural wife in a distant desert territory, to one of the country's leading women. Her belief in women went beyond country, beyond nationality. Why should she not fight for all of them? There was no place for revenge, for slights in payment for the years of humiliation she and her colleagues had experienced from Washington, D.C. There should be no reserve in the work she would do to emancipate all American women. Perhaps one day she would even go beyond American women. Perhaps this work would take her to England too, where the women there were waging their own lengthy campaign.

The thought thrilled Emmeline. Even at her age, she felt a burst of energy when she considered the work she could continue to do on behalf of women. The writing yet to be done. The petitions to promote and sign. The speaking on behalf of women everywhere. The testimony she could give that enfranchisement didn't destroy the home or masculinize women, but rather enlivened society and enriched civic life, as it had in Utah once before and as she was confident it would do again. Perhaps Anthony would ask her to go to Idaho or California. Maybe she would work beside those dear figures, or alongside Emma DeVoe and help inspire a new generation of tactics, as Annie had envisioned. Or maybe she would focus on the nation's capital and try to reinvigorate the interest in a national amendment. The state-by-state approach might continue to work, but yes, bringing the proposed national amendment to the finish line would be so very exciting.

The idea of a national amendment enfranchising American women first germinated in the early 1870s, when tensions over the Fourteenth and Fifteenth Amendments' exclusion of women's voting rights led to the separation of the National Woman Suffrage Association and the American Woman Suffrage Association. Anthony had planted the seed of the idea during a train ride with California senator A. A. Sargent in 1872. Sargent officially introduced a proposal for a constitutional amendment in 1878, but it didn't move out of committee and reach the Senate for a vote until 1887, at which time it was roundly rejected. By that time, the proposed amendment was known casually as the "Susan B. Anthony Amendment," but support for it languished as both the NWSA and the AWSA decided it was more effective to focus their efforts on the state-by-state approach. Both groups refocused their resources on the individual territories and states.

Could this be the time, Emmeline wondered, to reinvigorate the discussion of a national amendment? As much as she wanted Mel and all the women of Idaho to enjoy the same rights she and the women of Wyoming and Colorado enjoyed, her heart wasn't in pursuing the fight over and over again in each new state. Anthony's vision as she had described it the day before—of tackling Idaho and California, and then Oregon and

Washington and the Dakotas—didn't give Emmeline the big stage she craved. And she did think Annie was right; using the same polite tactics in each state would require too much patience and take too long. She was awake now, and she wanted to help her country—her entire country—in its hour of need.

She determined to bring up the amendment with Anthony that very day.

9:30 in the morning

Learning from the Monday morning crowds, clever Ruth May Fox had shown her problem-solving acumen and arranged for the Tuesday morning session to be held in the Assembly Hall. Although this final session of the conference, scheduled to begin at ten o'clock, was originally planned for the Convention Room of the Salt Lake City and County Building, Ruth had alerted the evening papers that the Assembly Hall on Temple Square would be the morning's location instead. She had appealed directly to the President of The Church of Jesus Christ of Latter-day Saints, Wilford Woodruff, for last-minute use of the building. Woodruff happily complied.

The Assembly Hall was the perfect venue, thought Emmeline as she approached the building well ahead of the crowds. Not as big as the Tabernacle, where the eight thousand had crammed in for the first session on Sunday afternoon, and not as small as the Convention Room. It stood on the exact spot where the original tabernacle had stood, the Old Tabernacle where Anthony had spoken when she'd first come in 1871. That building had been demolished in 1875 when the new, current Tabernacle was finished, and then the Assembly Hall had been built on the spot. So there was a kind of poetry to ending this conference on the same plot of land, if not in the same building, where Anthony had first fostered her connection to Utah so many years before. Emmeline had not selected the building as a conference location initially because it was inextricably tied to the LDS Church, and she had instead wanted "neutral ground," free from religious ties. But because yesterday's meetings had been held in the Convention Room in the Salt Lake City and County Building and the need for a larger space had been obvious to all, she was less concerned today about hosting the conference on Church property.

The Assembly Hall looked like a small Gothic cathedral, with twenty-four spires dotting the cross-shaped perimeter. As though to underscore that it shouldn't be confused with a traditional Christian worship space, the Latter-day Saint building incorporated a Star of David above each entrance, symbolizing the Latter-day Saints' belief that they were spear-heading the regathering of the biblical tribes of Israel. With seating for approximately 1,400 people, Emmeline was satisfied that while the building might not be full this morning, attendees would certainly be more comfortable than they had been the day before.

"Good morning, dear Miss Anthony," greeted Emmeline upon seeing Anthony already on the dais when she entered the building and made her way past the rows of wooden pews to the front of the cavernous room. The inside of the main room felt similar to the Tabernacle: a single oval space with a perimeter balcony, capped with a domed ceiling that gave an effect of endless expanse. The Assembly Hall, like the Tabernacle, was presided over by a vast pipe organ whose pipes shot straight up like a regimen of brass bedecked soldiers. "I trust you slept and ate well at Mrs. Beatie's home last night?"

"Good morning! Yes, she has been a most gracious hostess. And this morning over breakfast, she was quite forthcoming about her youth as a daughter of your President Brigham Young and her childhood in the Beehive House. It is quite fascinating to me. And then her poor mother died when she was three years old, and Aunt Zina simply folded her into her own brood right there in the same home. Quite remarkable."

"Well, it was a different time." Emmeline hesitated to respond to Anthony's romanticizing of the most prominent polygamous household in the nation. "She was blessed to have Zina rear her. She avoided being sent away or being put into an orphan home. But of course, there were other things that weren't so simple in that household at the time."

"I do not doubt it. Do not take my interest in the Young household as anything but academic, my friend. You know I have very little respect for the institution of marriage generally, and I have always stood by the position that I don't care who is married to whom or how, because I plan to avoid the whole thing myself. But let's not let Reverend Shaw hear us speak of it. She would be scandalized, even though she herself is not married. She is quite close to my niece Lucy, though, and I would not be surprised if the two keep each other company for the rest of their days. They are quite thick. Well, look here. It appears the Reverend has roused herself successfully."

Reverend Shaw ascended the stairs and approached the pair. "Such a fine day to conclude our work here, do you not agree, ladies?" she beamed. "And I do approve of this venue. It feels quite grand. I do hope we have a chance to hear that organ at work this morning, Mrs. Wells."

"I am not certain we can muster a proper organist for this morning, Reverend. We did not plan to meet here or have the opportunity to enjoy it. Happily, the crowds that you draw have forced us into this larger venue."

"Yes, I am aware." The Reverend's plump smile revealed the dimple in her cheek. "Such a delightful surprise. I'm very much looking forward to this concluding session and the reports from various local associations. I am sure we will be impressed by your productivity and resourcefulness here in Utah."

"With our own work here in Utah completed," said Emmeline, "you can rest assured that we will continue to raise funds for the national association's work in Idaho and California and support those campaigns there. You inspired us with your rally cry yesterday, Miss Anthony, and you can count on the women of Utah to do their part in welcoming Idaho and California to the elevated platform of liberated women."

"I know we can count on you, Emmeline. We always have." Anthony clasped her friend's hand as Emmeline wondered if this was the moment to bring up the national amendment. No, she decided. This was not the time to bring up her hesitations about Idaho or her desire to work on a broader stage. That would simply detract from the morning's momentum. She would wait.

Anthony called the meeting to order from the podium at exactly ten o'clock in the morning as Emmeline sat behind her to her right and Shaw to her left. Because the move to the Assembly Hall was made with such short notice, there was no chance to liven the meetinghouse with any of the characteristic bunting or yellow drape with which Ruth had beauti-fied the conference's various other meeting spaces. Still, the audience was a colorful and radiant assembly, basking in the energy and optimism of the past two days. There were the usual suspects in the crowd: the Utah leaders, a core set of younger women led by Annie, the representatives from other states, and several hundred other women. Additionally, there were a few dozen men, including the Honorable John T. Caine, a former Representative of the Territory of Utah to the United States Congress who had been given a special seat on the stand next to Anthony, and about twenty reporters who were also men. Emmeline noted Elizabeth Taylor in the back of the hall, standing behind the pews with a notebook in her hand. Emmeline admired the young woman's tenacity and made a note to herself to add the *Utah Plain Dealer* to the papers whose conference cover-age she would review.

Anthony seemed especially pleased to welcome Elmina S. Taylor to the podium to say the opening prayer. As president of the Church's Young Ladies' Mutual Improvement Association, Elmina had recently traveled to Washington, D.C., with a delegation of seven other Utah women to join with Anthony in leading the National Council of Women, an organization dedicated to supporting the advancement of women in education, philan-thropy, reform, and social culture. The NCW sought to bring under one umbrella all efforts to uplift women, not just suffrage campaigns. In keep-ing with this focus, Elmina's prayer included a supplication to God to bless all benevolent efforts on behalf of women, not just the purposes of their specific gathering that day.

After Elmina's prayer, the time was largely devoted to receiving re-ports from representatives from the various counties in attendance.

Dr. Ellen Ferguson reported on the financial health of the Salt Lake City suffrage association, and she publicly committed that association's financial support to the national efforts soon to unfold in Idaho and California. "We will answer our sister's call," declared Dr. Ferguson. "Let our bounty here in Utah be shared with our neighbors."

Representatives from suffrage associations in Weber County, Davis County, and Utah County echoed the sentiments and the dedication to the cause. Mrs. Emma McVicker offered summary remarks to the local associations' reports. Emmeline watched Emma DeVoe, seated near the front of the audience, as each representative pledged their financial resources to the campaign's next battles. Was Mrs. DeVoe pleased at this show of solidarity? Perhaps, but Emmeline couldn't help but smile at the thought that the Utahns who had so scandalized Mrs. DeVoe with their remonstration of her polite tactics would help finance her Idaho efforts.

The reports complete, Anthony again took the podium.

"Utah will be a banner state in its support of our national efforts. The effects of your work and generosity will be felt in Idaho and California today, and Oregon, Washington, and Nevada tomorrow. When you hear the shouts of emancipation ringing from your neighbors, you will say, 'We played a part.'"

A great cheer arose from the audience.

"I am delighted to invite to return to the podium today Mrs. Bradford of Colorado, who reminded us yesterday with her eloquence that even after woman has voted, she is woman still. She has prepared a resolution that she will share with you that shall mark the final proceedings of this conference, cementing the unity we have felt here this weekend and enshrining our commitment to move forward. The opportunity to support a resolution and present it to governing bodies is one of the civic outlets available to women today and which we should seize with vigor. Through it, we express our gratitude to the men who have opened the doors through which we enter public life. We reaffirm our commitment to keep those doors open to those who follow us. And we pave the way through official declaration the sentiments and visions that we hope will be codified by those men into our constitutions and legislation. No other tool, save the petition, can speak so eloquently and concisely for the voice of women as the resolution. It seems only fitting that, at this historic conference, we eloquently formalize the sentiments of goodwill and unity that have existed here this weekend. As a representative of one of Utah's neighbors, and anticipating the gratitude that will be shown hereafter by Utah's other neighboring governments, Mrs. Bradford has been invited to draft and present to us here her resolution."

Mary Bradford approached the podium and read her prepared document in her clear, clipped voice.

"Whereas, Great gains in the suffrage sentiment and achievement have made the last year memorable; and

"Whereas, The women who have struggled so long in order that the Ideal American Republic might become real, have reason to hope that the final incarnation of justice in American institutions is near at hand; and

"Whereas, The women of Wyoming and Colorado already possess full suffrage, and the school suffrage is enjoyed by the women of twenty-five States; and

"Whereas, The men of Utah have seen fit to build the foundation of their new State upon absolute justice, equality and freedom: therefore be it

"Resolved, That the sentiment of this conference is one of unity in pressing forward with the cause of suffrage, committing energy, financial resources, and support in spirit to the forthcoming efforts in Idaho and California; and therefore be it

"Resolved, That this conference express profound gratitude to the men of Utah who have so unequivocally and practically witnessed to their faith in the principle of exact justice to all the citizens of this new and glorious commonwealth."

Mrs. Bradford looked up from her paper. "Those in support of this resolution, say 'aye.'" Along with the shout of affirmation, many of the ladies in the audience threw in the air yellow flowers they had been holding in their skirts: daffodils, daisies, and a rare early rose. The flowers speckled the air with cheery punches of the national movement's symbolic color. From her seat on the podium, Emmeline thought it was the most beautiful sight in the world.

CHAPTER 16

Freedom's daughter, rouse from slumber,
See, the curtains are withdrawn
Which so long they mind hath shrouded;
Lo! Thy day begins to dawn.
Woman, 'rise, thy penance o'er.
Sit thou in the dust no more;
Seize the scepter, hold the van,
Equal with thy brother, man.

"Woman, Arise!" Words by Louisa Greene Richards, sung to the tune of
"Hope of Israel"; from the *Utah Woman Suffrage Songbook*

Tuesday, May 14, 1895
2 o'clock in the afternoon

The regular two fifteen afternoon train to Saltair was almost ready
for the group of 150 suffragists to board. Two additional cars were being
secured to it to provide ample room for the special guests. Emmeline and
Ruth had invited a select group of their out-of-town visitors to enjoy an
afternoon at "the lake." They were referring to the Great Salt Lake, the
largest saltwater lake in the western hemisphere, whose shores were mere
miles from the center of the city. With the business of the conference fully
concluded, the women lifted the brims of their hats and turned their faces
to the sun.

"It is practically impossible to believe there is a lake so nearby!" exclaimed Mrs. French, the conference attendee who had come one of the
farthest distances, all the way from Pittsburg, Pennsylvania, along with
her husband, who was joining the excursion too.

"It's not difficult to believe when the acrid salt air disturbs our noses,"
retorted Mrs. Trumbo, scrunching her nose, who, with her husband

Isaac, had just recently moved into the Gardo House, the most elaborate Victorian mansion in the city.

The striking lakeside resort on the shore of the Great Salt Lake, inspired by the design of a Moorish palace, was two years old and still a novelty in the area. Intended from its construction to serve as "Coney Island of the West," the resort quickly became the most visited family attraction west of the Mississippi. Built on 2,500 wooden pilings driven into the lake, it was home to the largest dance hall in the country, 600 bath houses, and a pier over a thousand feet long jutting into the briny water. Trains carried people from Salt Lake City to Saltair every forty-five minutes from 9:30 in the morning to midnight. A round-trip ticket and admission to the resort cost fifty cents.

With the 2:15 afternoon train finally outfitted to transport the guests of honor, Emmeline invited the men and women to find seats and settle in. A brief twenty-minute ride through the barren outskirts of the city revealed the magnificent pavilion, a revelation to the out-of-town guests. "What a remarkable place!" exclaimed Reverend Shaw as the train slowed. "It almost makes one want to take to the skies on a magic carpet!" Murmurs of marveling echoed throughout the cars.

"Last year's paint refreshing certainly added a measure of beauty," Margaret Salisbury commented to those in her train car as they examined one of the Utahns' most famous points of pride.

Reporters who had followed the party to the resort reported for the evening papers on the group's activities: "The hour at the beach was spent in strolling about the pavilion, or enjoying the luncheon from well-filled hampers, and about a score, most of them ladies, took to the water. The temperature was 72 and the bathing as pleasant as in some of the cooler days of July."

Anthony did not choose to swim. Emmeline had counted on this, and she found her friend seated on a wicker chair on the salt-encrusted beach, while the cheery Reverend Shaw exclaimed how the salt burned her eyes as she waded into the water. Drawing a chair close to her friend, Emmeline considered how to broach the subject of the national amendment.

"The Idaho campaign will be in strong hands with Mrs. DeVoe," she began. "Such refined manners and respectful approach will go far, if she is able to earn the trust of Mrs. Marshall and the WCTU, as well as Mrs. Duniway." Emmeline did not mention that she, like Annie, thought the "still hunt" tactics would eventually run their course. "I believe I've told you that my daughter Melvina lives there with her husband."

"Yes, I thought of her yesterday as we were discussing support for Idaho. I suppose they have suffered because of the ostracism of the Mormons there?"

"Mel has actually distanced herself from the Church, so she lives quite a different kind of life than she might if her husband Will had to succumb to the Test Oath." Emmeline looked out across the water to the carefree bathers. "To be distanced from her spiritually as well as physically feels like quite a burden."

"I'm sorry for it, Emmeline," said Anthony sincerely. "I admire your willingness to support a neighboring government that perpetuated the hardship among its own people that the federal government forced upon you. But just imagine: an effective and successful equal suffrage campaign in Idaho might prompt both the men and women of that state to put past hostilities behind them. The campaign could be the perfect opportunity for the sizeable Mormon population there to join in unity with those who might once have been foes. I foresee very positive engagement in our cause by both the Mormons and non-Mormons there. Perhaps Mel and Will might even consider rejoining your faith."

"I suppose that is possible," Emmeline smiled weakly. "But I do admit that the Idaho campaign remains fraught for me personally. I worry about engaging myself in a community Mel has cultivated for herself. She is capable and engaged; I do not think she would appreciate me involving myself too heavily in her new home's governance."

"I understand."

Emmeline took a deep breath before continuing. "It has made me consider if there might be a broader stage on which I could contribute. Could I be of some use beyond this western region? With my husband now deceased and my children grown, I should very much like to spread my wings even further. I still have responsibilities at the *Exponent*, but I should like to deliver more of my messages in person now, rather than just writing about them. I know I shall always be viewed with some degree of suspicion because of my marriages. It is easy to comprehend the prejudice I will meet, when everyone I meet wants to know directly if I am a Mormon and would not think of asking a woman from any other state what church she belonged to. But I have to hope that someday soon I shall be looked upon first and foremost as a self-made woman who would like to see more self-made women in the future."

Emmeline was relieved to see Anthony responding with a warm smile. "I have had you in my sights for some time, my friend, as someone we could employ more thoroughly in the cause. I wanted to allow you to complete your work here in Utah first, and now with polygamy set aside, statehood imminent, and your women free, the time might be just right. I see a bright future for you working on broad issues with women throughout the country, not just equal suffrage. In particular, the National Council for Women needs to be fortified and expanded. Elmina Taylor has offered a steady hand thus far, but she doesn't have the national experience or recognition you have to be an effective executive.

"I can envision a role for you as we lend greater aid to our colleagues abroad," continued Anthony. "The International Council of Women is also of the highest priority, and its leaders will be traveling to England shortly to confer with the leaders of the movement there. There are many fine countesses and noblewomen who promise to host us quite lavishly when we descend upon them!"

"Oh, that does sound quite wonderful." Emmeline thought of the British poets and novelists that had inspired her own writing for decades, and her mind also touched on the fact that Daniel had served twice as an officer for the Church in England, leaving his wives and children for years at a time in the 1860s and 1880s. She would walk where he had walked.

"I would very much love to contribute to broader issues, now that we have helped create momentum for the equal suffrage movement specifically. And England sounds heavenly. But, I do feel my particular passion for the ballot must continue to be of use here. Could I serve as an advocate for the national amendment?"

"Ah, the amendment," sighed Anthony. "We are like gardeners trying to cultivate a desert, Emmeline, finding water for each flower individually to satisfy each's own thirst. What we most need is a storm from heaven that would water all equally and abundantly. I have been so focused on finding water for one state to the next, that I have failed to maintain the momentum of poking the storm cloud."

"Not failed, Susan, certainly," said Emmeline gently. "The local approach is prudent, and it is bearing fruit. I only ask to do my small part to poke the storm cloud while you continue to focus on the flowers."

"My dear, I will put you on a train to Washington, D.C., tomorrow to speak with senators, if that is what you wish. You offer an example of the enabling effects of civic participation on women, as one who voted many years ago and will vote again after statehood is official. The gentlemen need to see that a woman with the ballot is still indeed a woman, and not a masculinized monstrosity who abandons home and family."

Emmeline laughed. "Yes, I carry that banner quite well."

"But as I consider it," continued Anthony, "will not statehood for Utah mean the opportunity for women to run for political office? You may do your greatest service yet by becoming the first female elected official of Utah. It would allow you to remain close to your *Exponent* office while still contributing on the grand scale you desire."

Emmeline had of course considered running for office since female candidacy would be an option under the new state constitution, but she let Anthony continue.

"And, Emmeline," Anthony turned to face Emmeline in her chair, leaning forward with a sense of sudden alarm. "Representative Caine mentioned to me this morning that Mr. Brigham Roberts is already expressing his interest in running for a seat in the House of Representatives. I need not tell you that cannot happen. After his behavior last month at your constitutional convention, elevating that man to the ranks of the federal government would set all of our efforts—in the states or on behalf of the national amendment—in jeopardy. Not to mention the backsliding it would cause for Utah in the minds of the nation. To elect a polygamous anti-suffragist to represent Utah in the highest chambers of our nation would do irreparable damage. "

Emmeline sighed. "I heard gossip of the subject circulate after the convention, but I pushed it aside as simply the grumblings of a dejected loser. Of course, if I continue to be needed here in Utah, I will do it gladly."

She wasn't entirely convinced she would do it gladly, but she would do it if it would allow her to be useful.

The reporters from the evening papers didn't notice Emmeline's reflective mood as the train returned the visitors to Salt Lake City. "Lively chat," the *Salt Lake Herald* reported, "made the ride home seem all too short, and the train arrived at the depot at 4:30 p.m., bearing as jovial a company of equal suffragists as ever held a public or private conference."

"I have had so many firsts just in these past several days, Mrs. Wells," gushed Reverend Shaw on the train back to the city. "I was the first woman to preach in the Tabernacle; Sunday was my first time speaking to such a large audience. It is the first time I have set my feet in salt water so far from the nation's coast! What an adventure you have given us here."

The ladies' Utah adventure was not quite over. That evening, Anthony and Shaw returned to the train station with packed bags to proceed northward to the city of Ogden, where they spoke again that evening and were hosted at a reception by the ladies of that city. From there, they would continue to Reno, Nevada, and then on to San Francisco.

This time, only a small group gathered on the platform to see off Anthony, Shaw, and Emma DeVoe, who would now be joining the national advocates on the rest of their western journey.

"You will always be engaged in a field of usefulness, Emmeline," said Anthony, clasping Emmeline's hands. "I know it is your fondest wish. You communicate your resolve with every word you write and every lecture that you host. I am getting old, Emmeline. I hope to see this work to its culmination before I die. But I must know that there are women like you—and Ruth and Martha Cannon and Emma McVicker and your own daughter Annie—who have the vigor of mind and force of personality to finish whatever I cannot. And, truthfully, our work will never be finished. Political equality is but the stepping stone to civil, educational, religious equality. The ballot is but the weapon by which we will bring all good things to ourselves and our children. I know you understand this. Your greatest work may be in ensuring the next generation understands it too."

Emmeline's friend Margaret Salisbury and her daughter Annie stood aside, giving the two women their space as they exchanged parting embraces. The small group was like a still eye in the midst of the train platform's storm of travelers. As Anthony picked up the valise beside her and turned to board her train, Annie stepped to Emmeline's side to put her arm around her tiny mother. For a moment, mother and daughter watched Anthony approach the train. Then, mid-step, Anthony stopped.

"Take this." Anthony set down her valise and hastily returned to Emmeline while pulling at a finger on her right hand. "My gold ring. I want you to have it." Anthony pressed a slim gold band into Emmeline's palm as Emmeline gave her friend a surprised look.

"No, I can't possibly take this."

"Take it as a token of the esteem and love I hold for you, my friend. Women in this little mountain state vote and hold office before they do in the rich and powerful states of the seaboard. You have my eternal respect."

Emmeline hesitated, but shook her head again. "I've worn many tokens of esteem on my finger throughout my life. Tokens given me by men to whom I have linked my life. I do not want you to be bound to me or I to you by anything but the bands of freedom. Let me earn this ring from you. Only when all of our women have been emancipated will I accept this final token as a symbol of the bondage we have cast off together."

She handed the ring back to Anthony with her chin up so there would be no more debate. Without knowing what victories or defeats still awaited, the two women took a final moment to clasp hands and revel in the triumphs that were behind them. And then Anthony boarded the train to find out what lay ahead.

EPILOGUE

I think civilization is coming Eastward gradually.
—Theodore Roosevelt, June 1913

On November 5, 1895, the men of Utah voted to accept the new constitution of the State of Utah, with suffrage included. 31,305 voted to ratify; 7,687 voted against ratification. Although the women couldn't yet vote and thus relied on the men, once again, to deliver their freedom, they showed their support for the process by serving lunch in all of the voting precincts.

On January 4, 1896, President Grover Cleveland officially made Utah the forty-fifth state in the Union.

The state-by-state approach validated by Wyoming, Colorado, and Utah did indeed bring triumph to Idaho. The partnership of the Women's Christian Temperance Association and Idaho's Equal Suffrage Association, led by women such as Emma DeVoe and Abigail Scott Duniway, delivered a victory on November 3, 1896, when an amendment was added to the Idaho constitution allowing for equal voting rights. The vote was 12,126 in favor of the amendment; 6,282 against. Idaho became the fourth state to enfranchise its women.

Aside from the Idaho victory, the years immediately following the Utah and Idaho victories proved disappointing personally to Emmeline. The two-party political system, new to Utah with its statehood, caused rifts among some of the Utah women as they chose to join either the Republican or Democratic party. Most of the suffrage leaders of Utah chose to become Democrats; Emmeline chose to become a Republican. Few of her colleagues chose to follow her example. Ruth May Fox was one of those few, giving her reason: "When the women who had been ardently working for suffrage arrayed themselves for the political battle [between the political parties], most of them seemed to be Democrats while Aunt Em stood almost alone, a Republican. To even things up a bit, I joined hands with that great leader."

Additionally, Emmeline did choose to run for elected state office 1896 in the first Utah election open to female candidates, as predicted by her colleagues. But it was a disappointing experience for her. She ran on the Republican ticket, along with four other Republican candidates, including local Church and civic leader Angus Cannon. Cannon's wife, Dr. Martha Hughes Cannon, also chose to run in the election but on the Democratic ticket. Martha had been a typesetter at the *Woman's Exponent* in her youth before receiving four degrees in medicine, pharmacology, and oration. Despite running against both her husband and her mentor, Martha Cannon won the election, becoming the first female state senator in the nation and leading an ambitious public health agenda while serving in the legislature. Emmeline never did attain an elected office.

One bright spot in this period for Emmeline was her participation in the International Council of Women (ICW), which did in fact take her to London and give her experience advocating for women outside of her home nation. In June 1899, Emmeline joined other Utah colleagues such as Susa Young Gates, Margaret Caine, Elizabeth Claridge McCune, and Lucy Bigelow Young in London for an ICW meeting. In addition to attending presentations and receptions with leading suffragists of the United States and Great Britain, Emmeline was among those who paid a social call to Windsor Castle to Queen Victoria. On the ship returning home, Emmeline reflected on the "many amusing incidents, the great fund of information[,] the stigma of Mormonism." In a rare example of existential contentment, Emmeline mused, "My life seems wonderfully changed and developed. What further changes are yet to come I know not. Certainly a remarkable destiny and a most romantic life."

But disaster befell the suffrage community when, in September 1898, Brigham H. Roberts announced his candidacy for U.S. Congress on the Democratic ticket. In the wake of his anti-suffrage performance at the Utah Constitutional Convention, his campaign became a national media story and a source of severe embarrassment for Emmeline personally. Not only had Roberts been the main stumbling block to including suffrage in

Utah's state constitution, but he was also still blatantly living with his three wives from the pre-Manifesto era. Despite a vast coordinated effort by the Utah suffragists to remind the people of their new state how close Roberts had brought the women to continued political captivity, Roberts won the congressional seat, 32,316 to 27,108.

It was clear to Emmeline that women's votes had contributed to his win. "It is a great disappointment to me that Roberts was elected," she wrote in her diary. "It cannot but be detrimental in every way. My heart is very sad. I cannot understand how the women of the State can be so unscrupulous as to vote for such a man."

The selection of Roberts by Utah's citizens strained the Utah suffragists' relationships with the national suffrage organizations. Group after group put forth resolutions demanding Roberts not be seated. Emmeline and the Utah leaders were pressured to also renounce Roberts's election, but their loyalty to the legitimacy of his election, their religion, and the principle for which he was being denounced prompted them to withhold their official complaint. Anthony joined in the Utahns' claim that Roberts had the right to be seated. Still, by the time Congressional hearings debated the question of Roberts's seating in 1900, seven million Americans had signed a petition protesting Roberts. He was not appointed to the House of Representatives, and a special election was held to elect another candidate to take his place.

Although bitter about his experience on the national stage, Roberts went on to be one of the most colorful and influential thinkers within the Church at the beginning of the twentieth century. His *Comprehensive History of The Church of Jesus Christ of Latter-day Saints* and his work as assistant Church historian shaped the scholarly approach to LDS history for almost a century. The women with whom he had sparred did not fare so well. The move away from women-led political work—through clubs, petitions, and suffrage associations—into the two-party political system proved to be a challenging transition for many Utah women.

The unifying and optimistic spirit of the Rocky Mountain Suffrage Conference didn't last for Susan B. Anthony and Anna Howard Shaw, either. Upon arriving in San Francisco, the two leaders were feted as they had been in Salt Lake City, and California's Woman's Congress began meeting in Golden Gate Hall on Monday, May 20, 1895. The mood at the meeting was ebullient: despite several previous attempts at enfranchisement in the state, a date had finally been set for a popular referendum vote to approve revising the California state constitution to include suffrage. The women had more than a year before the vote to raise funds and implement Anthony's "all-partisan" approach, which aimed to gather supporters from all constituencies, similar to the Colorado strategy. Anthony felt the best approach for California was to gain endorsements from all parties in order to neutralize partisan attacks.

The California referendum vote took place on November 3, 1896, the same day as Idaho's. But in a devastating loss to California and the national suffrage movement, the referendum did not pass: 110,355 voted for the amendment; 137,099 voted against.

That day marked a turning point in the course of the American suffrage movement. It marked the end of the initial Western triumphs. Between 1869 and 1896, the movement had seen equal suffrage laws embraced by Wyoming Territory and then the State of Wyoming, the State of Colorado, Utah Territory and then the State of Utah, and by the State of Idaho. But the momentum summoned by these triumphs that culminated in the optimistic gathering of the Rocky Mountain Suffrage Conference met the end of the road with the California defeat.

Instead, the movement transitioned into a new era that day: the Doldrums, a period of frustration that conspicuously lacked public victories for fourteen years.

"The doldrums" is an old term, dating at least as far back as colonial sailors, that refers to an area in the Atlantic where sailing ships were often caught in inconsistent winds and ended up drifting for weeks before escaping. The label for the time period was given later by historians in the twentieth century who noted that no referendums to amend existing state constitutions were won during this period, nor did any state come into the Union as a suffrage state. The implication is that for fourteen years, from 1896 to 1910, the suffrage movement spun in place, unable to progress.

But other historians look back on that fourteen-year period differently: they see a period of reorganization, new strategies, and new leadership, leading to the flood of successes in the 1910s and, eventually, to the passage of the Nineteenth Amendment in 1920. For example, the Doldrums forced a reexamination of the "still hunt" tactic practiced so expertly by Emma DeVoe. Suffragists emerging from the Doldrum period took a decidedly different approach to their public visibility than their nineteenth-century counterparts. They embraced the media, no longer just newspapers but also film, photography, and mass market magazines, appealing to the Progressive Era's amplification of consumerism as a dominant social force.

The suffragists took control not just over where and how often they were portrayed, but how they were portrayed. With the goal of appealing most broadly to both the male voting public and their wives, public perception was key. The suffragists recognized that the vision of a civically engaged woman as a destroyer of hearth and home had to be put to rest once and for all. Historian Emily Scarborough explains, "In order to win both the support of women who embraced the newness of the twentieth century and those who held onto old Victorian visions of motherhood and womanliness, the suffrage cause compromised its radical vision of the future, and instead drew heavily on the past for much of its campaign in the media. Instead of framing suffrage as liberating for women, suffrage became a way to protect gender distinctions by promoting domesticity, morality, and femininity."

Pedestalization (putting women on a metaphorical pedestal of moral superiority to men) and the concept of the "angel mother" (a woman of untouchable goodness and sweetness) had always provided arguments for enfranchising women: women would civilize the political process and apply their housekeeping skills to cleaning up the mess men had made, while focusing on stereotypically feminine civic issues such as education. But in the twentieth century, this emphasis on women's domesticity and morality as a boon to civic life took a much more prominent role.

Leadership changes during the Doldrums facilitated this strategic shift. Elizabeth Cady Stanton died in 1902 and Susan B. Anthony died in 1906, making way for new figureheads for the movement. Carrie Chapman Catt emerged as the National American Woman Suffrage Association's new leader, taking over from Anthony in 1900. (Anna Howard Shaw actually assumed the presidency of the group from Catt in 1904, but she did not prove to be as effective a leader as she was delightful a speaker. She resigned in 1915, returning the leadership to Catt, who led again from 1915 to 1920.) Catt expanded the ranks of NAWSA leadership so that power wasn't concentrated in so few, and she also was instrumental in bringing in the support (and money) of many Northeastern socialites. Heiresses such as Alva Vanderbilt Belmont and Katherine Mackay hosted suffrage gatherings at their Manhattan clubs and Newport mansions, mailing out the embossed invitations to exclusive guest lists. A journalist noted in 1910, "Woman suffrage, once the cause forlorn and rejected, has entered the drawing room. And the women who have invited it there are those who may lead . . . in a cause as in a cotillion."

Alice Paul also emerged as a new force, joining the NAWSA in 1912 but quickly realizing that the group had not moved as far from the "still hunt" tactics as she would like and bristling at the pedestalization strategy. She was also frustrated by the state-to-state approach the national organization still favored. She founded the National Woman's Party to embrace the more militant approaches practiced by the suffragettes in England and work specifically toward a national amendment extending equal suffrage to all American women in all states.

The Doldrums came to an end in 1910, and it was once again the western United States that led the way. That year, despite many national suffragists having given up on state campaigns as possible victories, Washington state approved the first equal suffrage amendment in fourteen years, bringing the first suffrage triumph of the twentieth century. With the geographic, financial, and leadership loci of the national movement having moved decisively east since Idaho's triumph in 1896, the Washington victory was both a surprise and an inevitable conclusion to a decades-long fight in that state. (Washington's long fight included a four-year period between 1883 and 1887 when Washington women were enfranchised and actively voted, but the Washington Supreme Court then invalidated the equal suffrage law on a technicality.) But in 1910, it was partly that very distance from the mainstream campaign that made the Washington victory possible.

A new generation of suffrage leaders in the Pacific Northwest rejected the interference of the NAWSA, formed partnerships with the Progressive and socialist movements, and disassociated themselves from the temperance movement, which they believed was now a liability. Strong links with the labor movement, which was fighting for an eight-hour workday for women, were also crucial. Emma DeVoe had continued to work tirelessly in the region and was still crucial to the success, but she was joined in the new generation by women like Dr. Cora Smith Eaton, who led a cadre of suffragists up Mount Rainier to stake a green pennant banner with the words "Votes for Women" on the peak. A special train, the "Suffrage Special," transported suffrage activists from Spokane to Seattle, and along the way they conducted whistle-stop rallies. Washington represented a hybrid of older, conservative tactics paired with the flashier, more media-based approach of the new generation.

Fifty-six years after the first attempt to enfranchise Washington women, the amendment to the state constitution passed with nearly 64 percent of the vote. It was the first triumph of the twentieth century, although qualified in its success: the amendment stipulated that only those who read and spoke English could vote, presaging a whole new campaign for people of color that would last another fifty years.

In California, a massive, modern campaign preceded a 1911 vote to add an amendment to the California state constitution. The old ways were almost entirely discarded: local leaders, eschewing NAWSA assistance, produced suffrage parade floats, stereopticon shows to rapt audiences, and suffrage posters on every surface. The 1911 California campaign also embraced the diversity of the vast state: Suffrage articles appeared in Spanish, Chinese, German, Portuguese, and Italian. Coalitions were built between the white suffragists, the Colored Women's Suffrage League, Latina coalitions, and Chinese Americans. And these coalitions delivered, but just barely. Equal suffrage passed with 50.7 percent of the vote. But it was enough to make California the sixth suffrage state.

As in California, Oregon's success came from that state's leaders' ability to embrace parades, publicity, and coalitions. Leading up to a 1912 referendum vote, at least twenty-three suffrage clubs existed in Portland alone: Colored Women's Equal Suffrage Association, Chinese American Suffrage Club, Men's Equal Suffrage Club, a Quaker club, a stenographers' club, and more. Using similar techniques, by the end of 1912, Kansas, Arizona, and the new territory of Alaska had also joined Wyoming, Colorado, Utah, Idaho, Washington, and California as states in which women were equally enfranchised.

Those nine western states, still the only states with full equal suffrage laws in 1912, accounted for six and a half million American women voters. This fact was not lost on Alice Paul, leader of the National Woman's Party, a political party with only one agenda: passage of the Nineteenth Amendment. The pressure her party put on U.S. President Woodrow Wilson was unrelenting. NWP members were the first women in history to picket the White House, becoming the legendary "silent sentinels." Over the course of two and a half years, over two thousand women picketed silently. They were harassed and arrested and even tortured by U.S. authorities. Paul's militant approach had a cost, but it also got results.

Paul's efforts contrasted with Carrie Chapman Catt's mastery of drawing rooms and tea rooms and hotel lobbies, where key legislators made their deals. But by approaching the American public by every possible angle, the two leaders eventually prepared a nation for what finally came on June 4, 1919: the United States Congress agreed to send a suffrage amendment to the states for ratification. The amendment needed the acceptance of thirty-six states to be included in the U.S. Constitution and made national law—a law that benefited not only the women of specific states or territories but of the whole nation. On August 26, 1920, after Tennessee had cast the final vote to accept the amendment, the Nineteenth Amendment was officially made law.

The story did not end there, however, for American women of color, who although technically enfranchised continued to face barriers to their equal participation at the polls. Additional leaders rose within communities of color, including Utah's Elizabeth Taylor who, as a founder of the Western Federation for Colored Women, cemented herself as a leading voice in the African American community not only in Utah but all of the West. In addressing the federation in 1904, Taylor explained, "This is not our struggle alone, because we are only bearing the brunt of the battle of others to come, who will realize the necessity of organization. If the Western Federation of Colored Women can do the work that it intends to do, it will not only better the condition of homes, our girls and ourselves, but the entire West will be cherished, helped and respected by every good, fair-minded citizen."

While the formation of the federation was significant in the West, Taylor's optimism wasn't immediately rewarded on the national stage. Although the NWSA and the AWSA joined forces again in 1890, ostensibly putting aside their differences over the Fifteenth Amendment's enfranchisement of black men, the white suffragists continued their racially discriminatory practices in the early twentieth century as ratification of the Nineteenth Amendment became more likely. White suffragists feared that including African American women in their cause would offend white Southern voters, whose votes were crucial to receiving the two-thirds state majority needed to ratify the amendment.

When the Nineteenth Amendment technically enfranchised all eligible American women, in reality the outcome was entirely unclear for women of color. African American women voters in the Jim Crow South encountered the same disenfranchisement strategies and violence that contributed to the disenfranchisement of black men. Continued advocacy by women of color, including African Americans, Asians, and Native Americans, secured additional legislative measures that protected civic rights.

Native American women, for example, were not considered U.S. citizens at the time of the Amendment and thus were not able to vote. Zitkála-Šá, a Lakota writer and activist who lived much of her adult life in the western United States, lobbied Congress to secure equal suffrage for indigenous Americans. In 1924, Congress passed the Indian Citizenship Act, which defined Native Americans as U.S. citizens. Even after passage of this law, however, many western states continued to prevent Native Americans from voting. Zitkála-Šá then cofounded the National Council of American Indians, which focused on civil rights for native peoples.

Similar advocacy measures were needed for people of Asian descent, who benefited from the 1952 passage of the Immigration and Nationality Act. This law finally allowed immigrants of Asian descent to become U.S. citizens and gain voting rights. And in 1965, the Voting Rights Act prohibited poll taxes, literacy tests, and other racially discriminatory state voting regulations. President Lyndon B. Johnson signed the Voting Rights Act into law, putting protections in place so that both men and women of color could actually exercise the civic rights that had been technically granted to them decades before.

On March 13, 1906, Susan B. Anthony died in her home in Rochester, New York. The adoption of the "Susan B. Anthony Amendment" into the U.S. Constitution was still fourteen years away. Although unfulfilled in her lifelong dream of seeing all American women enfranchised, she didn't forget her friends in the West. She treasured, for instance, a dress made of the famous black Utah silk that the women of Utah gave on the occasion of her eightieth birthday. "This is the finest dress this former Quaker lady has ever owned," she declared, because it was made by "free women." Hours from death, Anthony slipped the gold ring—the same gold ring she had offered to Emmeline years before—off of her finger and in-structed those around her to send it to Emmeline. The ring was sent to Utah with a note that read, "In recognition of her esteem and love for Mrs. Emmeline B. Wells, Miss Anthony sent one of her gold rings on the day of her death to Mrs. Wells in Utah. The bond between these two women was very strong and the friendship had continued for nearly thirty years." Emmeline accepted the ring publicly at a memorial service for Susan B. Anthony held in Salt Lake City on March 17, 1906.

Fourteen years later, on October 3, 1919, Emmeline likely wore the ring on the steps of the Utah State Capitol building, her tiny, hunched, ninety-one-year-old frame draped in ghostly white, to witness the gover-nor of the State of Utah, Simon Bamberger, announce Utah's ratification of the Nineteenth Amendment. Almost fifty years had passed since women had stepped into civic life with the first female vote, and Emmeline was a living testament to the self-reliant western women who had first opened the door.

AUTHOR'S NOTE

One of the joys of writing this account was digging into the primary sources that record the proceedings and presentations of the 1895 Rocky Mountain Suffrage Conference. Because the sources—newspaper articles, diaries, and meeting minutes—are substantial, they include a trove of details that made my descriptions of the events possible, such as what people were wearing and how the rooms were decorated. Also, thanks to these sources, the vast majority of the speeches I have presented are taken verbatim from the actual words offered on those days. I have taken some liberty in shortening the speeches and linking them together for the sake of the narrative—for example, I have combined Anna Howard Shaw's speech at the Tabernacle with a second speech she gave that same evening at the Salt Lake Theater. In addition, as much of the dialogue as possible is taken from actual writings, such as journal entries or the speakers' public writings, and the sources for these are indicated in the endnotes.

There are, however, several places where I manufactured dialogue in order to present background information or themes. I have noted these instances in the endnotes as well. For instance, no conversation between Emmeline Wells and Elizabeth Taylor is recorded in a primary source as far as I have discovered, but, as I indicate in the endnotes, it is most likely the two would have crossed paths.

The great mystery in the story of Emmeline and Utah women's suffrage journey is the question of whether or not Emmeline voted on February 14, 1870, on the same day as Seraph Young. As I noted in the endnotes, Seraph Young was the only woman recorded by the media that day, voting records from that day are lost, and Emmeline's journals from that year are lost too. So there is no certain proof that Emmeline participated that day. But there is no proof that she did not, either, and surrounding historical evidence suggests she would have been one of the voters that day. I have chosen in this account to cast Emmeline as a voter, although the truth on this particular point may never be known.

ACKNOWLEDGMENTS

In a series of emails in the summer of 2015, my friend Mandee Grant and I tentatively recognized that the year 2020 would mark the 150th anniversary of Seraph Young's first female American vote. Mandee had just read Carol Cornwall Madsen's *An Advocate for Women*, and I had become acquainted with Carol after the publication of my 2014 book, *Women at Church*. In personal conversations and discussions at her home, Carol had opened to me the remarkably prolific but privately lonely life of Emmeline B. Wells.

I say we "tentatively" explored the 2020 anniversary because we first had to assure ourselves that Seraph Young's vote was, in fact, the first. It seemed unbelievable to us that we didn't know this landmark fact before becoming familiar with Carol and her work. We were both transplants to Utah, and so we could be excused for not remembering it from our school years. But even the Utah natives we knew seemed not to know about or grasp the significance of Seraph's action. How had this history been lost? And how could we reignite its legacy for today?

I have since learned there are many ways to define "first," and we have become sensitive to the caveats requisite whenever describing Seraph's vote: the first female vote in the modern nation (i.e., after the Seneca Falls initiation of the cause); the first female vote under equal suffrage law (i.e., with women enfranchised to vote in all elections, not just school boards, etc.); the first female vote after the colony of New Jersey ended its suffrage era. And I have since learned that it is not just Utah's leading role in the national suffrage movement but the role of the western states and territories generally that has been largely overlooked or misunderstood by historians and scholars. But the sheer, incredulous delight I felt at discovering Seraph's—and Utah's—place in history has never left me in the ensuing years.

And so I would like to begin my acknowledgments for this book with a special recognition of Mandee Grant and Carol Cornwall Madsen, with whom it all began. My initial conversations with Mandee turned into the creation of a nonprofit organization, Better Days 2020, with a mission to popularize Utah women's history in preparation for 2020, which marks not only Utah's anniversary but the centennial of the Nineteenth Amendment. Through Better Days 2020, I have had the tremendous fortune to work with remarkable people who feel as passionately as I do about Utah and western suffrage history. Specifically, Katherine Kitterman and Rebekah Ryan Clark pointed me to a trove of newspaper articles and primary source documents that provided the backbone of my knowledge of the 1895 Rocky Mountain Suffrage Conference. They are consummate historians, and I've been grateful to have them as resources, although all errors are my own.

For proposing I write this book, I thank Heidi Taylor Gordon and Chris Schoebinger of Shadow Mountain Books. Katherine and I approached them, after an introduction by Marianne Monson, about the 2020 anniversaries, suggesting they consider adding a book about the western suffrage story to their editorial lineup. I am tremendously grateful to them for not only accepting our idea but then tapping me to shepherd its creation.

I relied on the efficient skills of Rachel Felt, who transcribed the newspaper articles and diary entries for ease of access and provided the initial drafts of the individual biographies. Emily Farnsworth dug into Wyoming, Colorado, and Idaho histories, as well as specific people I wanted to highlight in the narrative. Amy Jameson kept me goal-oriented and focused on deadlines. I've admired Anna Rolapp's skills in textile scholarship and restoration for years, and I was particularly excited to call on her for a description of Emmeline's 1895 dress. She has been endlessly generous to me and to Better Days 2020.

For reading drafts of the manuscript, I thank three dear friends: Anita Cramer Wells, Barbara Christiansen, and Chantal Dolan. It is a test of true friendship to ask someone to read a draft still pocked with holes and questions, and they all passed with flying colors.

My children and my husband, Elliot C. Smith, have been endlessly patient when I've looked up from my computer with glazed eyes as they have come to say goodnight. My mother-in-law, Jan C. Smith, never complained when I missed family events due to maximizing my work time.

Lastly, I express gratitude to Emmeline B. Wells herself, my personal hero. As a young girl growing up near Emmeline's own eastern home, I too prayed that I would "be useful." She has lent a voice through which, I hope, I have done just that.

SUFFRAGIST TIMELINE
IN AMERICA

1842 March 17: Female Relief Society of The Church of Jesus Christ of Latter-day Saints organized in Nauvoo, Illinois

1847 July 24: Latter-day Saint pioneers arrive in the Salt Lake Valley

1848 July 19–20: First woman's right convention held in Seneca Falls, New York

1850 September 9: Utah Territory organized

September 9: California becomes the thirty-third state, without suffrage

1861 Civil War begins

1865 Civil War ends

1869 May 15: National Woman Suffrage Association (NWSA) and American Woman Suffrage Association (AWSA) established separately

December 10: Wyoming Territorial Legislature grants women the right to vote

1870 January 13: The Great Indignation meeting held in Salt Lake City

February 3: Fifteenth Amendment grants all men the right to vote

February 12: Utah Territorial Legislature grants women the right to vote

February 14: Utah women are the first to vote in the United States under equal suffrage laws

February 14: Esther Hobart Morris sworn in as justice of the peace in Wyoming

September 6: Wyoming women are the second to vote in the United States

1871 June 28–July 7: Susan B. Anthony and Elizabeth Cady Stanton visit Utah

1872 June 1: First issue of the *Woman's Exponent* published

1882 March 23: Edmunds Act disenfranchises polygamous men and women

1883 November 22: Washington Territorial Legislature grants women the right to vote

1884 December 22: Idaho institutes Anti-Mormon Test Oath

1887 March 3: Edmunds-Tucker Act disenfranchises all Utah women

1888 August 14: Washington Territory revokes female suffrage

1889 January 10: Woman Suffrage Association of Utah founded
November 11: Washington becomes the forty-second state, without suffrage

1890 February 18: National American Woman Suffrage Association formed
July 3: Idaho becomes the forty-third state, without suffrage
July 10: Wyoming becomes the forty-fourth state, the first with equal suffrage in its constitution
October 6: Manifesto ends LDS plural marriage

1893 February 3: Idaho revokes Anti-Mormon Test Oath
September 19: New Zealand grants women the right to vote
November 7: Colorado becomes the second state with equal suffrage in its constitution

1895 March 4–May 8: Utah State Constitutional Convention
May 12–15: Susan B. Anthony and Anna Howard Shaw visit Utah for Rocky Mountain Suffrage Conference
November 5: Utah's men vote to accept the new Utah state constitution

1896 January 4: Utah becomes the forty-fifth state, the third with equal suffrage in its constitution
November 3: Idaho grants women the right to vote, the fourth state with equal suffrage in its constitution
November 3: Utah's Dr. Martha Hughes Cannon elected as first female state senator

1900 February 15: Anthony receives gift of Utah silk for her eightieth birthday

1902 October 26: Elizabeth Cady Stanton dies, age eighty-six
June 12: Australia grants women the right to vote

1906 March 13: Susan B. Anthony dies, age eighty-six
June 1: Finland grants women the right to vote

1910 November 8: Washington re-enfranchises women, the fifth state with equal suffrage in its constitution

1911 October 10: California grants women the right to vote, the sixth state with equal suffrage

1912 November 5: Oregon, Arizona, and Kansas grant women the right to vote

1913 March 21: Alaska Territory grants women the right to vote
June 11: Norway grants women the right to vote

1914 November 3: Nevada and Montana grant women the right to vote
World War I begins

1915 June 5: Denmark grants women the right to vote

1916 June 5: Alice Paul and Lucy Burn found the National Woman's Party

1917 January 10: National Woman's Party begins picketing at the White House
April 2: Montana Representative Jeannette Rankin becomes first woman to hold federal office
July 20: Russia grants women the right to vote
November 6: New York grants women the right to vote

1918 November 5: Oklahoma, South Dakota, and Michigan grant women the right to vote
November 28: Poland grants women the right to vote
November 30: Germany grants women the right to vote
December 18: Austria grants women the right to vote

1919 May 21: House of Representatives passes women's suffrage amendment
June 4: Senate passes women's suffrage amendment
September 18: Netherlands grants women the right to vote
October 3: Utah ratifies the women's suffrage amendment
November 1: California ratifies the women's suffrage amendment
December 12: Colorado ratifies the women's suffrage amendment

1920 February 11: Idaho ratifies the women's suffrage amendment
March 20: Washington ratifies the women's suffrage amendment
August 18: Tennessee becomes thirty-sixth (and final) state to ratify the women's suffrage amendment
August 26: Women's suffrage added to U.S. Constitution as Nineteenth Amendment

NOTES

EPIGRAPH

Martha Hughes Cannon Address to the House Judiciary Committee in Washington, D.C., 15 February 1898.

Sandra L. Myres Sandra L. Myres, *Westering Women and the Frontier Experience, 1800–1915* (UNM Press, 1982), 235.

CHAPTER 1

Union Pacific depot In her diary from that day, Emmeline refers to picking up Anthony at the "U.P. Depot." Additionally, "Two Celebrated Women" in the *Salt Lake Herald-Republican* refers to the "Union Pacific depot." According to "Day of the Suffragists" in the *Salt Lake Tribune*, the women took the Rio Grande Western Railway to arrive in Salt Lake City. Neither the Rio Grande nor the Union Pacific Stations that currently exist in Salt Lake City were built until several years later. The Union Pacific depot was built in 1908, and the Rio Grande Western Depot was built in 1910. So the 1895 depots would have been different buildings.

"Good old-fashioned love fest" "Day of the Suffragists," *Salt Lake Tribune*, 13 May 1895.

Recent triumphs Numerous newspaper articles gave preliminary reports of the conference. For one example, see "Two Celebrated Women," *Salt Lake Herald-Republican*, 12 May 1895.

400 and 500 East Emmeline's home was located at 429 Westminster Avenue, between 400 and 500 East. See Carol Cornwall Madsen, *Emmeline B. Wells: An Intimate History* (Salt Lake City: University of Utah Press, 2017), 323.

Utah Drag A report of the conference, including the use of the "Utah Drag," can be found at "The National Conference, National American W.S.A.," *Woman's Exponent* 23, 15 May 1895.

Templeton Hotel Details of the morning's events in "Two Famous Women," *Salt Lake Herald-Republican*, 13 May 1895.

23 inches around This measurement is taken directly from a dress Wells wore circa 1895, the year of the conference. The dress is owned by Wells's great-granddaughter Kathleen Cannon Knowlton and was restored by Anna T. Rolapp in 2017. Of this specific dress, Rolapp writes, "Emmeline's 'day dress' is very similar to one sketched in Arnold's *Patterns of Fashion 2*. The illustrated 1895 dress is from the Gallery of English Costume and is described as being 'taffeta . . . with flecked spots.' Emmeline's dress is additionally similar in that they both have extreme full sleeves 'lined with paper to stiffen them' and cuff details. Both dresses have high collars, bodices with gathered fronts, and waist bows. Emmeline would have been 67 years old when she wore this dress in 1895. Undergarments would have included a boned corset and a gored petticoat with frills at the hem (Arnold). Shoes worn with this dress would have been described as 'hand sewn turn shoes' priced from $2–$6 with a Louis XV heel. The shoes would have been found in both the Sears and Montgomery Ward catalogs. Rexford, Nancy E. *Women's Shoes in America, 1795–1930*." Many thanks to Anna Rolapp for access to the dress and this description.

Ruth May Fox Linda Thatcher, "'I Care Nothing For Politics': Ruth May Fox, Forgotten Suffragist," *Utah Historical Quarterly*, vol. 49, no. 3 (Summer 1981).

Utah silk Silk worms were cultivated in Utah as early as 1856. According to the *Encyclopedia of Mormonism*, "In 1856, Elizabeth Whitaker produced cocoons from worms that her husband brought from England as eggs; in 1858, Nancy Barrows planted mulberry seeds, feeding her worms on lettuce leaves until the mulberry trees matured. She reeled thread, wove it into fabric, and made the first silk dress in the territory of Deseret in 1859. . . . In 1867, President Young offered free eggs and mulberry leaves to any persons willing to 'undertake the work' of hatching, tending, and feeding the worms. He called George D. Watt to promote silk culture throughout the territory and Zina D. H. Young, of the newly reorganized Relief Society, to head the silk project. She traveled widely over the territory, delivering speeches, and organizing and teaching classes." See Elizabeth Hall, "Silk Culture," *Encyclopedia of Mormonism* (New York: Macmillan Publishing Company, 1992), 1312.

Anthony's first visit to Utah While it is likely that Emmeline met Anthony in 1871 when she visited Utah, there is no documented evidence of the meeting. Emmeline kept a journal continually from 1844 to 1920, but the journals between 1846 and 1874 are missing, so there is no way to corroborate the possible meeting from her own account. Anthony was hosted at Daniel Wells's home during the 1871 visit, so the likelihood of meeting is high, but Emmeline was not living in Wells's main house at the time.

Seneca Falls, New York The definitive history of the women's suffrage movement was collected into six volumes by Elizabeth Cady Stanton, Susan B. Anthony, Matilda Gage, Harriot Stanton Blatch, and Ida H. Harper. For specific history of the Seneca Falls era, see *The Complete History of Woman's Suffrage, Volume 1 (1848–1861)*.

Rights of woman Ibid., 1096.

The Sentiments The complete text of this report can be found in the original tract produced after the convention in the North Star Printing Office owned by Frederick Douglass, Rochester, New York. It was reprinted several times and circulated as a sales item at local and national women's rights conventions. See "Report of the Woman's Rights Convention," *NPS.gov*. https://www.nps.gov/wori/learn/historyculture/report-of-the-womans-rights-convention.htm.

No concept For the Report of the Woman's Rights Convention, Rochester, NY, 1848, see https://rbscp.lib.rochester.edu/2448.

Rochester, New York For information on additional woman's suffrage conventions held in the 1840s and 1850s, see https://www.nps.gov/wori/learn/historyculture/more-womens-rights-conventions.htm.

Abandoning the teaching Nancy Hayward, "Susan B. Anthony." National Women's History Museum, 2017. *WomensHistory.org*.

NOTES

CHAPTER 2

"At Last" Emmeline B. Wells, "At Last," *Musings and Memories* (Salt Lake City: The Deseret News, 1915), 68.

"Mrs. Wells?" There is no known evidence of Emmeline and Elizabeth Taylor meeting, but biographical details suggest the women would have likely crossed paths, if not at this time then slightly later. Taylor arrived in Salt Lake City in 1891 and started her newspaper (with her husband) in 1895. The Rocky Mountain Suffrage Conference may have been one of the first events covered in that newspaper. Additionally, both Emmeline and the Taylors were members of the Utah Press Association and may have associated through that organization. Emmeline doesn't share her views on race in her diaries or editorials, suggesting she almost certainly shared the biases of her time, which did not consider the equality of black women in the "equal" suffrage movement.

"We gather now to lay" "Day of the Suffragists," *Salt Lake Tribune*, 13 May 1895.

Convert the general public See "The History of Woman Suffrage In Utah, 1870–1900," by Emmeline B. Wells. First published as "Utah," chapter 66 in Susan B. Anthony and Ida Husted Harper, eds., *The History of Woman Suffrage*, Vol. 4 (Rochester: Susan B. Anthony, 1902), 3619–32.

Ida B. Wells Arlisha R. Norwood, "Ida B. Wells-Barnett." National Women's History Museum, 2017. *WomensHistory.org.*

"be useful" Aunt Em, "Midnight Soliloquy," *Woman's Exponent*, 15 April 1880.

"Two powers seemed to be warring" Emmeline B. Wells, "Hephzibah," *Woman's Exponent*, 1 February 1890.

In Nauvoo For the most complete biography of Emmeline B. Wells, see Carol Cornwall Madsen, *Emmeline B. Wells: An Intimate History* (Salt Lake City: University of Utah Press, 2017).

"something extraordinary" Minutes, "Nauvoo Relief Society Minute Book, 17 March 1842." The Joseph Smith Papers, *josephsmithpapers.org.* p. 12.

James left Nauvoo Madsen, *Intimate History*, 51–54.

collection of letters Ibid., 336–37.

"that tiny but mighty old lady" Geneva Kingkade, letter to Carolyn Chouinard, 24 August 1970. Quoted in Madsen, *Intimate History*, 336. The letter is in Madsen's possession.

"affected my whole after life" E. Wells, Diary, 28 July 1894.

Three years into the marriage Emmeline Whitney, letter to Newel K. Whitney, 10 October 1847, Winter Quarters, NE. N. Whitney Papers. Quoted in Madsen, *Intimate History*, 86.

happy home life For an example of one of Emmeline's letters expressing her happiness with Whitney, see Letter to Newel K. Whitney, 10 October 1847, Winter Quarters, NE, N. Whitney Papers. L. Tom Perry Special Collections, Brigham Young University.

the traditional gender structure For an exploration of marriage as a public contract and its ramifications for women, see Nancy F. Cott, *Public Vows: A History of Marriage and the Nation* (Cambridge: Harvard University Press, 2002).

20 and 30 percent Kathleen Flake, *The Politics of American Religious Identity: The Seating of Senator Reed Smoot, Mormon Apostle* (Chapel Hill: The University of North Carolina, 2004), 65. Flake quotes several reports describing widely varying numbers: "The extent of the practice of polygamy in the Latter-day Saint community was virtually impossible to calculate under the circumstances. Modern scholars have arrived at various estimates. A reliable summary is provided by Thomas Alexander: 'At present, perhaps the best estimates of the number of polygamous families among late-nineteenth-century Latter-day Saints range between 20 and 30 percent. Nevertheless, studies of individual communities show a wide variation in the incidence of plurality.' . . . [Joseph F.] Smith testified that 'only about 3 or 4 percent of the entire male population of the church have entered into that principle.' Senator and former federal marshal Fred Dubois argued that this was merely the number convicted." Flake continues to cite Thomas Alexander, *Utah: The Right Place: The Official Centennial History* (Salt Lake City: Gibbs Smith, 1995). "Using 1880 census data, geographer Lowell C. 'Ben' Bennion found the lowest percentage of polygamous families—5 percent—in Davis County's south Weber and the highest—67 percent—in Orderville. He found 15 percent in Springville. In a study of St. George, historian Larry Logue found nearly 30 percent of the families polygamous in 1870 and 33 percent in 1880."

Brigham Young famously stated Leonard J. Arrington, *Brigham Young: American Moses* (University of Illinois Press, 1985), 100.

divine reasoning In *A House Full of Females*, Laurel Thatcher Ulrich expounds on these reasons for the introduction and acceptance of plural marriage. Ulrich explains, "Latter-day Saints had contradictory ideas about sex. They simultaneous glorified reproduction and urged sexual restraint. Although they accepted the nineteenth-century notion that women were inherently less troubled by sexual passion than men, they vehemently denied that polygamy was an outlet for male lust. A man who married multiple wives in order to indulge his lascivious impulses was as guilty of adultery as a monogamist who strayed from his marital vows. Mormons understood that human beings were imperfect and that they lived in a fallen world. How, then, was prostitution to be prevented? In [Parley P.] Pratt's words, 'It is to be prevented in the way the Lord devised in ancient times; that is, by giving to His faithful servants a plurality of wives, by which a numerous and faithful posterity can be raised up, and taught in the principles of righteousness and truth.' A righteous man understood that his bodily desires originated in a Godlike drive to populate worlds. Latter-day Saint theology liberated male sexuality by transforming lust into responsibility, and by giving every woman an opportunity to marry and become a mother." Laurel Thatcher Ulrich, *A House Full of Females: Plural Marriage and Women's Rights in Early Mormonism, 1835–1870* (New York: Alfred A. Knopf, 2017), 241.

"A plural wife has more time" Annie Laurie Black, "Our Woman Senator," *San Francisco Examiner*, 8 November 1896. Reprinted in the *Salt Lake Herald*, 1 November 1896.

CHAPTER 3

"We are now, politically speaking" Steven Waldman, *Sacred Liberty: America's Long, Bloody, and Ongoing Struggle for Religious Freedom* (New York: Harper Collins, 2019), 114, citing Wilford Woodruff to William Atkin, 18 March 1889, Woodruff Letterbooks Collection, LDS Archives.

"The doctrine of the Mormons" "The Mormons, Their Doctrine and Their Social Condition," *Boston Herald*, 1 March 1861.

"The duty of the Government" "Polygamy and a New Rebellion," *New York Times*, 19 June 1862.

"No one living in or practicing bigamy" A Bill in Aid of the Execution of the Laws in the Territory of Utah, and for Other Purposes, H.R. 696, 41st Cong., 2nd Sess. (1870).

"We, the 'Mormon' ladies of Utah" "Correspondence," *Deseret News Weekly*, 15 January 1868, 389. For the minutes of the Indignation Meeting, see Minutes of "Great Indignation Meeting," 13 January 1870, in "Great Indignation Meeting of the Ladies of Salt Lake City, to Protest against the Passage of Cullom's Bill," *Deseret Evening News*, 14 January 1870, 15 January 1870.

"Only the Mormons would suffer" New York Times, 17 December 1867.

"the plan of giving" Deseret News Weekly, 24 March 1869.

"If that word 'male'" Letter from Elizabeth Cady Stanton to Gerrit Smith, 1 January 1866, Gerrit Smith Collection, George Arents Research Library for Special Collections, Syracuse University.

"I will be thankful in my soul" Elizabeth Cady Stanton et al., eds., *History of Woman Suffrage, vol. 2* (1881), 384.

"Gold was the main attraction" For a comprehensive overview of the Wyoming equal suffrage movement, see Michael A. Massie, "Reform is Where You Find It: The Roots of Woman Suffrage in Wyoming," *Annals of Wyoming* 62, no. 1 (Spring 1990), 2–22.

"Reports after the legislative session" Sidney Howell Fleming, "Solving the Jigsaw Puzzle: One Suffrage Story at a Time," *Annals of Wyoming* 62, no. 1 (Spring 1990), 22–65.

"Once during the session" Editorial written by Edward M. Lee, *Wyoming Tribune*, 8 October 1870.

Esther Hobart Morris For a contemporary perspective on Esther Hobart Morris, see Jessica Anderson, "Overlooked No More: She Followed a Trail to Wyoming. Then She Blazed One," *New York Times*, 23 May 2018.

Morris did not bite right at first Accounts of Hobart's reluctance can be found in Lynne Cheney, "It All Began in Wyoming," *American Heritage*, vol. 24, no. 3 (April 1973).

The county clerk telegraphed Karin Marcy, "Esther Morris and Her Equality State: From Council Bill 70 to Life on the Bench," *The Journal of American Legal History*, vol. 46, no. 3, (1 July 2004) 300–43.

"The women of America" Quoted in Cheney.

CHAPTER 4

"The agitation of the [suffrage] question" "Female Suffrage in Utah," *Deseret News*, 16 February 1870.

"Omaha Herald" Deseret Evening News, 14 February 1870.

"Eliza R. Snow called" All of the quotations from this section are taken from Minutes of "Great Indignation Meeting," 13 January 1870, in "Great Indignation Meeting of the Ladies of Salt Lake City, to Protest against the Passage of Cullom's Bill," *Deseret Evening News*, 14 January 1870. Accessed via *First Fifty Years of Relief Society* (Church Historian's Press, 2017).

On January 27th Utah Territory Legislative Assembly papers, 1851–1872; Nineteenth Session, 1870; House minutes, 1870 January 20–31; Church History

Library. https://catalog.churchofjesuschrist.org/assets?id=33aabb69-59b3-49af-bbc4-90dd78f3ad24&crate=0&index=32.

No woman had ever legally cast a ballot The colony of New Jersey allowed women to vote between 1797 and 1807. New Jersey's constitution gave voting rights to "all inhabitants of this colony, of full age, who are worth fifty pounds . . . and have resided within the county . . . for twelve months," although still only single women could vote because married women could not own property and thus could not be worth fifty pounds. In 1807, the New Jersey state legislature restricted suffrage to tax-paying, white male citizens.

City Hall "Salt Lake City Council Hall," Wikipedia. https://en.m.wikipedia.org/wiki/Salt_Lake_City_Council_Hall.

The twenty person legislative Council "Territory of Utah: Legislative Assembly Rosters 1851–1894." Compiled by Utah State Archives Staff, 2007. Archives.utah.gov.

a volunteer brass band For descriptions of the 14 February 1870 election, see "The Election," *Deseret Evening News*, 15 February 1870, and "The Woman Suffrage Bill," *Deseret News*, 16 February 1870.

Hooper was elected Gordon Morris Bakken, Brenda Farrington, *The American West: The Gendered West* (New York: Routledge, 2013), 350.

"the thing is all a hoax" This story is related in "William H. Hooper," *Phrenological Journal*, November 1870, 331.

CHAPTER 5

We are the people of Utah "Salutory," *Woman's Exponent*, vol. 1, no. 1 (June 1872), 4.

"Your subsequent writings" Carol Cornwall Madsen, *Battle for the Ballot: Essays on Woman Suffrage in Utah, 1870–1896* (Logan: Utah State University Press, 1997), 5.

You walked right past There appears to be no evidence that Emmeline actually was among the twenty-six women who voted on February 14, 1870. Her name is not mentioned in the newspapers (Seraph Young is the only name mentioned). Also, although Emmeline kept a journal continually from 1844 to 1920, the journals between 1846 and 1874 are missing. Thus, there is no way to check Emmeline's own reflections of the day. However, as she was engaged in civic life in Salt Lake City by 1870 and was married to Daniel Wells, a prominent civic and Church leader, it is very likely that Emmeline was among the "leading ladies" of that day.

"Brief visits" "The Election," *Salt Lake Herald*, 2 August 1870.

She thought marriage Anthony commented on her distaste for the contractual ownership of a woman implicit in marriage on several occasions. In a speech in 1877, Anthony predicted "an epoch of single women. If women will not accept marriage with subjugation, nor men proffer it without, there is, there can be, no alternative. The woman who will not be ruled must live without marriage." "Homes of Single Women," by Susan B. Anthony, 1877, quoted in *The Elizabeth Cady Stanton—Susan B. Anthony Reader*, edited by Ellen Carol DuBois (Northwestern University Press: Boston, 1981), 148.

Liberal Institute Susan B. Anthony, Diaries, 2 July 1871.

"if there were henceforth any slavery" Quoted in Lola Van Wagenen, *Sister Wives and Suffragists: Polygamy and the Politics of Woman's Suffrage, 1870–1896*. (PhD. diss, New York University, 1994), 24.

After the Indignation Meetings For an exploration of Wells's intellectual flowering, see Madsen, 177–81.

"Let our daughters" "Our Daughters," *Deseret News*, 27 August 1862.

"train my girls" Emmeline B. Wells diaries, 21 May and 27 June 1876.

twelve suffrage newspapers Sherilyn Cox Bennion, *Equal to the Occasion: Women Editors of the Nineteenth-Century West* (Reno: University of Nevada Press, 1990), 57.

"anomalyous condition of affairs" Van Wagenen.

CHAPTER 6

Is there then nothing worth living for Editorial by Blanche Beechwood (Emmeline B. Wells), *Woman's Exponent*, 1 October 1874.

"The Millennium" Susan B. Anthony and Ida Husted Harper, *History of Woman Suffrage*, vol. 4, chapter 17, 3142. Speaking before the National Woman Suffrage Association held 26–29 January 1897 in Des Moines, Iowa.

"[We learn] from the teaching" Wil A. Linkugel, *The Speeches of Anna Howard Shaw*, vol. 2 (University of Wisconsin, 1960), 84.

"Work and worship" *New York World*, 2 February 1896, quoted in Ida Husted Harper, *The Life and Work of Susan B. Anthony*, vol. 2, 859.

"Salt Lake will have some" "Two Celebrated Women," *Salt Lake Herald-Republican*, 12 May 1895.

The station clock chimed Detailed descriptions of the morning's meeting are offered in several newspaper reports, such as "Two Famous Women" *Salt Lake Herald-Republican*, 13 May 1895.

Charlotte was raised Beverly Beeton, "A Feminist Among the Mormons: Charlotte Ives Cobb Godbe Kirby," *Utah Historical Quarterly*, vol. 59, no. 1, Winter 1991, 23–31.

Emmeline had the megaphone Madsen, *Advocate for Women*, 150.

"little woman" Letter from Charlotte Godbe Kirby to President Wilford Woodruff, 5 February 1889. Quoted in Beeton, 24.

Woodruff's response Letter from Wilford Woodruff to Charlotte Godbe Kirby, 11 February 1889. Quoted in Beeton, 29.

CHAPTER 7

Mr. Caleb Walton West Governor West's involvement is described in "Many Ladies Meet," *Deseret Evening News*, 13 May 1895, and "Women of Three States," *Salt Lake Tribune*, 14 May 1895.

"most brilliant women" Kerry Drake, "Estelle Reel: First Woman Elected to Statewide Office in Wyoming." *WyoHistory.org*. Wyoming State Historical Society, 8 November 2014.

Jenkins was the only woman Ann Gordon, *The Selected Papers of Elizabeth Cady Stanton and Susan B. Anthony: Their Place Inside the Body-Politic, 1887 to 1895* (Rutgers University Press, 2009), 476.

"eloquent lady speakers" "Eloquent Lady Speakers," *Deseret News Weekly*, 11 May 1895.

Mrs. Emma DeVoe This apocryphal story about DeVoe is told in Jennifer M. Ross-Nazzal, *Winning the West for Women: The Life of Suffragist Emma Smith DeVoe* (Seattle: University of Washington Press, 2011), 3.

DeVoe's presence Newspaper articles do not mention DeVoe as being present during the Rocky Mountain Suffrage Conference, but Ross-Nazzal places DeVoe in Utah—and staying with Emmeline—in the spring of 1895. See Ross-Nazzal, 99. In the western states and territories DeVoe worked most closely with Carrie Chapman Catt, who deputized her to raise money and manage local suffrage organizations. For explorations of DeVoe's work in Idaho, see Ross-Nazzal, 95–107.

As the northern neighbor Julie VanDusky-Allen, "Trading Statehood for Votes: The Early Decline of the Democratic Party in the Idaho." *QuantitativePeace.com*. The Quantitative Peace, 15 August 2013.

Reynolds v. United States For a summary of the *Reynolds* case and link to complete judgment text, see *Reynolds v. United States* (1879), BillofRightsInstitute.org.

gave federal authorities the backbone For an exploration of the congressional debates around polygamy and the effect of *Reynolds*, see Stephen Eliot Smith, "Barbarians within the Gates: Congressional Debates on Mormon Polygamy, 1850–1879," Journal of Church and State, vol. 51, no. 4 (Autumn 2009), 587–616.

The Idaho legislature's Kathy Barnard, "Women's Suffrage, Right to Vote Came Early in Idaho." Lewiston Tribune, 3 July 1990, *LMTribune.com*.

After the constitution For a comprehensive summary of the history of the Mormons' involvement in the Idaho statehood campaign, see Colin Branham, "The Saints Were Sinners: The Mormon Question and the Survival of Idaho." *BoiseState. edu*. Boise State University. This article relies heavily on Merle W. Wells, "The Idaho Anti-Mormon Test Oath, 1884–1892," *Pacific Historical Review*, vol. 24, no. 3 (August 1955), 235–52.

elaborate breakfast for forty "Two Famous Women," *Salt Lake Herald-Republican*, 13 May 1895; and "Day of the Suffragists," *Salt Lake Tribune*, 13 May 1895.

"I came here opposed to woman suffrage," Frances Elizabeth Willard, "Mrs. Amalia Barney Simons Post," *American Women: Fifteen Hundred Biographies with Over 1,400 Portraits* (Mast, Crowell & Kirkpatrick, 1897), 583.

"respect the desires of the State Associations" Ross-Nazzal, 95. As an itinerant organizer for the NAWSA, Emma DeVoe was subject to criticism of meddling in local campaigns. The tension between state and national organizational efforts was particularly pronounced in her career.

CHAPTER 8

household tips to poetry Sherilyn Cox Bennion, "Nineteenth-century Women Editors of Utah," *Utah Historical Quarterly*, Summer 1981, 302.

"It is pitiful to see" "Woman Suffrage," *Woman's Exponent*, 1 April 1895.

"this little paper" Susan B. Anthony and Ida Husted Harper, *History of Women's Suffrage, Volume 2*, Chapter 66, "Utah." Quoted in Christy Karras, *More Than Petticoats: Remarkable Utah Women* (Guilford: Globe Pequot Press, 2010), 36.

"Aunt Em" For an exploration of Wells's various pen names, literary styles, and influences, see Madsen, *Intimate History*, 161–68.

"So long has custom" "Woman's Progression," *Woman's Exponent*, 15 February 1878.

"recognized as a responsible being" "Woman's Expectations," *Woman's Exponent*, 1 July 1877.

"preferable to the licensed social evil" "The Utah Ladies in Washington," *Deseret News*, 18 January 1879. Quoted in Madsen, *Intimate History*, 185.

"*Dear me,*" Zina Young Williams, Diary, 26 January 1879. Quoted in Madsen, *Intimate History*, 186.

Rutherford B. Hayes Wells's visit with President and Mrs. Hayes is described in Carol Cornwall Madsen, *An Advocate for Women: The Public Life of Emmeline B. Wells, 1870–1920* (Provo: Brigham Young University Press, 2006), 165–70.

"*They close no career*" Elizabeth Wood Kane, *Twelve Mormon Homes Visited in Succession on a Journey Through Utah to Arizona*, 5. Quoted in Madsen, *Intimate History*, 193.

"*It is not alone because of unjust taxation*" "Suffrage in Utah," *Woman's Exponent*, 1 December 1883.

"*the ladies of the Church of Jesus Christ*" "'Mormon' Women's Protest, 1886 (Excerpt)" *First Fifty Years of Relief Society* (Salt Lake City: Church Historian's Press, 2016), 517.

"*I wish you out there*" "Report," *Deseret News Weekly*, 2 June 1885. Quoted in *First Fifty Years*, 521.

They were right to worry For an exploration of the effects of polygamy's aftermath, see Lola Van Wagenen, "Sister-Wives and Suffragists: Polygamy and the Politics of Woman Suffrage, 1870–1896," *BYU Studies*, 2003.

CHAPTER 9

The society was limited Patricia Lyn Scott, "Jennie Anderson Froiseth and the Blue Tea," *Utah Historical Quarterly*, vol. 71, no. 1 (2003), 20.

"*holy modern home*" "The Gulf Between Them," *Salt Lake Tribune*, 11 January 1889.

"*to fight to the death*" "Our Policy," *Anti-Polygamy Standard*, April 1880.

Harriet Beecher Stowe The quotation was taken from Stowe's introduction to Mrs. T. B. H. Stenhouse, "Tell It All: The Tyranny of Mormonism; or, an Englishwoman in Utah," (1880; reprint, New York: Praeger Publishers, 1971), vi. See also the front page of each *Anti-Polygamy Standard* starting April 1880.

"*in the midst of the enemy's camp,*" Scott, 33.

"*anomalous condition*" "The Gulf Between Them," *Salt Lake Tribune*, 11 January 1889.

"*foul blot*" "The Ladies Anti-Polygamy Society of Utah," *Anti-Polygamy Standard*, April 1880.

"*peculiar*" E. Wells, Diary, 9 October 1890.

"*a more universal sisterhood*" "Woman's Work," *Woman's Exponent*, 15 November 1875.

Board of Lady Managers See "Board of Lady Managers," *Deseret Evening News*, 7 September 1892. See also "Utah's Lady Managers," *Salt Lake Herald-Republican*, 24 December 1892.

"*The women of Utah*" Tiffany Greene, "Utah Women in the 1893 Chicago World's Fair," *UtahWomensHistory.org*, Better Days 2020, 4 April 2019.

Patented inventions "From the Utah Women," *Salt Lake Herald-Republican*, 8 April 1893.

"*confirmed on all hands*" "Utah Silks at the Fair," *Salt Lake Tribune*, 28 September 1893.

mulberry trees Elizabeth H. Hall, "Silk Culture," *Encyclopedia of Mormonism* (New York: Macmillan Publishing Company, 1992), 1312.

"vast army" "Women and the World's Fair," *Woman's Exponent*, 1 December 1892. Quoted in Madsen, *Intimate History*, 331.

CHAPTER 10

"Base and Meridian" "The Center of the City," *history.churchofjesuschrist.org*. LDS Church History Museum, 28 October 2014.

On Day 1 All accounts of the Constitutional Convention are taken from the minutes of the Convention: "Proceedings and Debates of the Convention Assembled to Adopt a Constitution for the State of Utah," Utah State Legislature, *le.utah.gov /documents/conconv/utconstconv.htm*.

"perfect toleration" Proceedings, Day 1.

active correspondences Madsen, *Advocate for Women*, 184.

Dr. Ellen Ferguson Madsen, *Intimate History*, 341–42.

"very ill with my heart" E. Wells, Diaries, 11 February 1894.

too caustic Madsen, *Intimate History*, 343.

Beaver County Woman Suffrage Association For details on the Beaver County association, see Lisa Bryner Bohman, "A Fresh Perspective: The Woman Suffrage Associations of Beaver and Farmington, Utah." *Utah Historical Quarterly*, vol. 59, no. 1 (Winter 1991).

"there will be a feeling of unity" Emmeline B. Wells to Mary A. White, 13, 14 January 1895, Beaver County Woman Suffrage Association Papers. Quoted in Madsen, *Intimate History*, 343.

"President Anthony" "Convention in Atlanta," *Woman's Exponent*, 15 February 1895. Describing the incident as it was related in the *Atlanta Evening Journal*.

"During the time" Salt Lake Tribune, 19 March 1895.

"To you, gentlemen" Proceedings, Day 15.

"Was it under" "Midnight Soliloquy," *Woman's Exponent*, 15 April 1880.

"The woman suffragists" Salt Lake Tribune, 19 March 1895.

separate submission For a comprehensive exploration of Roberts's arguments at the Constitutional Convention, see Jean Bickmore White, "A Woman's Place Is In the Constitution: The Struggle for Equal Rights in Utah in 1895," *Utah Historical Quarterly*, vol. 42, no. 4 (Fall 1974), 344–69.

"My appeal to you" Proceedings, Day 25.

"The adjective 'male,'" "Susan B. Anthony's Letter," *Woman's Exponent*, 15 August 1894.

"You are the queens" Proceedings, Day 26.

"I offer you three reasons" Proceedings, Day 26.

"Suppose a man" Proceedings, Day 30.

"A stream of language" "Women and the Ballot," *Salt Lake Herald*, 29 March 1895.

"Today, all is confusion," E. Wells, Diaries, 6 April 1895.

"It is pitiful" Woman's Exponent, 1 April 1895.

To an LDS Relief Society All Joseph F. Smith statements here are from "Relief Society Conference," *Woman's Exponent*, 15 August 1895.

"I want to tell you" Proceedings, Day 32.

"Generous, chivalrous" E. Wells, Diaries, 1 April 1895.

"Equal suffrage" Proceedings, Day 25.
"I do not care" Proceedings, Day 46.
"I have in my hand" Proceedings, Day 46.
"A little bitterness" E. Wells, Diaries, 18 April 1895.
"Hurrah for Utah" Woman's Exponent, 1 May 1895.

CHAPTER 11

"The large attendance" "At the Tabernacle," *Salt Lake Herald Republican*, 13 May 1895.

"Gentiles" Reverend Anna Howard Shaw also spoke at the Salt Lake Theater on the night of Sunday, May 12. "Dr. Shaw at the Theater," *Salt Lake Tribune*, 13 May 1895, describes the audience of multi-denominational leaders in attendance, although their representation wasn't as comprehensive as Emmeline would have liked. This description of attendees is a combination of both the Tabernacle event at 2:00 p.m. and the Theater event at 8:00 p.m. that night.

"O My Father" "At the Tabernacle," *Salt Lake Herald Republican,* 13 May 1895.

"Order is heaven's first law" Eliza R. Snow, "Celebration of the Twenty-fourth at Ogden," *Deseret News Weekly*, 26 July 1871. Quoted in Jill C. Mulvay, "Eliza R. Snow and the Woman Question," *BYU Studies* 16, no. 2 (1976).

"that class known as 'strong-minded'" Snow, quoted in Mulvay.

"it is only by obedience" "Miss E. R. Snow's Address to the Female Relief Societies of Weber County," *Latter-day Saints' Millennial Star*, 12 September 1871. Quoted in Mulvay.

"to extend the emancipation" "At the Tabernacle," *Deseret Evening News*, 13 May 1895.

Only Emmeline knew There is no known evidence that Cannon entrusted Wells with her plans in 1895, but Cannon had worked as a typesetter for Wells before receiving her medical degrees and looked to Wells as a mentor. Thus the connection is possible. For a contextualization of Cannon's feminism, see Jennifer L. Duqué, "'We Know How To Keep House and We Know How to Keep A City': Contextualizing Dr. Martha Hughes Cannon's Feminism," *AWE (A Woman's Experience)*: Vol. 2 , Article 5, 2015. Cannon's eventual run in 1896 was complicated by the fact that not only her husband Angus ran too, but also Wells, both on the opposing party from Cannon.

"My friends," Shaw recalled her western visits in *History of Woman Suffrage*, Vol. 4. Chapter 16: The National-American Convention of 1896, 3123.

"Yesterday, as the train" This speech is taken from accounts in "At the Tabernacle," *Deseret Evening News,* 13 May 1895 and "At the Tabernacle," *Salt Lake Herald Republican,* 13 May 1895.

"It is woman's destiny" Whitney's speech here is a combination of *Proceedings*, Day 33 and accounts given in "At the Tabernacle," *Deseret Evening News,* 13 May 1895 and "At the Tabernacle," *Salt Lake Herald Republican,* 13 May 1895.

CHAPTER 12

Equal suffrage is not an end "Ellis Meredith," Colorado Women's Hall of Fame, www.cogreatwomen.org/project/ellis-meredith/.

When she had appealed For an exploration of Daniel Wells's consideration of his responsibility to Newel K. Whitney, see Madsen, *Intimate History*, 106–11.

"closer than sisters," Annie Wells Cannon, "Mothers in Israel," quoted in Madsen, *Intimate History*, 115.

"How much pleasure" E. Wells, Diaries, 10 October 1874.

"Wilt thou not condescend" Madsen, *Intimate History*, 123.

"O my heart" E. Wells, Diaries, 5 December 1875.

"My home is a pleasant one" E. Wells, Diaries, 7 January 1875.

"dear old homestead" E. Wells, Diaries, 8 May 1883.

"rookery for owls" E. Wells, Diaries, 20 March 1891.

Templeton Hotel Madsen, *Intimate History*, 304.

"highest motive" "Woman's Expectations," *Woman's Exponent*, 1 July 1877.

"Self-made woman" "Self-Made Women," *Woman's Exponent*, 1 March 1881.

tremendous scandal For an exploration of the John Q. Cannon scandal, see Madsen, *Intimate History*, 230–42.

"I only moved to Colorado" Details from Bradford's life can be found in Heather Kleinpeter Caldwell, "Mary Carroll Craig Bradford: Providing Opportunities to Colorado's Woman and Children Through Suffrage and Education," Texas A&M University, December 2009.

Captain Howard Stansbury "Notable Assemblage," *Salt Lake Herald-Republican*, 14 May 1895.

"Mrs. DeVoe" Rebecca J. Mead, *How the Vote Was Won: Woman Suffrage in the Western United States, 1868–1914* (New York: New York University Press, 2004), 66.

CHAPTER 13

fancy financier "A Week of Conventions," *Salt Lake Tribune*, 12 May 1895.

By 10:30 a.m. Descriptions of the Monday morning session can be found in "Many Ladies Meet," *Deseret Evening News*, 13 May 1895. Also, "The Cause of Suffrage," *Salt Lake Herald Republican*, 15 May 1895.

"as pure as fair woman" "Women of Three States," *Salt Lake Tribune*, 14 May 1895.

"Emily [Richard's] birthday" E. Wells, Diaries, 22 April 1895.

"gala day" "Suffrage Convention," *Salt Lake Herald*, 14 May 1895.

The garlands Descriptions of the Convention Hall decor and seating arrangements can be found in "Women of Three States," *Salt Lake Tribune*, 14 May 1895.

Many of the decorations "The National Conference," *Woman's Exponent*, 15 May 1895.

thanked the Almighty "Women of Three States," *Salt Lake Tribune*, 14 May 1895.

After the prayer "Many Ladies Meet," *Deseret Evening News*, 13 May 1895.

discussed periodically Joseph G. Brown, *The History of Equal Suffrage in Colorado: 1868–1898* (Denver: New Job Printing Co., 1898), 16–29.

labor movement in Colorado For a comprehensive exploration of the Populist-supported victory in Colorado's referendum, see Mead, 53–72.

They did justice to all Much of this speech is taken from "Day of the Suffragists," *Salt Lake Tribune*, 13 May 1895, and "Evening Session," *Salt Lake Tribune*, 14 May 1895.

three bricks laid down "The Washington Convention," *Woman's Exponent*, 1 February 1896.

form a state association Ross-Nazzal, 88.

As for California Mead, 81.

And the facts are this This portion of Anthony's speech is taken from Anthony and Husted, *History of Woman Suffrage*, 5053.

What we would like better Anthony and Husted, *History of Woman Suffrage*, 3792.

They cut as wide "Former Brooklyn Society Woman a Leading Colorado Politician," *Brooklyn Eagle*, 1902. Quoted in Caldwell, 154.

"Just fancy coming" Bradford's speech is taken from "More Women's Work," *Deseret Evening News*, 14 May 1895, and "Many Ladies Meet," *Deseret Evening News*, 13 May 1895.

"In the equal suffrage victory" Mary C. C. Bradford, "The Equal Suffrage Victory in Colorado," 23 December 1893.

"Our presence has driven" "Evening Session," *Salt Lake Tribune*, 14 May 1895.

The Coloradan suffragists' Mead, 69.

"I am very glad that Aunt Susan" "Remarks by Mrs. E. M. Stansbury," *Woman's Exponent*, 15 May 1895.

"A man once said to me" "Evening Session," *Salt Lake Tribune*, 14 May 1895.

CHAPTER 14

Abigail Scott Duniway Susan B. Anthony and Ida Husted Harper, eds., *The History of Woman Suffrage*, Vol. 4 (Rochester: Susan B. Anthony, 1902), Chapter 15.

festooned in yellow The reception, including décor, invited guests, and reception line, is described in "A Brilliant Event," *Salt Lake Tribune*, 14 May 1895, and "Notable Assemblage," *Salt Lake Herald-Republican*, 14 May 1895.

Her three-story Victorian home The Richardses' home still stands on A Street in Salt Lake City, but is in a seriously dilapidated condition.

"the guests of honor" "A Brilliant Event," *Salt Lake Tribune*, 14 May 1895.

South Dakota to Montana Ross-Nazzal, 99.

"The current WCTU president" Cheryl Cox, "Ghost of an Old Town," Idaho Falls Magazine, 1 July 2012, *www.idahofallsmagazine.com*.

"Such unsuccessful efforts" Sarah Rounsville,"Women's Suffrage and Temperance in Idaho," Intermountain Histories, *www.intermountainhistories.org*.

'Always be good-natured' Ross-Nazzal, 14.

The New Northwest Bennion, 62–64.

Making the ground "fertile" Ross-Nazzal, 94.

'still hunt' tactics Ross-Nazzal, 94–95.

CHAPTER 15

From her bed Madsen, *Intimate History*, 324.

Woman, awake! Emmeline B. Wells, "The New Era," *Musings and Memories*, 1915.

"What it Means to be an Enfranchised Woman" Ellis Meredith, "What It Means to be an Enfranchised Woman," *The Atlantic Monthly*, 102 (August 1908), 202.

The Assembly Hall Newspapers reporting on the conference alerted their readers to the change in location in the previous evening's editions. For example, see "Evening Session," *Salt Lake Tribune*, 14 May 1895. Anthony reported on the location change in her diary on 13 May 1895.

She had appealed "More Women's Work," *Deseret Evening News*, 14 May 1895.

Mrs. Beatie Anthony's hostess is noted in "Society Notes," *Salt Lake Herald*, 12 May 1895. Also, Susan B. Anthony, Diaries, 12 May 1895.

And this morning over breakfast Phoebe Louisa Young Beatie, www.findagrave.com/memorial/24624504/phoebe-louisa-beatie.

"She was blessed" "Bishop W. J. Beatie," *Biographical Record of Salt Lake City and Vicinity* (Chicago: National Historic Record Co., 1902), 316.

She is quite close "Reverend Dr. Anna Howard Shaw," National Park Service, 27 June 2019, www.nps.gov/people/anna-howard-shaw.htm.

Anthony called the meeting For coverage of this meeting, see "The Cause of Suffrage," *Salt Lake Herald*, 15 May 1895. Also "More Women's Work," *Deseret Evening News*, 14 May 1895, and "Evening Session," *Salt Lake Tribune*, 15 May 1895.

National Council of Women Madsen, *Advocate for Women*, 278.

"Whereas, Great gains" The text of the resolution is recorded in "Evening Session," *Salt Lake Tribune*, 15 May 1895.

CHAPTER 16

The regular 2:15pm The trip to Saltair is described in "The Cause of Suffrage," *Salt Lake Herald*, 15 May 1895, and "More Women's Work," *Deseret Evening News*, 14 May 1895.

Mrs. French The key participants and their home cities are listed in "The Cause of Suffrage," *Salt Lake Herald*, 15 May 1895.

The striking lakeside resort Nancy D. McCormick and John S. McCormick, *Saltair* (Salt Lake City: University of Utah Press, 1985).

"The hour at the beach" "The Cause of Suffrage," *Salt Lake Herald*, 15 May 1895.

"To be distanced from her spiritually" Madsen, *Intimate History*, 322.

"It is easy to comprehend" E. Wells, Diary, 23–24 October 1898.

"Lively chat" "The Cause of Suffrage," *Salt Lake Herald*, 15 May 1895.

Ogden Additional coverage of Anthony and Shaw's Ogden visit can be found in "Miss Anthony and Miss Shaw," *Ogden Daily Standard*, 14 May 1895. See also "Miss Anthony and Miss Shaw," *Salt Lake Herald*, 15 May 1895, and "Junction City Notes," *Deseret Evening News*, 15 May 1895.

My gold ring While there is no evidence that Anthony promised her ring to Emmeline during her lifetime, Anthony did bequeath a gold ring to Emmeline on her deathbed. See Madsen, *Intimate History*, 420.

Little mountain state Margherita Hamm, a correspondent for the *New York Mail and Express*, recorded Emmeline saying these words about Utah in "The Woman Suffragists," *Journal History*, 23 January 1896, 8.

EPILOGUE

serving lunch E. Wells, Diary, 5 November 1895.

The vote was 12,126 Idaho Women's Right to Suffrage, SJR 2 (1896), *Ballotopedia.com*.

Ruth May Fox Ruth May Fox, "My Story," 26, Utah State Historical Society, Salt Lake City. Quoted in Madsen, *Advocate for Women*, 302.

International Council of Women For an exploration of Emmeline's international efforts, see Madsen, *Intimate History*, 379–400. See also Madsen, *Advocate for Women*, 419–27.

"My life seems wonderfully changed" E. Wells, Diary, 7, 8 August 1899. Quoted in Madsen, *Intimate History*, p. 387.

Brigham H. Roberts Madsen, *Advocate for Women*, 396.

"My heart is very sad" E. Wells, Diaries, 10 November 1898.

seven million Americans Madsen, *Advocate for Women*, 412.

The move away from women-led political work Madsen, *Advocate for Women*, 341.

The mood was ebullient Ross-Nazzal, 80.

"All-partisan" Ibid., 83.

110,355 voted for the amendment California's Woman's Suffrage, Amendment 6 (1896), *Ballotopedia.com.*

The "doldrums" is an old term The "doldrums" was a term first used to describe this period by Aileen Kraditor in Aileen Kraditor, *The Ideas of the Woman's Suffrage Movement, 1890–1920* (New York: Columbia University Press, 1965).

They embraced the media Emily Scarborough, *"Fine Dignity, Picturesque Beauty, and Serious Purpose": The Reorientation of Suffrage Media in the Twentieth Century.* University of Southern California, http://scalar.usc.edu/works/suffrage-on-display/restaging-the-movement.

Historian Emily Scarborough explains Ibid.

Alice Paul Debra Michals, "Alice Paul." National Women's History Museum, https://www.womenshistory.org/education-resources/biographies/alice-paul.

Alva Vanderbilt Belmont and Katherine Mackay For an exploration of the New York socialites' impact on the suffrage movement, see Johanna Neuman, *Gilded Suffragists: The New York Socialites Who Fought for Women's Right to Vote* (New York: Washington Mews Books, 2017).

embossed invitations Neuman, 42.

"Woman suffrage, once the cause forlorn" Mabel Potter Daggett, "Suffrage Enters the Drawing Room," *Delineator,* January 1910, Alva Belmont Scrapbooks, vol. 3. Quoted in Neuman, 41.

A new generation of suffrage leaders Mead, 97–99.

Mount Rainier Ross-Nazal, 115.

"Suffrage Special" Ibid.

64 percent of the vote Mead, 116.

only those who read and spoke English Shanna Stevenson, "The Fight for Washington Women's Suffrage: A Brief History," Washington State Historical Society, *WashingtonHistory.org,* http://www.washingtonhistory.org/files/library/TheFightforWashingtonWomensSuffrageABriefHistory.pdf.

In California, a massive, modern campaign Mead, 135–37.

White suffragists feared Sharon Harley, "African American Women and the Nineteenth Amendment." National Park Service, *NPS.gov.*

Zitkála-Šá Barbara Jones Brown, "Zitkála-Šá: The Red Bird Activist," Better Days 2020, https://www.utahwomenshistory.org/bios/zitkala-sa/.

Indian Citizenship Act The Indian Citizenship Act was still limited in that it did not override individual state laws that prohibited Native Americans who resided on reservations from voting. Such a law was added to the Utah State Constitution, for example, soon after statehood. This law remained in place until 1957. For more on Utah's history of Native voting rights, see Jennifer Robinson, "Utah and Native American Voting Rights," Better Days 2020, https://www.utahwomenshistory.org/2019/03/utah-and-native-american-voting-rights/.

The ring was sent to Utah After Anthony died on 13 March 1906, the ring was sent to Utah with a note that read, "In recognition of her esteem and love for Mrs. Emmeline B. Wells, Miss Anthony sent one of her gold rings on the day of her death to Mrs. Wells in Utah. The bond between these two women was very strong and the friendship had continued for nearly thirty years." Emmeline accepted the ring publicly at a memorial service for Susan B. Anthony held in Salt Lake City on 17 March 1906. In addition, after Anthony's death, her secretary sent a copy of her biography to Relief Society leaders, inscribed with the words, "To the women who were loyal and helpful to Miss Anthony to the end of her great work."

PRIMARY SOURCES

"The Mormons, Their Doctrine and Their Social Condition." *Boston Herald*, 1 March 1861.

"Polygamy and a New Rebellion." *The New York Times*, 19 June 1862.

"Our Daughters." *Deseret News*, 27 August 1862.

"Correspondence." *Deseret News Weekly*, 15 January 1868.

"Female Suffrage in Utah." *Deseret Evening News*, 8 February 1870.

"The Election." *Salt Lake Herald-Republican*, 2 August 1870.

"The Utah Ladies in Washington." *Deseret News*, 18 January 1879.

"The Ladies Anti-Polygamy Society of Utah." *Anti-Polygamy Standard*, April 1880.

"The Gulf Between Them." *Salt Lake Tribune*, 11 January 1889.

"Board of Lady Managers." *Deseret Evening News*, 7 September 1892.

"Utah's Lady Managers." *Salt Lake Herald-Republican*, 24 December 1892.

"From the Utah Women." *Salt Lake Herald-Republican*, 8 April 1893.

"Utah Silks at the Fair." *Salt Lake Tribune*, 28 September 1893.

"Women and the Ballot." *Salt Lake Herald-Republican*, 29 March 1895.

"Eloquent Lady Speaks." *Deseret Weekly News*, 11 May 1895.

"Two Celebrated Women." *Salt Lake Herald-Republican*, 12 May 1895.

"Society Notes." *Salt Lake Herald-Republican*, 12 May 1895.

"A Week of Conventions." *Salt Lake Tribune*, 12 May 1895.

"Two Famous Women." *Salt Lake Herald-Republican*, 13 May 1895.

"Many Ladies Meet." *Deseret Evening News*, 13 May 1895.

"Dr. Shaw at the Theater." *Salt Lake Tribune*, 13 May 1895.

"At the Tabernacle." *Salt Lake Herald-Republican*, 13 May 1895.

"At the Tabernacle." *Deseret Evening News*, 13 May 1895.

"Day of the Suffragists," *Salt Lake Tribune*, 13 May 1895.

"Equal Rights in Utah." *San Francisco Call*, 14 May 1895.

"A Brilliant Event." *Salt Lake Tribune*, 14 May 1895.

"Notable Assemblage." *Salt Lake Herald-Republican*, 14 May 1895.

"Women of Three States." *Salt Lake Tribune*, 14 May 1895.

"Suffrage Convention." *Salt Lake Herald-Republican*, 14 May 1895.

"Suffrage Conference." *Provo Daily Enquirer*, 14 May 1895.

"More Women's Work," *Deseret Evening News*, 14 May 1895.

"Miss Anthony and Miss Shaw." *Ogden Daily Standard*, 14 May 1895

"For Equal Suffrage." *San Francisco Call*, 15 May 1895.

"Evening Session." *Salt Lake Tribune*, 15 May 1895.

"The Cause of Suffrage." *Salt Lake Herald-Republican*, 15 May 1895.

"National Conference." *Woman's Exponent*, 15 May 1895.

"Miss Anthony and Miss Shaw." *Salt Lake Herald-Republican*, 15 May 1895.

"Coming to the City." *San Francisco Call*, 16 May 1895.

"Our Woman Senator." *San Francisco Examiner*, 8 November 1896.

The Woman's Exponent Digital Collection (1872–1914), Harold B. Lee Library: Brigham Young University. https://contentdm.lib.byu.edu/digital/collection/WomansExp/id/17660/rec/2.

Anthony, Susan B., Elizabeth Cady Stanton, Matilda Gage, Harriot Stanton Blatch, and Ida H. Harper. *The Complete History of Woman's Suffrage, Volumes 1–6.* Web.

Biographical Record of Salt Lake City and Vicinity. Chicago: National Historic Record Co., 1902.

Reynolds v. United States (1879). BillofRightsInstitute.org.

"Report of the Women's Rights Convention Rochester, 1848." Rochester: University of Rochester. Digital collections.

"Proceedings and Debates of the Convention Assembled to Adopt a Constitution for the State of Utah," Utah State Legislature, *le.utah.gov/documents/conconv/utconstconv.htm.*

Minutes of "Great Indignation Meeting," 13 January 1870, in "Great Indignation Meeting of the Ladies of Salt Lake City, to Protest against the Passage of Cullom's Bill," *Deseret Evening News* (Salt Lake City, UT), Jan. 14, 1870, vol. 3, no. 44. Accessed via *First Fifty Years of Relief Society*, Church Historian's Press, 2017.

"Territory of Utah: Legislative Assembly Rosters 1851–1894." Utah State Archives, 2007. *archives.utah.gov.*

"William H. Hooper." *Phrenological Journal*, November 1870.

Wells, Emmeline B. *Musings and Memories.* Salt Lake City: Deseret Book, 1915.

_____. *The History of Woman Suffrage in Utah, 1870–1900.* (First published as "Utah," chapter 66 in Susan B. Anthony and Ida Husted Harper, editors, *The History of Woman Suffrage, Volume 4.* Rochester: Susan B. Anthony, 1902.)

_____. Diaries 1844–1919. Original in L. Tom Perry Special Collections, Harold B. Lee Library, Brigham Young University, Provo, UT.

Utah Woman Suffrage Songbook, https://catalog.churchofjesuschrist.org/assets?id=6f4aeb03–8d6f-4d52-bdda-6885e31522f2&crate=1&index=11.

SECONDARY SOURCES

Arrington, Leonard J. *Brigham Young: American Moses*. Chicago: University of Illinois Press, 1985.

Bakken, Gordon Morris and Brend Farrington. *The American West: The Gendered West*. New York: Routledge, 2013.

Barnard, Kathy. "Women's Suffrage, Right to Vote Came Early in Idaho." *Lewiston Tribune*, 3 July 1990. LMTribune.com.

Beeton, Beverly. *Women Vote in the West: The Woman Suffrage Movement, 1869–1896, American Legal and Constitutional History*. New York: Garland, 1986.

Bennion, Sherilyn Cox. *Equal to the Occasion: Women Editors of the Nineteenth-Century West*. Reno: University of Las Vegas Press, 1990.

_____. "Nineteenth-Century Women Editors of Utah." *Utah Historical Quarterly*, Summer 1981.

Bohman, Lisa Bryner. "A Fresh Perspective: The Woman Suffrage Associations of Beaver and Farmington, Utah." *Utah Historical Quarterly*, vol. 59, no. 1 (Winter 1991).

Branham, Colin. "The Saints Were Sinners: The Mormon Question and the Survival of Idaho." Boise State University.

Brown, Barbara Jones. "Zitkála-Šá: The Red Bird Activist." Better Days 2020.

Brown, Joseph G. *The History of Equal Suffrage in Colorado: 1868–1898*. Denver: New Job Printing Co., 1898.

Caldwell, Heather Kleinpeter. "Mary Carroll Craig Bradford: Providing Opportunities to Colorado's Woman and Children Through Suffrage and Education." Texas A&M University, December 2009.

Cheney, Lynne. "It All Began in Wyoming," *American Heritage*, vol. 24, no. 3 (April 1973).

Cott, Nancy. *Public Vows: A History of Marriage and the Nation*. Cambridge: Harvard University Press, 2000.

Derr, Jill Mulvay, Carol Cornwall Madsen, Kate Holbrook, Matthew J. Grow. *The First Fifty Years of Relief Society: Key Documents in Latter-day Saint Women's History*. Salt Lake City: The Church Historian's Press, 2016.

Drake, Kerry. "Estelle Reel: First Woman Elected to Statewide Office in Wyoming." Wyoming State Historical Society, 8 November 2014.

DuBois, Ellen Carol. *The Elizabeth Cady Stanton—Susan B. Anthony Reader*. Chicago: Northwestern University Press, Boston, 1981.

Duqué, Jennifer L. "We Know How To Keep House and We Know How to Keep A City": Contextualizing Dr. Martha Hughes Cannon's Feminism. AWE (A Woman's Experience): Vol. 2 , Article 5, 2015.

Flake, Kathleen. *The Politics of American Religious Identity: The Seating of Senator Reed Smoot, Mormon Apostle*. Chapel Hill: University of North Carolina, 2004.

Fleming, Sidney Howell. "Solving the Jigsaw Puzzle: One Suffrage Story at a Time." *Annals of Wyoming* 62, no. 1 (Spring 1990).

Fluhman, J. Spencer. *"A Peculiar People:" Anti-Mormonism and the Making of Religion in the Nineteenth-Century America*. Chapel Hill: University of North Carolina, 2012.

Gordon, Ann. *The Selected Papers of Elizabeth Cady Stanton and Anthony B. Anthony: Their Place Inside the Body-Politic, 1887 to 1895*. Rutgers University Press, 2009.

Greene, Tiffany. "Utah Women in the 1893 Chicago World's Fair." Better Days 2020, 4 April 2019.

Hall, Elizabeth. "Silk Culture," *Encyclopedia of Mormonism*. New York: Macmillan Publishing Company, 1992.

Harley, Sharon. "African American Women and the Nineteenth Amendment," National Park Service.

Hayward, Nancy. "Susan B. Anthony." *WomensHistory.org*, National Women's History Museum, 2017.

Iverson, Joan. "The Mormon-Suffrage Relationship: Personal and Political Quandries." *Frontiers: A Journal of Women Studies*, vol. 11, no. 2/3 (1990).

Karras, Christy. *More Than Petticoats: Remarkable Utah Women*. Guilford: Globe Pequot Press, 2010.

Kraditor, Aileen. *The Ideas of the Woman's Suffrage Movement, 1890–1920*. New York: Columbia University Press, 1965.

Linkugel, Wil A. *The Speeches of Anna Howard Shaw*. University of Wisconsin, 1960, Volume 2.

Madsen, Carol Cornwall, Editor. *Battle for the Ballot: Essays on Woman Suffrage in Utah, 1870–1896*. Logan: Utah State University Press, 1997.

_____. *An Advocate for Women: The Public Life of Emmeline B. Wells*. Provo: Brigham Young University Press, 2006.

_____. *Emmeline B. Wells: An Intimate History*. Salt Lake City: University of Utah Press, 2017.

_____. *"The Power of Combination": Emmeline B. Wells and the National and International Councils of Women*. BYU Studies 33, no. 4 (1993).

Marcy, Karin. "Esther Morris and Her Equality State: From Council Bill 70 to Life on the Bench," *The Journal of American Legal History*, vol. 46, no. 3 (1 July 2004).

Massie, Michael A. "Reform is Where You Find It: The Roots of Woman Suffrage in Wyoming." *Annals of Wyoming* 62, no. 1 (Spring 1990).

McCormick, Nancy D. and John S. McCormick, *Saltair*. Salt Lake City : University of Utah Press, 1985.

Mead, Rebecca J. *How the Vote Was Won: Woman Suffrage in the Western United States, 1868–1914*. New York: New York University Press, 2004.

Michals, Debra. "Alice Paul." *WomensHistory.org*, National Women's History Museum, 2017.

Mulvay, Jill C. "Eliza R. Snow and the Woman Question." *BYU Studies* 16, no. 2, 1976.

Neuman, Johanna. "Gilded Suffragists: The New York Socialites Who Fought For Women's Right to Vote." New York: Washington Mews Books, 2017.

Norwood, Arlisha R. "Ida B. Wells-Barnett." *WomensHistory.org*, National Women's History Museum, 2017.

Rea, Tom. "Right Choice, Wrong Reason: Wyoming Women Win the Right to Vote." *WyoHistory.org.* Wyoming State Historical Society, 8 November 2014.

Robinson, Jennifer. "Utah and Native American Voting Rights." Better Days 2020. UtahWomensHistory.org.

Ross-Nazzal, Jennifer M. *Winning the West for Women: The Life of Suffragist Emma Smith DeVoe.* Seattle: University of Washington Press, 2011.

Rounsville, Sarah. "Women's Suffrage and Temperance in Idaho." Intermountain Histories.

Scarborough, Emily. *"Fine Dignity, Picturesque Beauty, and Serious Purpose:" The Reorientation of Suffrage Media in the Twentieth Century.* University of Southern California, http://scalar.usc.edu/works/suffrage-on-display/restaging-the-movement.

Scott, Patricia Lyn. "Jennie Anderson Froiseth and the Blue Tea," *Utah Historical Quarterly,* vol. 71, no. 1, 2003.

Scott, Patricia Lyn and Linda Thatcher. *Women in Utah History: Paradigm or Paradox?* Logan: Utah State University Press, 2005.

Smith, Stephen Eliot. "Barbarians within the Gates: Congressional Debates on Mormon Polygamy, 1850–1879." *Journal of Church and State,* vol. 51, no. 4 (Autumn 2009).

Stevenson, Shanna. "The Fight for Washington Women's Suffrage: A Brief History." *WashingtonHistory.org,* Washington State Historical Society.

Thatcher, Linda. "'I Care Nothing For Politics': Ruth May Fox, Forgotten Suffragist." *Utah Historical Quarterly,* vol. 49, no. 3 (Summer 1981).

Ulrich, Laurel Thatcher. *A House Full of Females: Plural Marriage and Women's Rights in Early Mormonism, 1835–1870.* New York: Alfred A. Knopf, 2017.

Van Wagenen, Lola. *Sister-Wives and Suffragists: Polygamy and the Politics of Woman Suffrage, 1870–1896.* Provo: BYU Studies, 2011.

_____. *In Their Own Behalf: The Politicization of Mormon Women and the 1870 Franchise. Dialogue: A Journal of Mormon Thought,* vol. 24, no. 33.

VanDusky-Allen, Julie. "Trading Statehood for Votes: The Early Decline of the Democratic Party in the Idaho." *QuantitativePeace.com.* The Quantitative Peace, 15 August 2013.

Waldman, Steven. *Sacred Liberty: America's Long, Bloody, and Ongoing Struggle for Religious Freedom.* New York: Harper Collins, 2019.

Wells, Merle W. "The Idaho Anti-Mormon Test Oath, 1884–1892." *Pacific Historical Review,* vol. 24, no. 3 (August 1955).

White, Jean Bickmore, "A Woman's Place Is In the Constitution: The Struggle for Equal Rights in Utah in 1895." *Utah Historical Quarterly,* vol. 42, no. 4 (Fall 1974).

Willard, Frances Elizabeth. "Mrs. Amalia Barney Simons Post." *American Women: Fifteen Hundred Biographies with Over 1,400 Portraits,* Mast, Crowell & Kirkpatrick, 1897.

BIOGRAPHY SOURCES

ABIGAIL SCOTT DUNIWAY

Jean M. Ward, "Abigail Scott Duniway," *The Oregon Encyclopedia*, https://oregonency-clopedia.org/articles/abigail_scott_duniway/#.XXhbuJNKg1I.

AMALIA POST

D. Claudia Thompson, "Amalia Post, Defender of Women's Rights," November 8, 2014, https://www.wyohistory.org/encyclopedia/amalia-post-defender-womens-rights.

CHARLOTTE IVES COBB GODBE KIRBY

Tiffany Greene, "Charlotte Godbe Kirby, Champion of 'The Women's Era,'" https://www.utahwomenshistory.org/bios/charlotte-godbe-kirby/.

ELIZABETH ANNE WELLS CANNON

Max Binheim and Charles A. Elvin, eds., *Women of the West: A Series of Biographical Sketches of Living, Eminent Women in the Eleven Western States of the United States of America* (Shepardsville, KY: Publishers Press, 1928), 172.

ELIZABETH AUSTIN TAYLOR

Amy Tanner Thiroit, "Elizabeth Taylor: Newspaper Woman and Activist," https://www.utahwomenshistory.org/bios/elizabeth-taylor/.

ELLIS MEREDITH STANSBURY

Katherine M. Swafford, "Biographical Sketch of Ellis Meredith," *Alexander Street*, https://documents.alexanderstreet.com/d/1009860159.

EMILY SOPHIA TANNER RICHARDS

Andrea Radke-Moss, "Emily S. Richards, A Believer in Suffrage," https://www.utahwomenshistory.org/bios/emilysrichards/.

EMMA DEVOE

David Jepsen, "Emma Smith DeVoe: The Suffragist Who Wouldn't Back Down," *Women's Votes, Women's Voices* (Washington State History Museum), https://web.archive.org/web/20120313220751/http://stories.washingtonhistory.org/suffrage/People/edevoe.aspx.

ESTELLE REEL

Kerry Drake, "Estelle Reel, First Woman Elected to Statewide Office in Wyoming," *WyoHistory.org*, November 8, 2014, https://www.wyohistory.org/encyclopedia /estelle-reel-first-woman-elected-statewide-office-wyoming; http://www.herhat-wasinthering.org/biography.php?id=7451.

JENNIE ANDERSON FROISETH

Ami Chopine, and Rebekah Clarke, "Jennie Froiseth, A Passionate Suffragist and Anti-Polygamist," https://www.utahwomenshistory.org/bios/jennie-froiseth/.

MARY C. C. BRADFORD

Grace Napier, "Bradford, Mary Carroll Craig," *Biographical Dictionary of American Educators*, edited by John F. Ohles (Connecticut: Greenwood Publishing Group, 1978), 163.

RUTH MAY FOX

Brittany Chapman Nash, "Ruth May Fox, Equal Rights Proponent and Poet," https://www.utahwomenshistory.org/bios/ruth-may-fox/.

SARAH MELISSA GRANGER KIMBALL

Janelle M. Higbee, "Sarah M. Kimball, A Women's Rights Woman," https://www .utahwomenshistory.org/bios/sarah-m-kimball/.

ZINA D. H. YOUNG

Mary Firmage Woodward, "Zina D. H. Young," in *Encyclopedia of Mormonism*, edited by Daniel H. Ludlow (New York: MacMillan Publishing, 2007), 1612; "Zina Diantha Huntington Young," https://www.churchofjesuschrist.org/callings /relief-society/relief-society-presidents/zina-h-young?lang=eng.